THE MARKETING MATRIX

In the hands of the corporate sector, marketing has turned us into spoilt, consumption-obsessed children who are simultaneously wrecking our bodies, psyches and planet. Given the fiduciary duties of the corporation, notions like consumer sovereignty, customer service and relationship building are just corrosive myths that seduce us into quiescence, while furnishing big business with unprecedented power. Corporate Social Responsibility, the ultimate oxymoron, and its country cousin, Cause-Related Marketing, are just means of currying favour amongst our political leaders and further extending corporate power.

So it is time to fight back. As individuals we have enormous internal strength; collectively we have changed the world, and can again (indeed marketing itself is a function of humankind's capacity to co-operate to overcome difficulties and way pre-dates its co-option by corporations). From the purpose and resilience of Steinbeck's sharecroppers ('we're the people – we go on'), through Eisenhower's 'alert and knowledgeable citizenry' to Arundhati Roy's timely reminder about the wisdom of indigenous people who 'are not relics of the past, but the guides to our future', there are lots of reasons for optimism. If these talents and strengths can be combined with serious moves to contain the corporate sector, it is possible to rethink our economic and social priorities. The book ends with a call to do just this.

This compelling and accessible book will be of interest across the social sciences and humanities – and indeed to anyone who has concerns about the current state of consumer society. It will also be particularly useful reading for those marketing students who would prefer a critical perspective to the standard ritualization of their discipline.

Gerard Hastings is Professor of Social Marketing at Stirling and The Open University. He worked in market research before beginning his academic career, which has focused on researching the impact of marketing on society – especially the harm done by the alcohol, tobacco and fast food industries. This has involved him in advising Government, working with policy makers both nationally and internationally and acting as an expert witness in litigation – as well as publishing widely in both academic and popular outlets. His work also looks at the value of social marketing, and his first book was called *Social Marketing: Why Should the Devil Have All the Best Tunes?* He was awarded the OBE for services to health care in 2009.

'Gerard Hastings' masterful and ground breaking treatise on marketing is nothing short of a map out of the desert leading us all to Jericho. His challenge to the consumptive nature of the developed world and the unveiling of the "big lie", that the global corporate culture is working on the behalf of society, is nothing short of liberating...expect to be challenged...expect to be warned...then, expect to become hopeful...his prescription for healing is even more powerful than his diagnosis.'

James H. Lindenberger, *Director, Social Marketing Group, University of South Florida, USA*

'The cowboy and robber economy is back. There are even business schools that teach students that the sole mission of business is to maximize shareholder value. Finance is everything. Branding, however hollow, is everything. In contrast the new marketing theory of the 3rd millennium puts stress on customer service and value-in-use which is in line with Gerard Hasting's thinking. He has written a daring book. He calls a spade a spade, totally contrary to what advertising and other marketing does. So the conventional marketer will hate it. If they keep reading they will find that Hastings makes sense. We need business, but a nation needs fair business, not just windfall for the few. Marketing is also a tool for creating welfare in society – for everybody. Only then will business become efficient in the long run.'

Evert Gummesson, *Emeritus Professor, Stockholm University School of Business, Sweden*

'On the face of it, corporate marketing adds excitement and glamour to the most boring of everyday products and stimulates desire in the most jaded consumers. As consumers we are seduced by the power of this corporate apparatus with its seductive bargains, witty ads, myriad of choice with brand identity as the opiate of the people. As Hastings shows however, the powerful and ubiquitous behaviour change tools of modern marketing – i.e. "the marketing matrix" – actually create a false and superficial society based on more and more private consumption and less and less wellbeing and real satisfaction. In his ground-breaking analysis and searing critique of corporate marketing, Hastings brilliantly explains how this "matrix" works and also dedicates the second part of the book to setting out radical solutions for "marketing as if people mattered".'

Mike Saren, *Professor of Marketing, University of Leicester, UK*

'Gerard Hastings provokes long overdue debate and challenges us to consider the role commercial marketing has played in global catastrophes: deaths from tobacco, alcohol and junk food, among other problems. Yet he resists the temptation merely to demonise marketing and instead holds out the hope we might use the values that once underpinned marketing – reciprocity and mutual respect – to address these profound threats. If the fundamental re-evaluation of marketing that Hasting proposes succeeds, we might indeed understand the difference between being a consumer and a citizen, and take the first steps towards a sustainable, and more equitable, society.'

Janet Hoek, *Professor of Marketing, University of Otago, New Zealand*

'Wry, direct and disturbing. This book unceremoniously yanks the rug from beneath the feet of decades of marketing text books. It invites us gently, persuasively and passionately to take a long, hard and honest look at consumer capitalism. Drawing inspiration from John Steinbeck, Aldous Huxely, Dwight Eisenhower and Fritz Schumacher it calls for "full-on social change" through rethinking of economic and social systems and through co-ordinated community action. A "must-read" for anyone who cares about our future.'

Professor Agnes Nairn, *Co-Author of* Consumer Kids

'*The Marketing Matrix* is an in depth look at corporate marketing and how its power reaches into and limits our lives. As a marketing professor who has examined the inner workings of this power as wielded by alcohol, tobacco and food companies, Professor Hastings provides insight into the abuses of marketing and recommendations for how to combat them. The book is a grim reminder that, with few exceptions, customers, indeed, always come second.'

Craig Lefebvre, *Social Marketer*

THE MARKETING MATRIX

How the corporation gets
its power – and how we
can reclaim it

Gerard Hastings

Routledge
Taylor & Francis Group

LONDON AND NEW YORK

First published 2013
by Routledge
2 Park Square, Milton Park, Abingdon, Oxon OX14 4RN

Simultaneously published in the USA and Canada
by Routledge
711 Third Avenue, New York, NY 10017

Routledge is an imprint of the Taylor & Francis Group, an informa business

British Library Cataloguing in Publication Data
A catalogue record for this book is available from the British Library

Library of Congress Cataloging in Publication Data
Hastings, Gerard.
The marketing matrix: how the corporation gets its power and how we can
reclaim it / Gerard Hastings.
p. cm.
Includes bibliographical references and index.
1. Marketing–Management. 2. Consumption (Economics) 3. Consumer behavior.
4. Manipulative behavior. I. Title.
HF5415.13.H3653 2012
381.0973–dc23
2012009082

ISBN: 978-0-415-67861-2 (hbk)
ISBN: 978-0-415-67862-9 (pbk)
ISBN: 978-0-203-09955-1 (ebk)

Typeset in Bembo
by Saxon Graphics Ltd, Derby

MIX
Paper from
responsible sources
FSC® C004839
www.fsc.org

Printed and bound by CPI Group (UK) Ltd, Croydon, CR0 4YY

The Matrix

This 1999 science fiction film, written and directed by Larry and Andy Wachowski, depicts a near future in which human beings have become docile collaborators in their own exploitation. People are living in a seeming idyll, with all their wants and needs being satisfied. However, this turns out to be an illusion created by a sophisticated computer simulation called the Matrix; in reality they are being used by intelligent machines as a source of energy and sustenance. Things get interesting when a few people come to recognize that all around them is not as it seems, and start rebelling against the Matrix.

We too are living in a Matrix; one created by the power of corporate marketing. We too should learn to question and critique what is around us; we too should learn to rebel.

CONTENTS

FIGURES

TABLES

BOXES

FOREWORD

Why the matrix matters

Steve Connor

SCIENCE CORRESPONDENT – *THE INDEPENDENT*

In the early 1900s, when Sigmund Freud was finalizing his seminal theories on psychology, Americans typically ate a light breakfast of coffee, fruit juice and toast or a roll. Within thirty years, they were hooked on the idea of the 'All–American Breakfast' of bacon and eggs. Curiously, Freud's theories about people's innermost fears and desires had played a role in this gastronomic and cultural transformation. The near-universal popularity of bacon and eggs as the first meal of the day owes much to Freud's nephew, Edward Bernays, a pioneer of the public relations industry. It was Bernays – the father of spin – who was probably the first to understand the power of applying Freud's radical ideas about the human mind to business, and he did it by introducing his version of the scientific method. In the process he helped lay the foundation of the marketing matrix.

Although Bernays was brought up in the United States, he had spent his boyhood summers with his uncle in Austria and had eagerly imbibed the Freudian Zeitgeist of the time. Freud essentially believed that we were not always the independent, rational beings we like to think we are, but were subject to the deep, hidden urges of our subconscious mind which can influence the conscious decisions we make. Bernays had remembered his uncle's ideas when in the 1920s he became a young executive in the embryonic public relations business. He was faced with the problem of how to boost the sales of bacon, the main product of his client the Beech-Nut Packing Company of New York. He had to somehow persuade the American public to change their eating habits and so set about applying Freud's theories in what would become one of the best examples of early 'scientific' marketing.

Bernays first approached a friendly doctor about whether a 'light breakfast' or a 'hearty breakfast' is best for the human physiology. He asked a series of simple but leading questions, such as: does the human body expend energy in the night and does it need energy during the day? As a scientist, the doctor reasonably concluded that the body loses energy during the night and so it is better to start the day with a calorie-packed, heavy breakfast. Bernays then asked the doctor to write to 5,000 other doctors and see whether they concurred with his opinion. The doctor duly wrote the letter to his colleagues and received some 4,500 replies. The answer was unequivocal: a majority of American doctors believed a heavy breakfast was good for you.

Bernays then went public with the 'news'. Although the questionnaire to the 5,000 doctors did not specify the precise menu of the heavy breakfast, it didn't take long for some newspapers to assume that it meant a cooked breakfast of bacon and eggs. Within weeks, the sales of bacon shot up and the Beech-Nut Packing Company was making a handsome profit from its main product. Meanwhile, the American public had been convinced, with the ringing endorsement of the medical establishment, that a hearty breakfast of fried bacon and eggs was actually good for their health.

We live in an age of sophisticated marketing campaigns which owe much to this early exponent of the genre. As a science journalist I have over the years witnessed frequent examples of attempts to manipulate public opinion with the help of clever marketing gimmicks, whether it is the scientific evidence showing that chocolate is good for you (funded by the confectionery business), or the contrived mathematical formula for a perfect cup of tea (paid by the beverage industry). And as the marketing gets ever more sophisticated, then so do the dangers associated with the unregulated free market.

As I write this, in the spring of 2012, yesterday's newspaper tells me that the Academy of Royal Medical Colleges has warned the UK Government that it is failing to tackle the growing obesity epidemic because of its vacillation over irresponsible marketing by the junk-food industry. Why, for instance, have McDonald's and Coca-Cola, which have done more than most to foster today's calorie-rich, obesogenic environment, been allowed to sponsor the 2012 London Olympics? Deeper inside my newspaper there is a story about the Government's forthcoming consultation on plain packaging for cigarettes, which the tobacco industry is opposing with all its commercial might despite the fact that plain packs have wide public support.

When it comes to protecting their market, tobacco companies have shown themselves to be aggressive and litigious. I have myself experienced the chilling effect that Big Tobacco can have on the freedom of academics and journalists to delve into the cigarette business. In 2011 *The Independent* published a series of articles about how tobacco firms were using the UK's Freedom of Information laws to access academic records of confidential interviews with teenagers about their attitudes to smoking. Most subjects in science journalism are not of much interest to newspaper legal departments, but, as I soon discovered, unflattering stories about the antics of the tobacco industry most definitely are.

Modern marketing is no longer just about persuading people to buy things they never knew they needed. It is about understanding and manipulating the deeper fears and desires of the human mind, about protecting market share, lobbying governments and defending against restrictions and regulation. It pervades every sphere of life. This is why we need to understand the marketing matrix, and there is no better place to start than with this book.

London, April 2012

Perennial Monsters

Some of the owner men were kind because they hated what they had to do, and some of them were angry because they hated to be cruel, and some of them were cold because they had long ago found that one could not be an owner unless one were cold. And all of them were caught in something larger than themselves. Some of them hated the mathematics that drove them, and some were afraid, and some worshipped the mathematics because it provided refuge from thought and from feeling. If a bank or a finance company owned the land, the owner man said, The Bank – or the Company – needs – wants – insists – must have – as though the Bank or the Company were a monster, with thought and feeling, which had ensnared them. These last would take no responsibility for the banks or companies because they were men and slaves, while the banks were machines and masters all at the same time. Some of the owner men were a little proud to be slaves to such cold and powerful masters.

John Steinbeck (1939)[1]

We have unleashed a monster that no one can control, even that minority that profits from it. Unashamed self-interest is a vice, not a virtue. We must recognise that the usefulness of an activity is not necessarily measured by its profitability, and that what someone earns is not an indicator of their talents and abilities, still less of their moral stature.

Michael Thomas, Professor of Marketing (1999)[2]

PREFACE

Power and manipulation

This book is not an attack on business; on the contrary it respects and applauds business. It is an attack on power and manipulation: the power that business acquires when it gets too big; and the manipulation modern marketing makes possible. When a supermarket chain attains such dominance that it covers every corner of a country the size of the UK, threatens farmers' livelihoods with its procurement practices, undercuts local shops and bullies planners into submission, it becomes reasonable to ask: does every little really help? Once the 100 billionth burger has been flipped and yet another trouser button popped it is sensible to wonder: are we still lovin' it? As the planet heats up in response to our ever increasing and utterly unsustainable levels of consumption, it is fair to question: are we really worth it?

This book raises these and many more questions about the use by the corporate sector of the powerful and ubiquitous behaviour change tools of modern marketing; what I have termed 'the marketing matrix'. Given the impact that our consumption behaviour has on ourselves, our fellow human beings and our planet it argues that there is a need for much greater vigilance. In the seventy years since Steinbeck castigated the banks for their treatment of Dust Bowl farmers, and the fifty since Eisenhower warned us of the growing power of the military industrial complex, things have got steadily worse. Corporations have grown ever bigger, transcending national boundaries and dwarfing regulatory institutions. In one sense this is unsurprising: as many commentators, from Joel Bakan to Naomi Klein, have noted, a ruthless regard for the shareholder, corporate wealth and the bottom line is written into corporate DNA, and this in turn makes continuous growth a necessity.

What is surprising is that we have all remained so unruffled about this catastrophic state of affairs. As boardroom salaries rocket, companies outgrow countries and these largely undemocratic organizations become some of the most powerful on the planet, we have remained remarkably quiescent. In recent times, the financial crisis and the obvious outrages perpetrated by financial institutions have generated some protests – Occupy is a welcome case in point – but given the transgressions of corporate capitalism they are not nearly as widespread as might be expected. Also, vociferous and refreshing though Occupy might be, remember that each day that protesters camped out in Wall Street or in front of St Paul's, Tesco was turning over around 268 million dollars, McDonald's 65 million and L'Oréal 72 million.[3] Meanwhile the much reviled Royal Bank of Scotland has 40 million customers (that's several million more than the population of Canada).

Such is the success of the marketing matrix in selling the depredations of the 1 per cent to us, the 99 per cent, that we don't just fail to protest; we continually give them our money, and with it massive power.

If, for example, an unelected government were to kill millions of people there would be an outcry, UN resolutions and serious talk of military intervention; yet the world's five big tobacco companies have been doing this for half a century and no one talks of invading Philip Morris International or arraigning the CEO of British American Tobacco in The Hague. On the contrary, we show them tolerance and treat them as civilized entities. We live comfortably with their brands in our corner shops where our kids spend their pocket money; we are accepting of the reality that these same children, our children, will deliver up the next generation of smokers for them to exploit; we make no demur as they continue to make massive profits from addicting and killing those who are credulous enough to fall into their clutches.

Now if we pan out and think not just of the harm that the consumption of tobacco products does to smokers' lungs, but the harm that the consumption of all products is doing to the planet, the full import of corporate power becomes clear.

The secret of this corporate impunity is the remorseless – yet soft – power of the marketing matrix. We are won over by the faux charm of witty ads, seductive bargains, captivating ubiquity and an Aladdin's cave of choice – all wrapped up in the opiate of the brand. We buy their products, however damaging they might be to us or our planet; we buy their empty rhetoric of consumer sovereignty. And, because corporate marketers recognize that context matters, our political leaders are also seduced by glitzy Corporate Social Responsibility and Cause-Related Marketing campaigns, the easy option of voluntary codes and the attraction of being associated with those same evocative brands. Meanwhile, statutory regulation and proper corporate accountability are quietly forgotten. More prosaically, our leaders are all too often wrong-footed and pre-empted by the single-minded focus, massive resources and sheer nerve of the corporate marketer – who then turns on the charm to magic away any unease.

It brings to mind a scene from *Watership Down*, Richard Adams' parable about a community of rabbits forced by developers to find a new place to live. At one point the homeless rabbits arrive at an attractive warren with plentiful supplies of fresh food – lettuces, carrots, parsnips appear near their holes every morning seemingly by benign magic. The new arrivals feel in their water that something is wrong, but cannot work out what it is; the current inhabitants are close-lipped. Then it emerges that the food is being left by men, to tempt the rabbits into their snares.

For us too something is badly wrong and we have to start looking beyond the tempting offerings and heeding what are now time-honoured warnings. We already know that consumption does not bring satisfaction and material possessions do not deliver happiness, even without the countless studies proving this to be so. We know our lifestyles are foolishly unsustainable. But we keep on walking into the corporate marketers' snares and carry on shopping. It is time to fight back against the marketing matrix.

Fighting back

To find solutions, we have to look both internally and externally. First, it is necessary to examine our own behaviour and question why we consume so much; why we persistently fall for the tricks of modern marketing; and why we use the one remaining power many of us have – our purchasing power – with such profligacy and lack of thought. So *caveat emptor*, let the buyer beware, but not in the traditional sense of looking after our own interests, which for most of us in the rich countries are already being all too well met, but in the interests of our fellow human beings, our species and our planet. This will take resolve and determination – the marketing matrix perpetually pushes us to stay in our role of passive, spoilt consumers – but, as we will see, there is ample evidence that we have more than enough strength to resist.

Nonetheless we also need to recognize the power that marketing has and respond in two complementary ways. First, as some 'social marketers' have begun to realize, a discipline focused on behaviour change has the potential to do much good. Most human problems can be traced back to our behaviour – eating, exercise and substance use are the three pillars of public health. Just persuading smokers to stop killing themselves would save millions from a premature demise. More broadly our respect for the law, treatment of other people and contribution to the commonweal are all major determinants of social welfare. From self-harm, through intolerance to full-on violence, how we behave collectively defines the line between a society's success and failure. If marketing can really influence behaviour (and commerce shows all too well it can) we should invest in it properly – not to enrich already wealthy shareholders and CEOs, but to make the world a better place.

This social marketing, however, will surely fail if it becomes a top-down attempt at social engineering; a sort of well-intentioned version of the corporate marketing matrix. Rather it should harness the traditional wisdom of ordinary people and our innate capacity to improve our own lot. Both Steinbeck and Eisenhower recognized that salvation resides at a grassroots level; so should we. Indeed marketing itself can be seen as part of this traditional wisdom; in its purest form it is all about doing the deals that enable human cooperation – which depend on reciprocation and mutual understanding. Corporations did not invent it; they just co-opted and corrupted it.

But all the social marketing in the world will get nowhere until we tackle the excesses of the marketing matrix which underpins corporate power and drives our unsustainable lifestyles. This matrix has to be re-engineered so that instead of incessantly boosting sales, it deliberately reduces them, and actively encourages responsible – that is ethical and sustainable – consumption. This will require statutory measures; the corporation's relationship with the idea of market shrinkage is identical to that of the turkey with Christmas. If I can mix my poultry metaphors a little, the 1 per cent will not like the idea of the 99 per cent gaining control of their golden goose. But ultimately it is in everyone's interest to change course in this way: even the wealthiest merchant banker needs a planet to live on.

These three strands of change – personal reflection, the harnessing and empowerment of existing wisdom through social marketing and the containment and redirection of commercial marketing – will begin a much needed process of transformation. To reach its full potential we have to come together as a species and think through how we want to organize a world that recognizes the vital distinction between being a consumer and being a citizen. The former is an occasional necessity in a complex post-industrial world, the latter is a birthright in a civilized world – and maintaining the distinction is essential if we are ever to realize a sustainable world.

ACKNOWLEDGEMENTS

I have to thank many people for their help. To my good friends Alastair, Andy, Barry, Ian, Iain, Jim, Mark, Mary, Ray, Renata, Robert and Rémi who read drafts and gave invaluable comments, many of which have greatly improved the quality of this volume; to my colleagues Aileen and Kathryn, for vital technical support; to Diane who has, time and again, gone the extra mile in offering help, making suggestions and road-testing the text; to Sarah, my wife, who has been there throughout discussing the ideas, strengthening the arguments and tackling that most important but tedious of tasks, tracking down the sources and sorting the referencing; and to Xavier, who at four years of age is much the youngest contributor, but who provided an irrefutable reminder that a better future is well worth the struggle.

I also want to thank all of the people – friends and strangers – with whom I have discussed the issues examined in the book at every opportunity – on trains, in cafés, at work – even on one occasion while waiting to see the dentist. Everyone I spoke to was supportive; they all gave me encouragement; to a man and a woman they agreed that the status quo is untenable and that somehow we have to get off the consumption treadmill.

Finally, like many before me, I have stood on the shoulders of giants. Three in particular I would mention: John Steinbeck, who reminded me that polemic has an honourable literary tradition; Aldous Huxley, who elegantly parses the difference between religion and spirituality, showing that whilst the former is optional, the latter is an essential dimension of any fulfilled human life; and finally Fritz Schumacher, who provided a powerful critique of our way of life a generation ago and, just as importantly, began the process of offering an alternative vision.

Without the help of all these people this book would not have happened. Thank you.

The work of John Steinbeck has been reproduced by permission of Penguin Books Ltd.

Brave New World by Aldous Huxley is published by Vintage Books and reproduced by permission of The Random house Group Limited.

PART I
Out of control

The Lifeboat

It was just over half an hour since the passenger ship had gone down and the eight strangers found themselves shocked but safe in a lifeboat. Their condition was better than might be expected, after all the boat was designed for fourteen, so they had plenty of blankets and supplies to go round. Then someone noticed that there were still people clinging to wreckage near where the ship had sunk and suggested they row over to pick them up. This caused a lively debate. It was pointed out that, whilst this would certainly be a nice thing to do, it would make things more difficult and dangerous for them all. At the moment they were warm and well catered for, but if others got into the boat there would be less to go round. And if there were a lot of newcomers they might even swamp the boat. After some toing and froing it was decided to keep well away from the other survivors and concentrate on enjoying the energy dense biscuits and really rather good medicinal rum.[1]

1

THE SOFT POWER OF MARKETING

Power

Business is an important and valuable part of our society, but like most human endeavours it runs into a dangerous territory when it gets too powerful. This chapter starts by discussing the benefits of business, but then goes on to consider its downsides. It shows that these have been recognized and warned of for many decades and, despite the inclination to identify villains when things go obviously and badly wrong – as in the recent banking crisis – the problems are systemic not individual. Most notably, the corporation, with its separation between ownership and executive decision making, and the compensatory duty to put shareholders' interests above all others, has generated particular concern. The problems are so serious that the corporation has even been diagnosed as psychopathic.

This begs the question why so little has been done to treat this psychosis. This reticence can be explained by the soft power of modern marketing to charm and please us. It seems churlish to criticize a business approach that presents itself as the consumer's champion; looking after our interests and making sure our every whim is addressed. But the realities of shareholder focused corporations give the lie to this comforting myth. From this perspective the many skills and tactics of the marketer begin to look sinister rather than endearing.

There is a consequent need for vigilance, and for both internal and external reflection to find a way forward.

Size matters

The ability to do business is one of the things that separates us from the other animals. Barter, trade and the doing of deals is at the core of our capacity to operate collectively. This cooperation is also essential for our survival. We cannot possibly cater for all our worldly needs without the help of others, so we need a way of harnessing this help. Friends and family may well contribute voluntarily, but in a complex world their efforts will not suffice: strangers have to be brought into the equation. Business provides a mechanism for doing this.

Michael, the greengrocer in my Scottish hometown, epitomizes the benefits of business. He provides a good range of the foods we need – from apples to zucchini – and, if asked, will happily try and source items he doesn't normally stock. His prices are competitive, although most people would probably guess (incorrectly) that he charges more than the local supermarket. Michael also provides a pleasant service, expertly modulated to his customers. The dowager ladies from up the hill get the personal touch and their bags packed, the children are handled with kindness and respect and those customers who show a taste for it get a fine line in Scots wit and repartee. He even offers a home delivery service. Michael's business acumen is matched only by his unerring diplomacy: he never risks offending his customers. His adroit fencing of the inevitable anti-English jokes (many of his best customers come from south of the Tweed) is a joy to behold. When he retires from the shop, a job at the United Nations beckons.

What is more, Michael has succeeded in moving across the commercial border and becoming a real friend. He surely likes what we do for his bottom line, but he also genuinely likes us – and we him. Being his customer not only keeps our store cupboard well stocked, it warms the cockles.

Contrast this small town bliss with another Scottish business: the Royal Bank of Scotland. Superlatives and invective have been worn out describing the harm Fred Goodwin and his colleagues caused. Fred Goodwin was CEO of RBS and his calamitous leadership epitomizes the worst of the 2008 financial crisis: macho management, hubris and greed. His crude attempts to destroy evidence about the mistakes made on his watch earned him the sobriquet 'Fred the Shred'. Cupidity and insane excess brought the bank to the brink of ruin – and came close to taking the whole country with it. It is tempting to see this as an anomaly, driven by particularly toxic business models in a temporarily out of control financial sector.

Neither comfort blanket survives closer inspection, however; the problem is neither new nor a one-off. Steinbeck wrestled with exactly the same issues back in 1939 when writing about the predations of the banks on Dust Bowl farmers. He characterized the bank as a monster which 'needs – wants – insists – must have':

> those creatures don't breathe air, don't eat side-meat. They breathe profits; they eat the interest on money. If they don't get it, they die the way you die without air, without side-meat. It is a sad thing, but it is so. It is just so.[2]

Systemic flaws

It is painful to admit it, but the problem here is not Fred Goodwin's greed (palpable though this remains), any more than the solution is somehow moored in Michael the greengrocer's good nature. The problem is systemic. As Steinbeck suggests, individuals just get 'ensnared' – some more willingly than others. And here the monster analogy breaks down; it personalizes the situation too much. Banks are not creatures at all; they do not have feelings or thoughts; they are institutions with rules and operating procedures. They are governed by these rules, just as climate is governed by the rules of nature. Complaining that a bank puts profit before people is like criticizing a dog for chasing the butcher's van. It is just what they both do.

However the dog and the company differ in the size of their appetites. The dog will be single-minded in the pursuit of food and if necessary will fight hard to get it; but it also has its limits. It will eat until it is full (or in the case of my friend's dog, sick), then stop. A finance company has no such delicacy: 'the bank – the monster has to have profits all the time. It can't wait. It'll die. … When the monster stops growing, it dies. It can't stay one size.'[3] It brooks no limits. Steinbeck is not attacking business any more than this book is; after all his sharecroppers were business people. They too had to turn a profit; indeed it is their failure to do so that has got them into the parlous position described in *The Grapes of Wrath*. He is simply showing what happens when business gets too big and ownership becomes separated from real lives. He is introducing us to the realities of the modern corporation – whether in the finance or any other sector.

The essence of the corporation is that executive decision making is separated from ownership: CEOs spend other people's – shareholders' – money. Because of this, very strict rules are put in place by government to make sure that shareholders' interests (and therefore profits) always come first. This 'fiduciary imperative' ensures that the focus never leaves the bottom line. Even the excessive levels of bonuses and executive pay that we have witnessed in recent years are justified in terms of shareholder returns: 'it's the only way we can get and keep the best people'.

This does not mean that everything corporations do is wrong; they do, for example, bring employment, promulgate safe working practices, stimulate infrastructure development, warn their customers about faulty products, improve food hygiene and support good causes. The key point, though, is that they do these things either because they are compulsory (e.g. providing safety gear in factories or obeying food hygiene laws), where not doing so would harm their brands (witness Nike's sensitivities about sweat shops) – or where the costs are outweighed by the business benefits that result. In other words they do them because they are good for profits as well as the rest of us. And when there is a conflict, the former will always win out. Always.

On the psychiatrist's couch

This is what leads Joel Bakan to diagnose the psychopathy of corporations.[4] This may seem like a harsh judgement, but certainly when things go wrong it is difficult to disagree. When, for example, Ford hid the fault on its rather too hastily launched Pinto model which caused the petrol tank to explode in an entirely predictable way, and a leaked memo showed that management had reasoned that it was cheaper to pay what the lawyers estimated to be the likely damages than re-engineer the car. They even calculated a cost per death figure. Or when inadequate maintenance led Union Carbide's chemical plant to leak massive quantities of lethal methyl isocyanate into a heavily populated suburb of Bhopal killing 8,000 people and exposing up to half a million others to the toxic gas and the resulting congenital illnesses, deformities and lingering death. A quarter of a century later, Union Carbide is now the wholly owned subsidiary of another corporation, Dow Chemicals, but the poisoning continues. Chemicals at the aging plant, which has now been offloaded on the public sector, are still leaching into the drinking water of 30,000 local people.

In such cases criminal selfishness seems to be a fair assessment.

However psychopaths are not always that obvious. A paper in *Scientific American* explains how, because they are 'superficially charming, psychopaths tend to make a good first impression on others and often strike observers as remarkably normal'.[5] As we will see, corporate marketers are very good at 'superficial charm' so we have to be alert. Nonetheless it is fairly easy to spot psychopathic symptoms in specific industries.

The tobacco industry has for decades knowingly sold a product that kills one in two of those customers who do not manage to quit. It gets them young – in the US for instance 88 per cent of smokers start as children – and then, thanks to nicotine, holds on to all too many. We all know this: just think how daft it would be to push an adult non-smoker into trying a cigarette, as you might if he or she refused a chocolate – 'go on, these are really tasty... it's a new menthol flavour ... you know you want to ... '. We all just take it for granted that adults do not start smoking; that smoking is a paediatric epidemic. In the UK at least, people are gradually prising themselves free from tobacco, but 100,000 Britons still die needlessly early every year – and tobacco companies continue to do all they can to encourage them to continue doing so. And in the rest of the world – especially poor countries with few tobacco control policies – Big Tobacco continues to ride roughshod. The World Health Organization (WHO) estimates that tobacco will be killing more than eight million people a year by 2030.[6]

Then there is the beverage alcohol industry. WHO estimates that alcohol kills 320,000 young people (aged 15–29) every year and is responsible for 4 per cent of all deaths – even in a world where the majority of adults are teetotal.[7] Add to this drink driving, domestic violence and crime (most of which in 'wet' countries like the UK and the US is drink fuelled). The point is not that all of the problems of alcohol use can be laid at the industry's feet; humans were getting drunk for millennia before Diageo or Miller Brewing came into existence. It's just that the corporation, with its compulsion to grow and feed its shareholders, jet-fuels the process. It is permanently programmed to put the business case before the social cost. How, for example, could alcopops – the unholy cross-breeding of a children's soda with a powerful narcotic – ever be deemed the product of a socially responsible company? Or toffee flavoured vodka? Or lemon meringue shots?

Or indeed, given our collective weight problem, a burger that gives you half your daily salt, sugar and calorie intake all in one go (even before you count in the fries and the shake)? Given that over a third of Americans are now not just overweight but clinically obese, at an estimated medical cost of $168 billion[8] a year, space in the psychiatrist's consulting room also has to be found for fast food companies. Again, not that the world's expanding girth is all their fault – increasingly sedentary lifestyles are, for instance, partly to blame. But given the problem, the largely untrammelled existence of organizations whose *raison d'être* is to sell ever more fat, salt and sugar to the exclusion of all other priorities seems, at best, perverse.

And we haven't yet considered the arms industry. Remember that one of the reasons the US and UK governments were so convinced that Saddam Hussein had contraband armaments was because he had been supplied by American and British arms manufacturers in the first place. Half a century ago a Republican president and former soldier, Dwight D. Eisenhower, warned the world of the growing power of what he evocatively labelled the 'military industrial complex'.[9] He saw its 'unwarranted influence – economic, political, even spiritual' – being 'felt in every city, every Statehouse, every office of the Federal government', warning that 'we must not fail to comprehend its grave implications. Our toil, resources, and livelihood are all involved. So is the very structure of our society.'

His words were prophetic: think Blackwater, Halliburton and Bechtel in Iraq – and they also have traction way beyond the arms industry. He warned against the lure of a 'miraculous solution to all current difficulties' – from international relations to the farmyard. He used the term 'balance' no fewer than ten times in the fifteen minute address, calling for

> the need to maintain balance in and among national programs, balance between the private and the public economy, balance between the cost and hoped for advantages, balance between the clearly necessary and the comfortably desirable, balance between our essential requirements as a nation and the duties imposed by the nation upon the individual, balance between actions of the moment and the national welfare of the future.

His final words bring us to ecology and harm to the environment. Again there are obvious manifestations of the problem: the Mexican Gulf oil spill, the North Pacific 'trash vortex' (an island of discarded plastic the size of Texas), the proliferation of SUVs. In each case, shareholder interests have, one way or another, come before wider communal ones. But Eisenhower's speech takes us way beyond individual malefactors: he is raising the much broader concern of the toll on our eco-system of the spiralling consumption which infinite corporate growth inevitably demands. Again he does not mince his words: 'We cannot mortgage the material assets of our grandchildren without risking the loss also of their political and spiritual heritage. We want democracy to survive for all generations to come, not to become the insolvent phantom of tomorrow.' Even in the early 1960s he could see the power of big business beginning to eat away at the foundations of democracy.

What Eisenhower foresaw is now clear to all but the most blinkered. In writing this book I have talked to many people from all walks of life about these issues. No one, from any point of the political compass, has doubted that we are getting things wrong; that we are consuming too much, working too hard to pay the resulting bills and depleting ourselves and the planet – and usually both – in the process. The spectacular failure of the banks has jolted even the most conservative out of any complacency.

This begs questions about why we let corporations get away with such egregious behaviour. Why didn't we listen to Steinbeck and Eisenhower?

Enter the marketer

In one sense Steinbeck had it easy: the banks of Dust Bowl America were guileless in their predations. He is able to describe in chilling detail the bulldozers crossing the prairies and demolishing the sharecroppers' houses, almost literally pushing the people off the land, even as they prepared it for industrial planting. Modern corporations are just as ruthless in the pursuit of their stockholders' interests, but they are infinitely more subtle, for they have harnessed the astonishing possibilities, the soft power and ubiquity, of the marketing matrix.

At its heart marketing, like business, is an attractive concept. It is about seeing the world through your customers' eyes, so you can better understand and cater for their needs. A perfect illustration of this precept occurred recently in my local pub. My friend Bethany was waiting for her husband, Steve, who was late for their rendezvous. As time passed with no sign of Steve she got crosser, and by the time he arrived she had steam coming out of her ears. I was by the door when he rushed in, looking hunted – he knew he was in trouble. But he had forgotten Mary, the pub landlady, and her acute marketing skills. She had seen what was unfolding and when Steve arrived she drew him across to her at the bar before he could go to his wife. He was anxious to make his domestic peace, but Mary insisted. She then said one simple phrase to him: 'remember, Bethany has had her hair done'. Steve's face relaxed and his eyes smiled in gratitude: Mary had provided his 'get-out-of-jail-free' card. He floated across to Bethany and swept aside her irritation with an unanswerable 'Darling, your hair looks lovely'. Mary is a consummate marketer. She had worked out what her customer needed and provided it just in time. As a publican one might assume that she sells beer; in reality, on this occasion, she was selling marital harmony – but rest assured the beer sales will follow. Her sensitivity and customer focus will result in deep loyalty from Steve (with Bethany also acquiring pleasant associations with her pub); as a result he won't just buy Mary's beer tonight but for weeks and probably years to come.

In Mary's hands marketing is a benign enough approach to business, not because she has a kindly personality (though she has), but because her power is contained. Her resources are limited and there are three other pubs nearby, so we customers have bags of choice. This is a crucial point. Notwithstanding my good retail experiences, small businesses can be far from perfect.

A few years ago BBC television produced an immensely popular comedy series called *Open All Hours*, set in a corner shop, which was built on the running joke of owner Albert Arkwright's proverbial meanness – the finger on the scales, the out of date tins, the short change; week after week. A hundred years ago E. M. Forster quipped of the shopkeeper: 'I complain about the quality of his sultanas and he answers in one breath that they are the best sultanas and how can I expect the best sultanas at that price?'[10] The sitcom and the quip work because we know them to be true.

So it is not, as Schumacher[11] put it, that small is beautiful, but rather that small is relatively harmless because it lacks the power to cause major problems. In the hands of Albert Arkwright marketing is containable. As with business more generally, the problems only emerge when it is practised on an industrial scale and in corporate structures. And for most of us this is the much more familiar face of modern marketing – an approach to business that was in its infancy in Steinbeck's day and barely toddling when Eisenhower gave his farewell address.

The myth of marketing

Business textbooks laud marketing, arguing that it is the driving force, 'the beating heart' of a commercial model built around the sacred concept of consumer sovereignty. They regretfully recall the days of Henry Ford, when demand outstripped supply, and the customer had to suffer under the inflexible maxim 'any colour you want as long as it's black'. Then, after the Second World War, the economic balance changed – supply increased and began to outstrip demand. This might have been a good point at which to rethink the model; after all supply was only outstripping demand in the affluent north – much of the globe ('the majority world') was (and still is) living a life of hardship. An enlightened stance might have been to look for ways of spreading the plenty in the minority world more widely. The lifeboat story at the outset of this chapter is shocking and one is inclined to get very indignant about the disgraceful behaviour of the eight survivors. The story comes from a book on moral philosophy, and the lifeboat is a metaphor for the world. The 1950s, when supply began to outstrip demand in our bit of the globe, marked the time when we in the rich minority countries rowed away from our planetary fellow passengers.

Instead of wrestling with problems of redistribution and inequalities, the emphasis of business simply switched from production to selling: 'faced with stagnant markets and the spectre of price competition, producers sought to stimulate demand through increased selling efforts'.[12] A generation of Willy Lomans[13] stepped up to the plate and the growth of mass advertising gave them enormous reach. Vance Packard famously tore the mask off this world in *The Hidden Persuaders*,[14] uncovering a vast array of in-depth 'psychological' market research methods and correspondingly unscrupulous selling techniques.

But the 'spectre of price competition' remained:

> if all the products are perceived as being the same then price becomes the distinguishing feature and the supplier becomes a price taker, thus having to relinquish the important managerial function of exercising control. Faced with such an impasse the real manager recognizes that salvation (and control) will be achieved through a policy of product differentiation.[15]

The use of the word control is an interesting harbinger of the corporate marketers' relationship with power, which we discuss in more detail in Chapter 8.

The marketers' version of history continues with the decline and fall of this flawed era of high-pressure selling, and the dawn of the enlightened age of marketing. In effect, they pick up where Arthur Miller stops off, not exactly proclaiming the death of the salesman, but arguing that he has been superseded by a far more sophisticated and enlightened modus operandi. Many of us might question this transformation – especially if we have been mis-sold an endowment mortgage, had (yet another) cold call or tried to understand all the software we have somehow bought for our new laptop – and argue that, as with Mark Twain's death, that of the salesman has been exaggerated. Marketers have no such qualms; for them business simply came to see the error of its ways in the glare of their marketing insights and, instead of trying to sell what it produced, inverted the process and began making what it could sell. This has saved them from ruin and transformed dinosaur-like monoliths into responsive handmaidens. All because, the comforting narrative continues, marketing puts the consumer at the apex of the pyramid and focuses the whole business effort – from receptionist to CEO – on the Holy Grail of his or her complete satisfaction. We the consumers are now in charge. From this perspective, marketing begins to seem like an enlightened, almost democratic business model. It is like the scene in Orwell's *Animal Farm* when Boxer and friends throw out the humans and take control of their own lives.

Except that, as we have already noted, the corporate structure gives this the lie – we are not in charge; the shareholder is. And we all know how *Animal Farm* ended.

The reality of marketing

From a worm's eye view, then, notwithstanding its attempts to charm us, corporate marketing is much less appealing. In the first instance it is synonymous with mass media advertising. Although we are all inclined to see ourselves as immune to Madison Avenue's blandishments (anything less would be tantamount to confessing to being a mug) we also know it to be a powerful tool. Industry estimates of a global adspend of $481 billion in 2011[16] suggest the business sector is equally aware of advertising's potential to mould our behaviour. Billboards do dominate our lives, and television ads insert themselves endlessly into our homes, our minds and our hearts. Ronald McDonald and the Marlboro Cowboy have easily outdone the Pied Piper in their seduction of our children. Furthermore these are just the most obvious manifestations of marketing. The commercial, the clown and the cowboy are the visible tip of a beguiling and persuasive iceberg.

Billboards and television ads are combined with a host of other less obvious communications, including sports and arts sponsorship, product placement, merchandising, point of sale display and pack design. The less obviously commercial these platforms are the more persuasive they become. Sponsorship and product placement, for example, are much better at getting under our critical radar. A UK government enquiry[17] into alcohol marketing in 2010 found drinks companies rejoicing in the subtlety of music sponsorship – 'ultimately, the band are the heroes at the venue and Carling should use them to 'piggy back' and engage customers' emotions' – and gloating that 'they [young men] think about 4 things, we brew 1 and sponsor 2 of them'.[18] *Caveat emptor* really does ring hollow if we don't realize we are being sold. And all despite voluntary agreements which clearly state that youth culture, in the UK at least, is a no-go area for booze companies.

These real world communications platforms have recently been joined by a plethora of virtual ones: pop-ups, websites, viral campaigns and social networking sites and mobile media all provide additional ways for brands to interpolate themselves into our lives. In 2011, for instance, Diageo announced a multimillion dollar deal to link forces with Facebook. Kathy Parker, Diageo's senior vice-president of global marketing and innovation summed up the strategy as follows:

> Facebook are working with us to make sure that we are not only fan collecting but that they are actively engaged and driving advocacy for our brands. We are looking for increases in customer engagement and increases in sales and [market] share.[19]

That's right, the company isn't satisfied with selling its products to young people, it wants them to sell booze to each other – to become brand advocates – with, as the press release adds, a particular interest in developing countries.

The *Invasion of the Body Snatchers* has been remade once again: this time as a marketing communications strategy.

This mix of marketing communications is nested within the rest of the marketing effort of product design, distribution and pricing, with the combined aim of making us offers that are as attractive, ubiquitous and affordable (or exclusive) as possible. So young and old are perpetually tempted to try, and continue consuming, an appealing array of beautifully packaged, displayed and promoted products. If the mafia gives us an offer we can't refuse, the marketer gives us one we can't resist. This effort has been strategically and coherently deployed for many years (Coke, Ford and Lucky Strike are, for instance, each over a hundred years old and the ageless Ronald McD is on his fourth generation of children) and the physical offering is developed into a much broader and emotionally satisfying brand. Hence a bit of dried leaf in a paper tube or a plastic bottle of brown sugar water becomes an evocative lifestyle choice and a powerful statement of identity – and the alchemists' dream of turning base ingredients into gold is fulfilled.

Relationships from hell

So time has become a crucial dimension in all this. Marketers have long since moved on from the ad hockery of mere transactions. They don't just want us to buy things once, they want us to do so again and again – continually (or ideally continuously). If I buy one Kit Kat, Nestlé makes a few pence; if I buy one a day for forty years those pence turn into a significant number of pounds, and if I can be persuaded to do the same for my family ... well, the pot overflows. Then there is the possibility that I will like Kit Kat so much I will be attracted to larger bars or other Nestlé chocolates (or indeed other Nestlé products) – in marketing parlance the opportunity is there to 'up sell' and 'cross sell'.

Market research also shows that it is much easier (not to say cheaper) to hang on to existing customers than perpetually win new ones. Loyalty programmes – club cards, airmiles, reward schemes and the like – are the result. It also makes sense to get to know your customers really well; the algorithms that enable Amazon to make uncannily appropriate suggestions to you about additional purchases are the latest manifestation of this. Even mistakes become an opportunity – you can apologize and get to know your customer a bit better in the process. Dissatisfied customers certainly whinge a lot, but satisfied ones will tell their friends and family of your qualities and that is invaluable public relations. You know a billboard is out to sell you, and that a company is in it for the money – but your brother or best mate you trust. They have what the corporate marketer calls great 'source credibility'.

The chilling reality behind Diageo's deal with Facebook is that it enables a massive corporate body, selling an age-restricted drug that causes extensive, well-documented harm, to masquerade as a friend. Social networking is supposed to be about exactly that – getting to know people, connecting with your friends, finding romance. In reality it is just a corporation providing, for a fee, a camouflaged channel for another corporation to sell us their products and services. And remember, camouflage really works. The less we know we are being sold, the less we are on our guard.

For the corporate marketer this isn't a matter of acquisitiveness on the part of Nestlé, let alone anything as grubby as greed. No, this is about relationships: they want to become our friends and confidants. The concept of relationship marketing has swept away all previous marketing paradigms in the business literature over recent decades.

From a consumer's point of view, there are many upsides to this. We do get an enormous range of products to choose from, these are honed to match our preferences as far as is humanly possible, mistakes are rectified, customer service is increasingly obliging. In material terms, assuming you have the money, life is good. It seems like we have all moved to the Sugar Rock Candy Mountain, albeit a newly commercialized one.

Unfortunately the dream founders on a different rock: that of corporate reality. Nestlé, along with any other corporation, is only interested in us in so far as this interest benefits its shareholders. You don't really need to think any further than its disreputable record in the infant formula business to realize that this has the makings of a relationship from hell. Similarly, a tobacco company like Philip Morris International really gets marketing: its Marlboro brand is a global leader, the red chevron has become iconic and it commands remarkable brand fealty (you can't blame the nicotine – though it is the ultimate loyalty scheme – because PMI competitors all benefit from this as well). And yet, along with its competitors, it kills one in two of its most loyal customers.

The problem is that corporate marketers only pretend to be our friends. Marketing relationships are a parody of the real thing. Like that of a courtesan they are built on the pocketbook, not genuine attraction. If you are in any doubt about this, try ringing your bank and saying you are a bit short of cash so could they let you off this month's mortgage payment. A real friend would say yes. If you are lucky your bank will say 'it'll cost you' (though, if you are deemed to be a good bet, they may well say it in a more roundabout way).

Back to the system

Even now, the marketers' work is not complete. They have read John Donne and understand that no man (or woman) is an island and that social context has a big impact on the individual. They therefore put just as much effort into influencing the behaviour of stakeholders, policy makers and power brokers as they do into shaping ours. In this case, though, the aim isn't to push consumption directly, but to encourage pro-business policy and boost corporate image – and thereby push it indirectly.

At the heart of this stakeholder marketing are two core tools. The first is 'Cause-Related Marketing', where corporate marketers select good causes to support and then tell the world about their seeming generosity. These causes are invariably heart-warming, whether it be computers for British school children or indigenous rights in Central America, but they are chosen on strictly business grounds. The primary purpose is not to help the less well-off but to make the company look good.

The second tool is 'Corporate Social Responsibility' which adds in a strategic dimension. As well as supporting self-evidently good causes companies undertake to behave well on sustainability for instance, or human rights. Once again it looks impressive, but the purpose is self-serving; as Christian Aid put it in a highly critical report:

> corporate enthusiasm for CSR is not driven primarily by a desire to improve the lot of the communities in which companies work. Rather, companies are concerned with their own reputations, with the potential damage of public campaigns directed against them, and overwhelmingly, with the desire – and the imperative – to secure ever greater profits.[20]

Ultimately, as we will discuss in Chapter 8, this is not about behaving well or doing good, but fending off regulation, currying favour and cosying up to power.

In this way the corporate marketer recruits not just consumers, but the system to its cause. That's the same system that in a democracy is supposed to be at the beck and call of voters, not CEOs and shareholders.

Solutions

It is always easier to find fault than provide solutions. However there are useful indications of the route ahead, which have been pointed out to us frequently not just over the last century but for millennia. First of all we must dispel the miasma of corporate marketing and, in the words of the Chinese general Sun Tzu, get to know both ourselves and our enemies much better. That, he tells us, will make it possible to 'fight a hundred battles without disaster'. [21]

Knowing ourselves

Marketing has been with us forever. Michael the greengrocer and Mary the publican have been making a living for thousands of years by the simple and essentially benign process of working out what people need and selling it to them. This can, of course, be subverted by the unscrupulous – we have all been overcharged on occasion, or been sold the proverbial pig in a poke. But such behaviour is self-limiting in a competitive environment – we will only buy the fake pig once.

The real problems only begin when marketing is harnessed to big business – and especially the corporation. It injects 'superficial charm' into power, providing the mask that gives capitalism its acceptable face. It is this charm that has blinded us to the burgeoning problems that inevitably result from unbridled growth: the continued consumption of harmful goods and the over-consumption of all goods.

The first crucial step to finding a solution is to tear off this mask and look critically at what lies behind it. Eisenhower argued that 'only an alert and knowledgeable citizenry can compel the proper meshing of the huge industrial and military machinery of defence with our peaceful methods and goals, so that security and liberty may prosper together'.[22] Steinbeck's tenant farmer expressed the same point in simpler language: 'We all got to figure. There's some way to stop this. It's not like lightning or earthquakes. We've got a bad thing made by men, and by God that's something we can change.'[23]

Both injunctions carry with them the need for us to examine our own behaviour and use one of our few remaining powers – our purchasing power – much more effectively. We should indeed invoke *caveat emptor*, but not as is traditionally meant, to look after our own interests; instead we should use it to consider the wider implications behind everything we buy. If it's cheap, does that mean someone has been short-changed or some animal maltreated in the supply chain? (It almost certainly does.) If it's far-flung, how has it got to us? Who is selling it? Do they deserve our business (however good the deal)? And likewise who made it, do they deserve our money? Most fundamentally, do we really need to make the purchase at all? Is it worth the carbon it will inevitably cost?

Chapter 9 will take this thinking a little further.

The gentle herbivores of social marketing

Twenty years ago we had a conference at my then University of Strathclyde in Glasgow. We were lucky enough to attract a star from the marketing firmament, Philip Kotler, as keynote speaker – who generously donated his time. Indeed, truth be told, we organized the whole event around him. He pulled in a massive crowd and gave a delightful explication of the concepts of social marketing, a term he had coined some twenty years previously.

I still remember the story with which he opened his talk. He told of how, when he first began exploring the idea of using methods that business had devised to influence consumption behaviour to address other sorts of human activity such as safer sexual practices or exercise, he submitted a paper on it to a conference. The paper was accepted but the novelty of his subject meant that only one person turned up to hear his talk. He quelled an initial impulse to quietly creep away, and decided one person was still an audience and he owed it him to present as if the room was packed. He duly did, the audience was attentive – and even asked a couple of polite questions. Our keynote speaker then began packing away his papers and heading off. 'Oh you can't leave,' said his audience, 'I'm the next speaker.'

Perhaps it was this story that led Steve McGrail, the journalist who was covering the event, to call social marketers the 'gentle herbivores' of marketing. Or perhaps it was the resonant notion that the service ideals of Michael the greengrocer and the people skills of Mary the landlady – which patently made life better as well as benefiting Michael and Mary – could make a contribution beyond the marketplace. And when you add to this the thought we explored in the Preface, that so much human suffering can be put down to our behaviour, the potential is as impressive as any diplodocus.

A key proviso though, is that this benign version of marketing must build on the insights of Eisenhower's alert and knowledgeable citizenry and Steinbeck's sharecropper, as well as the time-honoured wisdom of Michael and Mary. This cannot be about one group of people (however well-meaning) doing things to another group of people (however deserving); it has to be about partnership, mutual respect and joint working.

We will revisit our diplodocus in Chapter 10.

Controlling marketing

Our diplodocus will have little chance, however, unless we start to tame the tyrannosaurus of corporate marketing. In the early days of the industrial revolution workplace accidents were a commonplace because people did not appreciate or attempt to contain what rapidly became obvious risks. Given that, in the hands of the food, drink and tobacco corporations marketing kills children and in the hands of all the other corporations it is killing the planet, it is surely time we had an equally strict health and safety regime in place.

These three strands of internal reflection, grassroots mobilization and taming the tyrannosaurus will not solve all our problems, but they do provide a starting point. Further progress will depend on us all coming together and engaging in an intelligent debate about how we should rethink our lives. In New Zealand the Maori have a tradition called the *Hui*, where the community comes together to discuss impending threats and potential opportunities; the world now needs a *Hui* to respond to the threat of over-consumption and the opportunity of post-industrial plenty.

There will be more of this in Chapter 11.

Back to the jungle

This chapter began by noting that it is the ability to do business that separates us from the other animals because it helps organize and facilitate our collective welfare. This good is now threatened by the sheer size of big business, especially in its corporate manifestation, and the power it is able to wield through the ingenuity of modern marketing. Paradoxically then, business may separate us from the other animals but unless we take radical action it will rapidly return us to the jungle – if our marketing-driven rush to consume hasn't led us to chop it all down first.

The Dream

1. I had a dream the other night
    Of a special court of law
    The corporations' CEOs
    Were pleading one and all
    That they'd seen the error of their ways
    And they would sin no more

2. First up before the jury
    Big Tobacco craved 'we rue
    Addicting all those children
    And then killing one in two
    So smokers send your invoice in
    We'll make it up to you'

3. Contrition is contagious
    And Dow has caught a dose
    They're fessing up for Bhopal
    And all their dealings gross
    Now the villagers are cheering
    But investors look morose

4. And who is this now in the dock
    But the lovely BAE
    They say they've made too many guns
    And WMDs
    So they're going to switch production to
    Hot buttered toast and tea

5. Now oozing through the court room
    Comes repentant Mr Oil
    He says he's very sorry that
    He's caused the earth to boil
    And to make it up for Gaia's grace
    He will now sweat and toil

6. And so the wondrous cavalcade
    Comes laying out its shame
    The corporations one by one
    Each humbly take the blame
    And offer restitution
    All in the people's name

7. But what is this? The mood has changed
    My dream it turns to dust
    They're pointing at the calendar
    And laughing fit to burst
    The month it seems is April
    And it is the sodding first

(Can be sung to the tune of 'Nicky Tams')

2

THE CUSTOMER ALWAYS COMES SECOND

Shareholder orientation

Consumer orientation is the clarion call, the first commandment of marketing. We the consumers are at the centre of the marketers' universe, the focus of their attention. Our needs are their watchword; and satisfying them is their undimming priority.

If only. In reality, at least in the hands of the corporate marketer, consumer orientation is not only a myth, but a dangerous myth. It is a myth, because as we have already noted the corporate marketer's first duty is to the shareholder – and any marketer's is to the success of the business – not the customer. The over-riding concern is, and always will be, to sell us stuff at a profit to themselves. The consumer only gets a look in because marketers have worked out that they are much more likely to succeed if they can create the illusion of putting their customers' interests first (or get closer to doing so than their competitors); in reality we will always come at least second. Illusions are powerful of course, as we will discuss in Chapter 4, and second place can still feel pretty good. But it remains an illusion, and it is a profoundly damaging one. It harms us and our planet, and distorts the very market that gave it birth.

More importantly, though, corporate marketing has created a systemic problem by blurring the line between the citizen and the shareholder, and deliberately interfering with the political process by sweet-talking, bullying and pre-empting our leaders.

Follow the money

Textbooks on marketing wax lyrical about the consumer, and place great emphasis on him or her being at the heart of marketers' efforts. As one leading text rather touchingly expresses it: 'marketing-oriented companies get close to their customers so they can understand their needs and problems'.[1] Increasingly, as well, as we have noted, this interest has moved beyond the transactional and the marketer wants to build relationships with us. All of which makes the marketer sound like a cross between an agony aunt and a confidant.

Successful businesses, the argument runs, take the time and trouble to find out what we need first, then set about producing it. They contrast this empathetic approach to the seeming insensitivity of Henry Ford who, with the newly developed power of mass production, could treat the consumer with 'any-colour-as-long-as-it's-black' disdain. The marketing texts reassure us that such hubris is no longer possible and, after a brief flirtation with high-pressure sales, sometime in the middle of the last century the enlightened day of the marketer dawned. But as with so much in the Panglossian world of marketing, all is not as it appears.

For a start Henry Ford was not being disdainful – he was giving consumers what they wanted: cheap, robust and easy to drive cars. That they had to be black was simply one of the factors that reduced the price. And he got obscenely rich in the process. So he was in fact a very good marketer. Furthermore, his business developed into the Ford Motor Company that still uses marketing (and sales) know-how to the nth degree. *Marketing Week*, for example, recently lauded its success at the cutting edge of marketing communications in its innovative use of social media.[2]

So Henry Ford, far from being a dinosaur of some bygone era, was in fact one of the key progenitors of modern business. The reality is much closer to Aldous Huxley's *Brave New World*, where 'Our Ford' has become the deity that sets the standards for society, with the T replacing the crucifix as icon in chief. Indeed, when Huxley pays a second visit to *Brave New World*, in 1958, thirty years after the original had appeared, the marketer takes pride of place in his analysis. But he is far from the benign confidant seeking 'to understand our needs and problems'. Rather his

> business is to study human weaknesses and failings, to investigate those unconscious desires and fears by which so much of men's conscious thinking and overt doing is determined. And he does this, not in the spirit of the moralist who would like to make people better, or of the physician who would like to improve their health, but simply in order to find out the best way to take advantage of their ignorance and to exploit their irrationality for the pecuniary benefit of his employers.[3]

Thus Huxley pinpoints the deception at the heart of marketing; a deception born of its motivation. The interest in our needs and wants – or in Huxley's more brutal assessment our 'failings and weaknesses' – is driven by a desire to exploit rather than resolve them. The marketer's solicitations are underpinned by avarice, not empathy. Or as the same marketing textbook I cited earlier transparently defines the 'marketing concept': 'the achievement of corporate goals through meeting and exceeding customer needs better than the competition'; and when building relationships these are strictly 'commercial' and 'profit remains an underlying business concern'. Our benign confidant is actually a cross between Scrooge and the Marlboro Cowboy.

What is the big concern, you might ask? After all, the world is full of people who are out to prioritize their own interests; we warn our children about them, take care to lock our doors and insure ourselves against malevolence as well as accident. The problem lies in the systemic nature of corporate marketing, which exacerbates the contradiction at its heart: how can a company simultaneously and continuously look after both its own and its customers' interests? There may be times when these interests coincide and mutual benefit is possible, but sooner or later a conflict will arise. A relationship that has one partner's advantage – the marketer's profit – as a hard-wired requirement is destined to get into problematic territory. It is like dating someone who is constitutionally selfish; there may be some great nights out along the way, but ultimately you either accept subjugation or you get out.

This brings us to the issue of power. Getting out of an unbalanced relationship is reasonably straightforward when the parties are on an equal footing, but it is much more difficult if one is manipulative, determined and well-resourced.

In the corporate marketplace our relationships will always be with partners who are constitutionally selfish, as well as extremely determined and well-resourced. But no one wants to date a psychopath, so the job of marketing – a job it does all too effectively – is to mask these uncomfortable truths by disguising the inanimate and ruthless corporate monolith as Prince Charming. It provides an introduction service, charm school and shape-shifting function all in one. In the process it greatly enhances corporate power at the expense of both the individual and the system. Such is soft power.

It's all in the plan

The marketers' self-centred purpose is confirmed by their strategic thinking. Strategic planning is accorded great importance, both by business academics and practitioners: courses are taught, textbooks are written and countless strategic planning documents are generated. The role of the marketing strategy is, as one leading exponent pithily expresses it, to determine 'how to recognize and achieve an economic advantage which endures'.[4] Not, you understand an economic advantage for the customer – just for the company. This is the same single-minded principle that has driven and continues to drive the financial sector (though in the case of Lehman Brothers at least, they forgot about the 'endures' bit).

It is perhaps no surprise, then, that the development of a marketing strategy does not actually begin with consumer needs, but with an analysis of the company's operating environment. Various acronyms are used to describe this exercise; PEST (Political, Economic, Social and Technological scanning) and SWOT (Strengths, Weaknesses, Opportunities and Threats analysis) are two common ones.

Whatever the precise configuration, the principle of all such strategic analyses is to take careful account of all the factors that might have an impact on the successful operation (i.e. profitability) of the company so that measures can be taken to exploit any opportunities, and either avoid, reduce or remove any threats. So business planning starts by asking what is in it for us, not what is in it for the customer. The latter only gets a look in when the former is well established.

For example, a couple of years ago the drinks industry saw a potential threat to its quest to 'recognize and achieve an economic advantage which endures' in Scotland, when the incumbent government proposed to raise the legal age of purchase for alcohol from 18 to 21. The measure would only apply to off sales (pubs and bars would remain accessible to the young) and was designed to protect young people from the dangers of the unsupervised and over-consumption of alcohol. The Wine and Spirit Trade Association (WSTA), a body which represents drinks giants such as Chivas Brothers and Diageo, expressed its displeasure both overtly and, using what we will see is a standard marketer's tactic, covertly – in this case through a third party. Specifically they funded a student protest group called CARDAS (Coalition Against Raising the Drinking Age in Scotland) enabling them to run an apparently independent publicity campaign comprising 500 posters, 5,000 leaflets and 500 constituency lobby cards. (Note: The agreement to pay the group's costs came after a meeting between CARDAS and the industry body in the Scottish Parliament building, showing how close big business is to the corridors of power – a phenomenon discussed further in Chapter 8.)

The CARDAS case illustrates three recurrent characteristics of marketing. The first is eternal vigilance. Companies like Diageo are massively powerful but they leave nothing to chance. The threat to the world's leading spirits producer from a minor legislative adjustment in a tiny northern market was miniscule, but still could not be countenanced. I had my own experience of this remorseless scanning a couple of years ago when I was unwise enough to say something less than flattering about Diageo in a newspaper interview. Again it was a tiny speck on the corporate map – a remark buried in the fourth column of a long piece in the second section of a minor British newspaper. My guess is no more than a dozen people read my irreverent reference; but one of them was a company lawyer and I received a warning letter the day after. Marketers are, then, eternally vigilant – and this vigilance is focused not on the much trumpeted interests of the consumer, but on those of the corporation.

Second, marketers play all sorts of games with identity. As we will discuss in Chapter 5, branding itself emerged as a subterfuge; a means of giving otherwise faceless companies a seemingly human identity. Philip Morris is just another profit seeking corporation, but the Marlboro Cowboy is a rugged individualist and a potential role model. In this instance, however, the aim was not to create an identity, but to hide one: the drinks industry wanted to make it seem like the protest was coming from a legitimate grassroots organization, not multinational companies with clear vested interests – and, but for some canny investigative journalism by the Glasgow-based *Herald* newspaper, it would have succeeded.

Third, notwithstanding their penchant for disguise, marketers are neither shy nor humble. Henry Ford's supposed hubris has become real and is alive and well. They will readily get involved in areas way outside their field of expertise if it suits their business interests. In the case of alcohol they strenuously insist that they have a legitimate role in the development of public policy, despite an obvious lack of public health expertise. For example, early in 2011 two leading public health NGOs in Scotland, ASH (Action on Smoking and Health) and AFS (Alcohol Focus Scotland) decided to put on a combined seminar to discuss what the two fields of tobacco and alcohol public health could learn from one another. They made an early decision that this should be an independent discussion, untrammelled by vested interest, so both the tobacco and alcohol industries were overtly excluded.

The tobacco companies did not demur; they are used to such treatment. One of the provisions of the WHO Framework Convention on Tobacco Control, which we touched on in Chapter 1, is that signatory governments (of which there are now over 270) must ensure that the tobacco industry is excluded from all public health policy planning. It might have come into being a full fifty years after tobacco's toxicity was first appreciated, but at least in this field of public health the need to separate the fox from the chickens has been understood.

Not so in alcohol: the protests of outrage were loud and indignant. This began with a letter to the Director of AFS (and simultaneously released to the press) from Diageo's unassumingly titled 'Corporate Social Responsibility Manager for Great Britain' who wanted 'to express' his 'profound disappointment that my colleague, … , has been refused a place at the upcoming Scottish Alcohol and Tobacco Policy Summit'. He continued: 'We have an obvious interest in the role that alcohol plays in our society and I firmly believe that as a key player in the industry, Diageo can and should contribute constructively to this debate.' The letter then reminded the addressee that AFS had, in the past, had funding from Diageo and concluded with an ill-disguised threat to remove this:

> If the position of AFS has fundamentally changed to the degree that the organization now believes the alcohol industry has no right of opinion or part to play in addressing Scotland's relationship with alcohol, then I believe we owe it to our stakeholders to explore this and our future relationship with you.

So once again we are reminded that there is no such thing as a free lunch and Diageo's support for the NGO is dependent on the provision of access to the policy-making process.

It was precisely this conflict of interest that had led AFS, some months previously, to change its policy, stop accepting the alcohol industry's shilling and adjust its strategic focus accordingly. This did not go down well with the Corporate Social Responsibility Manager for Great Britain. His next letter (again simultaneously released to the press) came straight to the point:

> I note with concern the apparent change in your policy direction set out in your recent 'Strategic Direction 2011–13' document in which your previously stated objectives of 'promoting responsibility, reducing harm and changing culture' have been replaced by 'reducing harm caused by alcohol'.

It takes a fair dollop of arrogance for a company focused on selling booze to feel it can tell an independent NGO, set up to ease the problems that result, what its strategic direction should be. Imagine for a minute how the Diageo board would react if AFS decided it wanted to set the company's sales targets and tinker with its brand strategies.

The Corporate Social Responsibility Manager for Great Britain also took exception to the idea, underpinning the conference and restated by AFS in the press, that the field of alcohol public health could learn much from the fight against tobacco. Sharing learning might generally be felt to be desirable, but not it seems when it threatens your sales – and, remember, this was the conference that the Corporate Social Responsibility Manager for Great Britain had previously been so keen to attend. He ended by saying that funding – which AFS had already decided should end – would discontinue.

The reality is that beverage alcohol corporations know a great deal about how to get us to drink and have an overwhelming incentive – indeed a legal imperative – to use every means at their disposal to hone and deploy these skills. By contrast they are not experts in the aetiology of cirrhosis, they have not mastered epidemiology; they do not understand the finer points of the spread of non-communicable disease – except to the extent that grasping these issues will help them further their core goals of increasing profits and enhancing shareholder returns. Far from having what they seem to consider is a God given right to contribute to the policy debate, they should be kept well behind a robust cordon sanitaire.

The linking theme in this vigilance, pretence and arrogance is the unflagging focus on the interests of the corporate entity – not the supposedly sacrosanct consumer. Indeed in this case their customers' needs were being met in a very real sense by the government's public health experts, who were all too aware of the harm that an overly easy access to alcohol, and its unsupervised consumption, were causing:

> In Scotland, the short term harms associated with impacts of alcohol misuse are higher in younger age groups than older age groups: e.g. alcohol-related attendances at Emergency Departments; alcohol-related assaults; and road accidents. The increased levels of harm from accidents are likely to be linked to higher rates of binge drinking and drunkenness amongst younger drinkers and links to other risky behaviours.[5]

Such official pronouncements can be shocking enough, but the human face of such data can be even more powerful. Just last year in my own home town a young man fell in the river and drowned after drinking far too much; the impact of this tragedy on his family, friends and the wider community was profound and remains to this day. The Scottish Government's concern is that similar calamities are hitting families across the country week in and week out.

Meanwhile, the corporate marketers, those self-proclaimed champions of the consumer, were doing all they could to ensure that Scottish youngsters stayed in harm's way simply because it would benefit their shareholders. So marketing becomes not just a potential threat to the individual, but our system of government. This political interference is, as with all corporate marketing, systemic. It is not accidental or the result of some aberration – it is inevitable.

Keep following the money

The aim of a marketing strategy then is to understand what is going on in the marketplace – what government, stakeholders and competitors are doing – and plan accordingly. What gaps are there in current provision, for instance, or might we be able to produce a cheaper, better, more ubiquitous version of product a or service b: 'simply find out whether it pays; simply investigate if there is an alternative that pays better. If there is, choose the alternative'.[6] Consumer needs are always secondary to this, and the result is a grossly distorted marketplace. This is not to suggest that consumer research is not important – it is, and marketers invest vast sums in countless forms of it, as we will discuss in later chapters. But the needs this research will examine are ones that have already been ear-marked as potentially profitable for its corporate sponsor, and the focus will be on confirming this viability and uncovering the best ways of ensuring the potential is fulfilled. That is, in confirming that we can and are inclined to buy the latest type of tyre/cigarette/vodka, and, crucially, how this inclination to purchase can best be encouraged.

So market research matters, but it is always subordinate to the strategic plan and the corporation's perpetual quest for the 'economic advantage which endures'.

New product ideas that are much needed by consumers, but unprofitable, will never see the light of day, whereas profitable ones of dubious worth will win through. This explains Bakan's observation that trivial Western ills such as baldness have had far more attention by pharma companies than lethal diseases of the poor such as bilharzia and tuberculosis:

> of the 1,400 new drugs developed between 1975 and 1999, only 13 were designed to treat or prevent tropical diseases and three to treat tuberculosis. In the year 2000, no drugs were being developed to treat tuberculosis, compared to eight for impotence or erectile dysfunction and 7 for baldness.[7]

Thus marketing is not driven by customer need, but customer money.

Similarly products that are harmful but nonetheless profitable will come winging through the strategic planning process. How else could we have tobacco companies

– which, as we have already noted, are consummate marketers – continuing to produce products that kill one in two of their most loyal customers? And tobacco companies don't just ignore the collateral damage from their products – they actively deny it and campaign to traduce it. Thus for years they hid their own internal research showing that nicotine is highly addictive, and as recently as 1994 the CEOs of the principal US tobacco giants stood in front of Congress and one by one swore an oath that nicotine did not cause dependence.[8]

This despite the fact that subsequent revelations have shown that at this time the tobacco industry had then been well aware of nicotine's addictive properties for at least three decades. As long ago as 1962 Sir Charles Ellis, the Science Advisor to the Board of Directors of British American Tobacco, stated unequivocally that 'Smoking is a habit of addiction', and later the same decade a memo to Helmut Wakeham, Philip Morris Vice President for Research and Development, confirmed his assertion and explained the reason for industry reticence: '[D]o we really want to tout cigarette smoke as a drug? It is, of course, but there are dangerous F.D.A. implications to having such conceptualization go beyond these walls.'[9]

The health effects of smoking have also been systematically downplayed and denied by the industry. In a UK court case over a decade after the infamous Congressional hearings, the CEO of Imperial Tobacco managed, on behalf of his company and its products, to evade responsibility for lung cancer. Despite being on oath and at the mercy of a highly trained Queen's Counsel his sophistry (see Box 2.1) prevailed.

Indeed Imperial Tobacco went on to win the case, which had been brought by one of its customers – Alf McTear – to seek compensation for his tobacco-related illnesses. To add insult to the all too apparent injury, Alf McTear had actually died of his smoking more than a decade before the case came to trial – around about the time that Mr Davis's US counterparts were lying to Congress. Thanks to a prolonged set of delaying tactics by the defendant the case had to be brought by his widow. Dickens would have appreciated the irony.

By what convoluted logic can any of this be described as 'consumer oriented' or 'putting people's needs at the centre of the business process'?

We will pick up this tunnel vision issue again in Chapter 8 when we discuss that most ironic of oxymorons: Corporate Social Responsibility, but for now the key point to note is that the business opportunity pre-dates and pre-empts any interest in consumer needs which, in any case, are more correctly defined as consumer capacity and preparedness to buy. Meanwhile, concern with consumer welfare doesn't just trail behind, but all too often becomes an obstacle to be overcome in the pre-eminent aim of realizing the business opportunity and delivering to the shareholder 'the economic advantage which endures'.

BOX 2.1 THE CROSS-EXAMINATION OF MR GARETH DAVIS (GD), CEO IMPERIAL TOBACCO BY THE QUEEN'S COUNSEL (QC) IN THE SCOTTISH HIGH COURT IN 2004

QC: So I think we have seen that on three of those there is the warning 'Smoking kills'?
GD: On the front on two and – yes, on the back on one.
QC: Does your company accept that?
GD: I think the answer is: we do not know. It may do, but we do not know.

Shown visual of Philip Morris accepting that 'there is no safe cigarette'.

QC: Do you agree with that?
GD: I think there are parts of it that I would agree with, but not in its entirety.
QC: Can you help us; what bits do you and Imperial agree with?
GD: I think it is fair to say that we believe smokers are far more likely to develop serious diseases, like lung cancer, than non-smokers, and we would agree there is no safe cigarette.
QC: If you agree that smokers are far more likely to develop lung cancer than non-smokers, does that not mean that you agree that smoking causes lung cancer?
GD: No, no, it does not mean that, Mr McEachran. What I would answer to that is that, over the years, there has been a significant amount of statistical association between smoking and certain diseases, including lung cancer, but I think most scientists would agree that statistical association does not equal causation. That is a judgmental call that Philip Morris have made here in the light of their work. I do not know the circumstances or the thoughts behind their position, but we have a different position. We have come to a different judgment.
QC: But your position as manufacturer is: you do not accept it as a fact; that smoking causes fatal lung cancer. Is that right?
GD: That is the situation … it may do, but we do not know.

The bigger picture

Wider social concerns are even further behind in the pecking order. The fact that a business opportunity is profitable (that a product can be made which genuinely meets the needs of a consumer who, in turn, can afford, and is willing, to buy it) does not make it good for society. As Schumacher points out this simplifies matters, but at a great cost:

Everything becomes crystal clear after you have reduced reality to one – one only – of its thousand aspects. You know what to do – whatever produces profits; you know what to avoid – whatever reduces them or makes a loss. And there is at the same time a perfect measuring rod for the degree of success or failure. Let no-one befog the issue by asking whether a particular action is conducive to the wealth and well-being of society, whether it leads to moral, aesthetic, or cultural enrichment.[10]

A Learjet, for instance, is an impressive product, marrying first rate engineering with cutting-edge design; the chief executive of a major car producer has both the desire and the means to buy one (or several), and in so doing will improve his quality of life (at least in the short term) by, for instance, saving his time and the need to jostle with the hoi polloi on commercial airlines. But the impact on the wider economy and indeed the planet will still be negative. Time and again these broader concerns – what are sometimes referred to as the externalities – are ignored, down-played or denied; after you have reduced reality to one only of its thousand aspects. In this example, the profligacy of the executive jet only caused alarm and despondency when three such auto executives – from Chrysler, Ford and General Motors – flew into Washington each in their own private jets, en route to ask Congress for a $25 billion bail-out.[11] Only then did the scales fall from our and the Congressional eyes. Congressman Gary Ackerman was clearly perplexed by the anomaly of their gold-plated begging bowls: 'It's almost like seeing a guy show up at the soup kitchen in high hat and tuxedo. It kind of makes you a little bit suspicious.'

Such extravagance, however, is not an anomaly; it is the natural end-point of corporate marketing which puts an over-riding emphasis on seeking out those needs that can turn a coin – the 'economic advantage which endures' – and then doing everything possible to satisfy them. The only limits are those of profitability, and in a world of spiralling wealth for the few these are puny indeed.

And the fact that marketers make these decisions also pre-empts and constrains policy makers. We are inclined to associate marketing with domestic niceties like baked beans or soap powder – but it is applied just as enthusiastically to much more obviously nasty products like armaments. If you have the slightest doubt about this just visit the BAE Systems website to learn about the company's 'Advanced Armor Solutions', 'Intelligent Munitions' and (presumably learning from the Walmart family) the 'Bradley Family of Vehicles'. This last is a set of particularly aggressive looking armoured cars which apparently 'provides the force protection required for today's conflicts and growth potential for tomorrow's conflicts' (aka 'economic advantage which endures'). The company's media strategy includes wraparound advertising on the homely London cab.

However, when UK arms companies use their marketing skills to push £4.7 million of 'wall and door breaching projectile launchers, crowd control ammunition, small arms ammunition, tear gas/irritant ammunition, training tear gas/irritant ammunition'[12] to a country like Muammar Gaddafi's Libya our concerns are pricked; when we learn that these figures refer to the third quarter of 2010 – just months before UK troops were fighting him – the myopia of free range corporate marketing is all too apparent. Except to the marketers of course, who will once again be 'achieving an economic advantage which endures' by supplying both sides; after each had a need and the ability to pay.

This victory of pay-off over patriotism is nothing new. In his forensic analysis of declassified government documents Charles Higham demonstrates with unnerving clarity that major US corporations – including the Chase Bank, ITT and our old friend the Ford Motor Company – were doing business with Nazi corporations like IG Farben (who built Auschwitz) throughout the war. He asks:

> What would have happened if millions of American and British people, struggling with coupons and lines at the gas stations, had learned that in 1942 Standard Oil of New Jersey managers shipped the enemy's fuel through neutral Switzerland and that the enemy was shipping Allied fuel? Suppose the public had discovered that the Chase Bank in Nazi-occupied Paris after Pearl Harbor was doing millions of dollars of business with the enemy with the full knowledge of head office in Manhattan? Or that Ford trucks were being built for the German occupation troops in France with the authorisation of Dearborn, Michigan? Or that Colonel Sosthenes Behn, head of the American international telephone conglomerate ITT, flew from New York to Madrid to Berne during the war to help improve Hitler's communications systems and improve the robot bombs that destroyed London?[13]

But, as he explains, all this was kept secret at the time, and has since been carefully hidden behind 'an ice cream mountain of public relations'. Corporate marketing has carefully and consistently applied and maintained the mask of respectability. Thus Higham concludes 'the bosses of the multinationals had a six spot on every side of the dice cube. Whichever side won the war, the powers that really ran nations would not be adversely affected.' It is called 'achieving an economic advantage which endures'.

In this way the greater good of society gets perennially forestalled by the marketing strategy. Scanning the business environment, conducting gap analyses and doing market research simply populates a chart with new product ideas and identifies whether or not they could be profitable. It does nothing to show whether or not they are desirable. The analytic effort is focused on market potential – not on whether the product or service in question is in the public or societal interest. A wider perspective may be taken into account, but only to the extent that social or public resistance may need to be addressed to benefit the project. This may result in abandonment: there is, for instance, plenty of demand and market opportunity to produce and sell cocaine, but the legal environment would preclude any legitimate company exploiting it. More often though it will involve a combination of marketing sail-trimming to avoid or reduce criticism, or the targeting of key stakeholders to make the environment more supportive (see Chapter 8).

Wicked

For example in the 1990s a chance new product in Australia helped alcohol companies uncover a gap in the market for alcohol drinks targeting juvenile palates. Marketers brought together a number of insights: that kids like sweet sickly flavours; that they enjoy irreverent (schoolboy) humour and fun; that they want to experiment with alcohol; and that conventional wines, beers and spirits are an acquired taste. This suggested that a new range of products that delivered to this need would succeed. Thus were alcopops, shots, shooters and flavoured alcoholic beverages (FABs) born. They come in a wide range of flavours, in garish colours and with childish names – such as Jaffa Cake flavoured Stiffy vodka and purple, flavoured WKD (pronounced wicked). They have been a roaring commercial success, transforming the alcohol market.

From society's perspective, however, as any sensible adult could have predicted, they have been catastrophic. A recent paper in the *American Journal of Public Health*, for instance, argues that they have transformed the youth alcohol market in the US. The author provides a forensic case study of Smirnoff Ice, a leading brand of alcopops, and explains how:

> Diageo developed a sophisticated marketing strategy to reenergize its Smirnoff Vodka brand using 3 key components:
>
> 1. Develop a beverage that tasted like soft drinks.
> 2. Use the Smirnoff Vodka brand name but market the product as a malt beverage to compete effectively with beer in terms of price, availability, and advertising in electronic media.
> 3. Reorient Smirnoff Vodka itself as a young person's brand by adding new fruit flavors and using other marketing innovations.[14]

Similarly, in England and Wales, alcopops have been linked with deeply problematic teen drinking.[15]

Why didn't a sensible adult intervene? Why weren't the obvious dangers of melding child friendly sodas with a dangerous adult drug the cause of an immediate public outcry? Why weren't public meetings called and laws passed? In essence, because marketers are far too fleet of foot: the tireless logic of the marketing strategy, and its remorseless search for 'an economic advantage which endures', will always outstrip politicians and civil society. Marketers have at least three advantages over the public servant.

First, they have enormous resources: Diageo alone boasts 'more than 20,000 talented people working with us to grow our business and nurture our brands'.[16] And these resources are bolstered by every purchase we make.

Second, the marketer is incentivized with Pavlovian precision: every bonus, every sales target makes sure they remain utterly single-minded. Just remember the toxic effects of the bonus culture in the banking sector. But the banks are not unique. In the late 1990s the Scottish government did an evidence gathering exercise on alcohol and public health. In one session a 'witness' was giving evidence to a duly appointed panel of the great and the good. The witness in question had worked as a brand manager for a drinks company, and one of the panel sat on the board of a major brewery. It had been a long hot day, people were tired and guards were down. The witness was explaining that he had sales targets to meet, and his focus on these was absolute because if he failed to meet them he would 'get his arse kicked'. At this point the brewery executive helpfully chipped in: 'yes and if I'd been your line manager, I'd have done the kicking'. Just for a moment the mask had slipped.

The marketers' final advantage over the public servant is the most important one. Theirs is an infinitely more simple task: they just have to sell us more stuff. As Bernstein says in *Citizen Kane*: 'making money is easy if all you want to do is make money'. Our politicians have to live with all the complexities of a democratic system. They have to listen to Eisenhower and his multiple calls for balance between public and private, the many and the few, 'the cost and hoped for advantages', now and tomorrow.[17] They have to weigh up competing priorities, address everyone's needs, not just those of their shareholders, and get re-elected every four years. This contrast of intricacy is writ large in the current euro crisis; the market is repeatedly calling for politicians to act, but representing the interests of an electorate of 450 million people, significant subsets of which have been at war with each other several times in the last hundred years, is much more challenging (and important) than pleasing shareholders. As one commentator put it:

> In the euro crisis, financiers chide governments all the time for their slowness "behind the curve" and their lack of leadership, as though the needs and wishes of electorates could be managed as swiftly and easily as a few million dollars on a trader's screen.[18]

This over-bearing superiority of focus and fire-power continues after the event, with the marketers moving in to air-brush away our disquiet with the deliberate efficiency of insects disposing of a carcass on the savannah.

As we have noted, alcopops emerged when a small producer in Australia hit on the idea of brewing alcoholic lemonade and named it 'Two Dogs' after a smutty schoolboy joke. Me-too products soon emerged with equally wacky names such as Hoopers Hooch and Moo (a short-lived alcoholic milk), varied flavours and the same irreverent anti-establishment imagery – and a whole new drinks sector was born. Common-sense disquiet was expressed, and academic research confirmed that this was justified.[19] The problem wasn't so much that children were drinking these new offerings (though many were, others rejected them as too expensive and awkward to carry); the real danger was in the symbolism. Alcopops with their childish jokes, silly names and fun advertising were saying something entirely new.

Previous generations of children had had to adapt to the unpleasant taste of traditional alcoholic drinks like beer and wine. Like the first cigarette, the first drink was unpleasant. At the very least they had had to add their own lemonade to the spirits and beer their parents drank to make them palatable. Now corporate marketers were doing the job for them, catering for their needs and producing bespoke products that suited their immature palates and minds. The subtext, plain for all to read, was that society, the adult world and the all-pervasive market now think it is fine for kids to drink booze.

But this is an awkward truth for the beverage alcohol industry and it is torn between the obvious profitability of teen drinking with its get-them-young promise of 'an economic advantage which endures', and the bad public relations such cynicism attracts. The solution is a makeover. No one in the industry talks about alcopops; the name has been excised from their language and replaced by the much more respectable sounding label 'Ready to Drink' or simply RTD. Brand leaders like Bacardi Breezer and Smirnoff Ice have been kitted out in much more sophisticated guise as pseudo cocktails. And the RTD sector is now sufficiently respectable for a company of Diageo's blue chip standing – and anxiety to burnish its corporate image – to boast that 'the RTD sub-category continues to provide a strong platform for new innovations' and that 'Diageo GB will continue to develop innovations to drive category growth'.[20]

We should not be fooled by the corporate marketer's sleight of hand: an alcopop dressed as an RTD is no more innocent than the wolf in granny's dressing gown, and plenty of unreconstructed alcopops remain, and continue to be launched on the market, as we noted above. The implicit thumbs up to youth drinking continues to reverberate.

Nor should we underestimate the extent to which the beverage alcohol industry has calmed the concerns of our political leaders. In the UK for example, astute marketing – this time targeted at cabinet ministers rather than young people – has been so successful in building mutually beneficial relationships with politicians that, far from being punished for the damage it has inflicted, the industry has been rewarded by being put in charge of alcohol health promotion (see Chapter 8).

More importantly, though, the die has been cast; no one can now put the alcopop genie back in the bottle. Once again the policy maker has been pre-empted by out of control corporate marketing.

Corroding democracy

The insidious influence of corporate marketing has profound implications for our society and where it is heading. In essence it conflates the interests of shareholders with citizens both individually and collectively, and whilst it might have entered through the pocket book, it has long infiltrated the ballot box. This may sound shocking or implausible, but, as we noted in the previous chapter, Eisenhower (a Republican president from a military background and hence conservative by nature) was warning fifty years ago of 'unwarranted influence – economic, political, even spiritual' – being 'felt in every city, every Statehouse, every office of the Federal government'.

And remember, the marketer's power to undermine government has long been accepted – and has often been portrayed as a benefit – when those governments are autocratic. Many have argued Coke and Levi's did more to open up China and destabilize the Soviet Union than Richard Nixon and the CIA combined. Rudolph Giuliani,[21] for instance, said that 'companies such as Pepsi, Coca-Cola, McDonald's, and Levi's helped win the Cold War by entering the Soviet market' and the label coca-colonization[22] was invented to express the powerful political influence of the spread of consumerist values.

In Latin America the marketer has also had a powerful political role, but few would argue that this has been anything other than calamitous for the local population. This has been documented many times, but most evocatively by Pablo Neruda in his poem 'The United Fruit Company'.[23] The poem speaks evocatively of the world being divided up by Jehovah at the dawn of time between *'Coca-Cola, Anaconda, Ford Motors, and other corporations'* and that *'The United Fruit Company reserved for itself the juiciest piece, the central coast of my world, the delicate waist of America'*. The poem goes on to list the *'bloodthirsty'* dictators, *'expert in tyranny'* that then emerged to dominate the resulting *'banana republics'*. Neruda concludes by focusing on the cheapness with which the company treated local Indian life: *'a body rolls down, a nameless thing, a fallen number, a bunch of lifeless fruit dumped in the rubbish heap'*.

This was written back in 1942, but political influence continues to this day. This is a journalist writing about the Costa Rican pineapple industry in 2011:

> this is an industry built on environmental degradation and poverty wages. Moreover, price cuts appear to have led to an immediate, sometimes brutal deterioration in conditions that were already poor .... I heard repeated allegations of chemical contamination, wage cuts, union-breaking involving mass sackings and accidental poisonings. Like many other local experts, Ramirez, who is the country's coordinator for the Pesticide Action Network fears that the pineapple boom has outpaced the government's ability to regulate it. "The fight now is against pineapples because there's been an explosion in production, but it's difficult because the owners of the plantations have very big political and economic influence." By now, the sprayer was bearing down on us and we reached for our masks. Then, out of nowhere, an armed guard rode up on his motorbike to inspect us. Costa Rica, with a population of just over 4m, has only 12,000 or so policemen and no army, but an estimated 17,000 gun-carrying security guards employed by private companies.[24]

Keep these words in your mind next time you consider buying a pineapple. Ignore the cheery logo, pay no heed to the innocent sounding name and look by the fruit's improbable perfection. Instead, ask yourself: which corporation is producing this, how many armed guards does it employ and in what pesticides does it dowse its workers? If the answer to the first question is one that subscribes to independently monitored Fairtrade standards, and to the latter two is none, then you can go ahead and enjoy your pineapple with an easy mind. If not, the nice branding may provide you with a conscience-salve for your purchase, but it will make life for Ramirez that bit harder.

In the liberal democracies of the developed world the impacts of corporate marketing are more subtle, but equally powerful. We have seen how the supposed focus on consumer needs is mere rhetoric: the primary and abiding focus is on the bottom line and shareholder value. Masquerading as our friends is just a 'superficially charming' way of achieving the crucial instrumental goal of selling us more stuff.

From this world view, the political system, the government of the day, is just one dimension of the business environment to be perpetually scanned for potential threats (such as public health regulation) and opportunities (such as international tensions). The former can then be suppressed, and the latter nurtured, using a combination of bullying, seduction and, most frequently, simple pre-emption. And time and again the corporate marketers succeed because they have enormous resources, unflagging persistence, perfectly targeted financial incentives and an enviably straightforward task.

Nonetheless, I hear you say, we do live in a democracy. No one is forcing us to consume carcinogens or bomb Gaddafi. Okay, kids are vulnerable and should be protected, but we are adults and we have a choice. And you are absolutely right. We do have a choice and we can and should exercise it. It is the choice to critically examine corporate marketing; the choice to question whether 'every little helps', or 'we are worth it'; the choice to challenge the motives behind 'superficially charming' marketing campaigns; the choice to side with Ramirez rather than the United Fruit Company's sinister successors. The great problem for corporate marketers is that soft power quickly diminishes once it is exposed; the ornate and carefully applied gilding of superficial charm soon tarnishes in fresh air.

That is why they are so keen to distract us with other choices.

The Mania of Owning Things

I think I could turn and live with animals, they are so placid and self-contain'd,
I stand and look at them long and long.

They do not sweat and whine about their condition.
They do not lie awake in the dark and weep for their sins.
They do not make me sick discussing their duty to God,
Not one is dissatisfied, not one is demented with the mania of owning things,
Not one kneels to another, nor to his kind that lived thousands of years ago,
Not one is respectable or industrious over the earth.

Walt Whitman[1]

It is preoccupation with possession, more than anything else, that prevents men from living freely and nobly.

Bertrand Russell

3
A TYRANNY OF CHOICE

Happy in our servitude

The idea of evermore extensive consumer choice, which is burnished and proselytized by marketers, is not a blessing, but a curse. While millions across the world have barely enough to live on, we in the minority world suffer an excess of choice between an unmanageable array of alternatives. A standard supermarket in the wealthy developed countries will offer us some 40,000 different products. It takes more than eleven hours just to count to 40,000, and heaven knows how long to work out what that number of different items are and appraise their qualities. Many of these offerings will differ only in the most trivial way – perhaps just in the brand name, or a miniscule variation in performance which we can barely detect. But we are flattered into thinking we can, and get churlish when our discriminatory skills and newly honed preferences are not met. This pandering to whims we didn't even know we had is turning us into hoity-toity prigs who must have things just-so. A British public that discovered wine little more than a generation ago, now demands specific grape varieties as a matter of course; where once black tea would suffice we now have endless variations on the theme (loose leaf, tea bags in numerous shapes and materials, varying strengths, different blends) as well as green tea, white tea and countless types of infusion.

The result is not customer satisfaction, but perpetual dissatisfaction. With forty different sorts of tea there is much more anxiety about whether you have made the 'right' choice, than if there is just one. It also encourages the delusion that we are at the centre of the universe; that our needs matter and should be prioritized. It makes us think, in the words of the L'Oréal strap-line, that we are worth it – when time and again we are not: forty different sorts of tea when millions cannot even access clean drinking water?

This over-indulgence furnishes the ground floor of an edifice built on greed. Given the state of inequalities both within and between nations, and the damage excessive consumption is doing to the planet, our forty sorts of tea or fifth generation iPhone, most of whose functions we won't even understand let alone use, is just as morally repugnant as the merchant banker's bonus.

Paradoxically all this spoiling does not liberate or empower us – it keeps us all in line. It ties us into earning ever more money to do ever more shopping for increasingly superfluous trinkets. All this dulls down our critical instincts, much as bread and circuses did those of the Roman mob; in Aldous Huxley's chilling phrase, it gets us to 'love our servitude'.

Choice overload

In 1982 I made my first visit to the United States. When I awoke in my Washington, DC bedroom I exercised my freedom of consumer choice, opted to forgo the hotel breakfast and headed out in search of a local café to have a coffee and a cream cheese bagel. I'd seen it on *Starsky and Hutch* and it seemed so cool. There were lots of coffee shops and choosing between them was tricky as I didn't know any of the brands. Remember this was 1982 and the Starbucks phenomenon was yet to reach my home in northern Britain. Eventually I found one that was simply called 'Coffee and Bagels', which kind of made the choice for me. I relaxed a little and went indoors. Then tricky turned to stressful as I queued at the counter. First there was the type of coffee to choose (there were six options – four I could understand: Americano, Latte, filter and Espresso), and the size of serving (four options, none of which I could understand; I would have to try 'small' and look hick in the hope this would win the server's heart). Then there were the bagels – five different flavours (plain, onion, sesame seed, poppy seed and raisin), toasted or fresh; the cream cheese – at least eight different options with four different possible accompaniments. At a rough count I had around 1,500 different options to choose from. And I just wanted a coffee with a bagel and cream cheese like on the telly.

Neither a plethora of choice nor the chance to be in a mutually beneficial relationship via a Coffee and Bagels loyalty card had empowered me or put me at the heart of the business process. I didn't feel in charge. I felt stressed and bewildered. And a little inadequate. Did I lack something that I couldn't even understand, let alone navigate, this menu? My fellow customers seemed to be doing it with ease. They articulated their orders with an impressive certainty and humbling efficiency. When it came to my turn I dithered and stumbled. I had to seek clarification from the cool Californian waitperson, and repeat my order three times because I mangled the coffee shop's argot. I was all too obviously an incompetent consumer and it felt like a damning inadequacy.

More troubling still, I began to think I must be some sort of philistine. The truth was that I just didn't care that much about what sort of bagel I got, or whether the cream cheese had herbs in it. I was pretty sure I would be utterly incapable of distinguishing between a filter coffee and an Americano. I not only lacked skills, I lacked taste.

I comforted myself that this was America, and they did things differently there. And they are so over the top. The café back home just served coffee or tea (add your own milk and sugar): two options, which suited me. I wasn't a fool, just a stranger – and a sensible one at that. Such nonsense would never happen back home.

Now fast forward thirty years. Four of us have just walked six miles through the deep rural countryside of North Yorkshire's upper Swaledale and are comfortably ensconced in a quaint little tearoom in an ancient farmhouse. My friend orders an instant coffee; I stifle a shudder and order an Americano (the other two go for tea). As the drinks are being brought to the table I can feel myself getting edgy: will the orders get mixed up? After all, they both look alike (black liquid), the place is busy and our waitperson isn't a cool Californian, but a moonlighting Yorkshire farmhand. Heavens, I might end up drinking instant coffee by accident. The thought is appalling; I can actually feel my blood pressure rising. When the coffees reach the table, there is indeed confusion. I am pretty sure that, horror of horrors, I have been landed with the instant coffee. I nearly make a fuss, but social courtesies just get the better of me and I sip sulkily at my coffee.

Two things are apparent in comparing 1982 Washington with present-day Yorkshire. First, bewildering choice has spread out from the States. Even in the backwoods of the rural north of England there is a Gaggia machine and multiple coffee options. Our two non-coffee drinking companions could also have chosen from a couple of dozen different teas and infusions. My local branch of Starbucks, which has now arrived in northern Britain, offers around 216 variations on a cup of coffee (Table 3.1), not including extras like chocolate sprinkles and marshmallows.

TABLE 3.1 Starbucks coffee choices (not including extras like chocolate sprinkles or marshmallows)

Beverage type (9)	Milk type (6)	Size (4)	Total options
Caffe misto/café au lait			
Flat white	None		
Caffe latte	Whipped cream	Short	
Caffe mocha	Skimmed milk	Tall	
Caramel macchiato (regular vanilla flavoured syrup)	Semi skimmed milk	Grande	9 x 6 x 4 = 216
Vanilla latte (flavoured latte)	Whole milk	Venti	
White chocolate mocha	Soya		
Hazelnut mocha (flavoured mocha)			
Peppermint mocha with drizzle			

It seems we are all living in Washington, DC now. Except this isn't an American phenomenon, it's a marketing phenomenon. This is the natural end point of sanctifying consumer choice and putting it at the centre of the business process – or at least purporting to do so.

I spent some time in Cuba a couple of years ago and the lack of retail choice was all too apparent: coffee or no coffee; rice or pasta; ham rolls, cheese rolls or ham and cheese rolls (actually it was always ham and cheese rolls). I am no advocate of this degree of restriction of choice, but it did serve to point up the ridiculous over provision when we returned home. The day after we arrived back in the UK I went to a local shop to buy my Sunday paper. It was a large 'CTN' (confectioners, tobacconist and newsagent), but nonetheless just a corner shop – yet it had a bewildering range. There must have been two hundred variations on the theme of chocolate for example, and more magazines than you could read in a month. It seemed silly in its own right, and, after Cuba, profligate and unfair. Anyone who has travelled outside the rich minority countries of the world will have experienced a similar unease.

The second lesson is that I have been successfully trained. I now know what I like (black Americano), can distinguish a venti from a grande and deliver my order with confidence and certainty. I treasure my new found skills, and am proud of my burgeoning good taste. My preference for 'proper' coffee shows that I am sophisticated, erudite and discriminating.

And I am not alone. Some of the earliest research on such consumer emotions actually levered this coffee snobbery.[2] Back in 1950 Mason Haire showed women in Boston two shopping lists that were identical except that one included a brand of instant and the other proper coffee. He then asked the respondents to describe the women who had written the two lists. The real coffee buyer was seen much more positively than her instant coffee using peer: she was an efficient, competent and admirable housewife compared to her instant sister who cut corners and kept house badly (these were unreconstructed times). Haire also realized that the women might be a little ambivalent about their judgemental attitudes, which is why he opted to quiz them in this elliptical way. He correctly deduced that simply asking them straight out 'are women who buy instant coffee slatterns?' might get an evasive answer. Interestingly in this case the marketers wanted to sell the instant coffee and were delighted to get this invaluable insight from which they could begin to build an acceptable image for instant coffee.

However their efforts have been wasted on me: I'm no slattern. Rather, thanks to adroit marketing by the coffee chains, I am now a skilled prig: unnervingly, my new found coffee know-how makes me feel superior to my instant coffee ordering friend. I have marked myself out as a sophisticate. Except that I am still anxious that I am drinking the wrong coffee. Then the awful truth dawns: I can't tell. I don't actually know whether I'm drinking the instant or the Americano. Pure illusion: pure marketing.

Customer dissatisfaction

The growth in coffee shop chains has been explosive, as has that of countless other consumer markets. My experiences are being replicated across developed economies and for every sector of consumption – food, cars, computers, furnishings, clothes, armaments – as well as coffee. Farcically over-stocked supermarkets now spread from Sydney to San Francisco, and their progenitors – Tesco, Wal-Mart, Carrefour – are looking to repeat their profitable strategies in developing countries, as are food producers (see Box 3.1) Stockholders are more than happy for them to do so.

This is the inevitable consequence of letting marketing rip and thereby releasing an army of bright executives who devote their every waking moment to devising new stuff, and new variations on stuff, to sell us. We will discuss their methods in more detail in Chapter 7, but at this point the wastefulness of this frenetic activity can best be illustrated by the 'me-too' product. This, as the name suggests, describes the marketer's inclination to copy other marketers: because a competitor has brought out a successful new product (i.e. one which sells) we will produce one as well. The result is endless replication. This may result in some perfecting of the product, but for the most it is just wasteful repetition. And the fact that marketers have given it a name speaks volumes for how common it is: a significant proportion of the 40,000 supermarket offerings will be 'me-toos'.

As with the coffee example, this superfluity of choice does not make our lives easier or better – it makes them more difficult and stressful. As a researcher I know

---

BOX 3.1 THE SUPERMARKET CULTURE OF RIDICULOUS CHOICE AND PROCESSED FOOD COMES TO THE AMAZON

Nestlé's floating supermarket

Nestlé's floating supermarket took its maiden voyage on the Amazon last year and has been distributing the company's products to around 800,000 isolated riverside people each month ever since. Christened Nestlé Até Você – Nestlé Comes to You – the boat carries around 300 of the company's processed lines, including ice creams and infant milk, but no other foods. The products are packaged in smaller pack sizes to make them more affordable.

The boat also acts as a collection point for the network of door-do-door saleswomen Nestlé has recruited to promote its brands. Targeting consumers from socio-economic classes C, D and E is part of the company's strategic plan for growth, it says.

Nestlé has also set up a network of more than 7,500 resellers and 220 micro-distributors to reach people in the slums of Rio de Janeiro, São Paulo and other major Brazilian cities.

Source: *The Guardian*, 24 November 2011, p.29

respondents find it very difficult to choose between multiple options, and if I ask a respondent to rank more than three – or at most five items – in order of preference, the data will rapidly degenerate into meaningless clutter. Try it yourself: list your ten favourite television programmes or pieces of music, starting with the one you like best. It is very difficult because there are multiple variables at play, your preferences will vary by time of day or your mood, holding ten positions in your head is challenging, and – perhaps most fundamentally – we frequently do not have such ready-formed opinions in our heads waiting to be downloaded on demand. Market researchers know all this well, as we saw with the coffee example, and so use far more sophisticated methods to get at our putative desires.

But as far as our discussion of choice is concerned, it suggests that we simply do not care that much. Again, a little personal reflection bears this out. Ordinarily we might well swither agonizingly between chicken oriental and the fish kedgeree on the restaurant menu, but if you haven't eaten since breakfast and have spent the day chopping logs the desire simply to eat comes to the fore. Similarly if we are cold the brand of the fleece we are offered ceases to matter, as does the make of car if we urgently need a lift.

Note this is not an argument for no choice – for a world of bland uniformity – just for less. To live fulfilled lives we do need variety, we just don't need the excess generated by corporate marketing; the 40,000 options. We cannot process them, the effort to do so makes our lives more difficult – and we just don't care that much.

For the marketer this indifference will not do at all; if we don't care we won't shop. Our indifference has to be tweaked into a whim, and from there into a want, then a need and, finally, the marketing heaven of a must-have. The perennial question 'do marketers create need or just respond to it?' is simplistic. Marketers do look for a grain of need (want/whim), but then focus all their efforts on stimulating and growing this. For example, conducting focus groups with eight-year-olds on their savoury snack eating preferences – about which years of marketing have given them lots of knowledge and opinions – might uncover a marginal preference for a crunchier potato chip. This could then be catered for with a new range of square crisps which are genuinely crunchier than the competition. To help the new product along, it will be backed by the full panoply of marketing tools we will discuss in Chapter 7 – including advertising (evocatively emphasizing their crispiness; a message reinforced on the pack), ubiquitous distribution and great value pocket money prices. And just to circle the wagons, parents will be targeted with reassuring nutrition messages (the crisps are lower fat thanks to a marginal reformulation – and they contain no sugar at all).

Thus a need is neither created nor imposed: it is encouraged, harboured and moulded. By definition, this process depends on customers being unhappy with current offerings; why else would the eight-year-old buy the new square crisp? Or why would you switch shampoos? Or trade in your car? More fundamentally, purchase depends on us being unhappy with and insecure about not just our current shopping habits, but our lives. Have we got BO? Is our car new enough to impress the neighbours? The kids will give me hell if I don't get that new breakfast cereal …

Thus marketing is not so much about satisfaction as dissatisfaction. Business textbooks extol the virtues of the satisfied customer as a route to 'the economic advantage which endures' because he or she will always come back for more. But we will only come back for more when we have a renewed need; in the short term at least, satisfied customers just stop consuming – which is an anathema to the marketer.

Ultimately, corporate marketing will always be about fostering discontentment – what Sennett calls 'the dramatization of the potential'[3] – because business depends on our perpetual neediness.

Fat chance

From our point of view the most tangible result of this faux spoiling is obesity. We are getting fatter by the day. It is no accident that, as we noted in Chapter 1, the USA – the home and still the capital of marketing – is leading the way. But others are following faithfully behind. Over 60 per cent of British adults are now obese or overweight,[4] while in Australia, the home of the outback and the surfboard, the rate is 61 per cent.[5] What better indication could there be that we are consuming too much?

You do not have to be a nutritionist to work out that we get fat when we take in more calories than we burn off. It is a simple variation on the Micawber principle: 'Daily calorific intake 2,000, daily expenditure 2,000. Result happiness. Daily calorific intake 2,000, daily expenditure 1,950. Result misery.' Nor does it come as much of a surprise that foods high in salt, sugar and fat are particularly bad for us – with the last two driving obesity and the first tempting our taste buds and cranking up our blood pressure. Your new burger isn't selling fast enough? Add bacon and cheese (fat and salt). Your brand of ice cream is languishing? Fold in extra chocolate (sugar and fat).

Processed foods have some or all of these three tempting but obesogenic constituents in common. They also benefit from massive marketing budgets. Indeed it is the processing that generates the money to spend on marketing. Plain old potatoes are currently selling in Tesco for 45 pence a kilo; a 150 gram pack of balsamic vinegar and sea salt Kettle Chips is £1.85 – which works out at £12.40 a kilo – approximately 25 times as much. (Unless you go for the special deal of two bags of Kettle Chips for £2, in which case they come down to the bargain price of £7 per kilo and the difference is merely a factor of 15. But then you will eat twice as many as you would have done, which is a really bad idea …)

So for the marketer the logic is irrefutable: if you add salt and fat to your potatoes, you massively multiply your profits and this forms the marketing strategy. As we noted in the last chapter, this is about profits and shareholder dividends, not our needs. Processing foods makes them far more profitable and the resulting money can be put into the sort of marketing strategies we will discuss in the next three chapters. The salt, sugar and fat that are added to tempt our whims actually harm our real needs; they provide transitory pleasure at the long term price of weight gain, hypertension and diabetes.

The perils of self-importance

At the same time as damaging our bodies, the pretence of focusing so devoutly on our needs and wants has a corrosive impact on our minds. David Foster Wallace, the American philosopher, reminds us of our tendency to see the world in an egocentric way.[6] What we see, hear, understand and experience is filtered through our own senses – through the 'lens of self'; everyone else's views and experiences come to us second hand; they have to be communicated to us. This creates a default position of perceiving everything as revolving around ourselves.

He goes on to highlight the dangers of this perspective. When things go wrong – the train doesn't arrive or the computer crashes – we take it as a personal affront, and give no allowance to the fact that other perfectly legitimate – indeed more important – priorities than our own might exist. We behave like over-indulged children. The truth of his words is brought home to me when I am in London and find myself getting dyspeptic about a delayed tube train – and every now and again the announcement will be made, using those awful words, 'there is a person under a train'. I am then forced, rather shamefacedly, to rethink my position.

Buddhists would agree with Wallace about the need to do such realigning on a more systemic basis: 'to conquer oneself is a greater victory than to conquer thousands in a battle'.[7] The alternative, Wallace warns, is fruitless and self-destructive:

> worship your own body and beauty and sexual allure and you will always feel ugly, and when time and age start showing, you will die a million deaths before they finally plant you[… .]Worship power – you will feel weak and afraid, and you will need ever more power over others to keep the fear at bay. Worship your intellect, being seen as smart – you will end up feeling stupid, a fraud, always on the verge of being found out.

The first and most daunting challenge is that we don't even realize we are behaving in this self-aggrandizing way. He illustrates this dilemma with the story of two young fish who are swimming along, and they happen to meet an older fish swimming the other way, who nods at them and says, 'Morning, boys, how's the water?' And the two young fish reply 'It is lovely, thank you.' They swim on for a bit, and then eventually one of them looks over at the other and asks: 'What the hell is water?'[8]

Wallace goes on to explain that the point of the story is that the most ubiquitous and powerful influences on our behaviour are those closest to us – the ones we take for granted, do not even realize are there and cannot discuss and describe. Our immediate environment is to us as the water is to the young fish, and it has an equally powerful impact on our lives whether we realize it or not.

The problem for us is that our water is increasingly polluted by marketing which, flying in the face of Wallace and the Dalai Lama, actively encourages us to be self-centred, vain and materialistic. Think for a minute how the cosmetics marketer lays waste to those stark warnings about worshipping youth and beauty. Oil of Olay, for instance, offers the opportunity of 'achieving younger-looking skin at any age' and the chance to 'fight 7 signs of aging' with a 'fragrance- and color-free daily facial moisturizer' which 'moisturizes to create visibly younger-looking skin'.[9] L'Oréal promises even more: 'Visible Lift' is their '1st anti-wrinkle foundation with a serum inside' so you can have 'instantly younger-looking skin'– no need to even wait for your eternal youthfulness to be created. (Notice, incidentally, the use of the word 'daily' by Oil of Olay – the promises may be fulsome, but you will need to make a long term commitment.)

Corporate marketers would have even less sympathy with Wallace's wider and equally blunt reminder that (discounting theology) 'pretty much anything else you worship will eat you alive. If you worship money and things – if they are where you tap real meaning in life – then you will never have enough.'

And here he skewers the toxic paradox at the heart of marketing. An Aladdin's cave of products and services are created for and offered to us to satisfy our every need – but we can never be satisfied. The problem is we are seeking happiness not stuff; and stuff brings us about as close to happiness as tinsel does to redemption. To quote the Dalai Lama again: 'happiness is not something ready-made. It comes from your own actions'. You cannot buy it any more than you can buy youth.

You have to work at it

Even if corporate marketers could genuinely deliver to our needs – if they really knew what was best for us, could commercialize it without jeopardizing our satisfaction and were not beholden to their shareholding paymasters – the resulting world would be mind-numbing.

Marketers are fond of proclaiming that consumerism is the shame of marketing: when marketing works as intended it becomes superfluous, because there is no dissatisfaction, no possibility of complaint. The customer pays the agreed price and gets exactly what he or she wants. Perfect harmony. But as with any earthly paradise, this is both unattainable and dangerous.

Somerset Maugham tells the story of a father explaining to his friend why he was worried about his son. Has his son got into difficulties, asks his friend? Is he in debt or ill? On the contrary, the story unfolds, he is doing extremely well: he has just taken a first class degree from Oxford, then spent the summer triumphing in a tennis championship in Monte Carlo, gambled and won at the casino and defeated a crude attempt to cheat him with his own ingenuity. So what on earth is the problem, asks the friend?

He has learnt nothing, replies the father.

As with Maugham's young man, the perfect market teaches us nothing about life. Even the promise of it is mind-warping, as it builds and reinforces a sense of unjustified entitlement. We have a right to satisfaction, we *are* worth it. It also strokes us into thinking such superficial satisfactions really matter, that retail therapy actually works. We know in our hearts this is nonsense, but the remorseless drip of modern marketing, with endless offers of easy tricks and hollow solutions, wears us down.

Marketers certainly fear the veil will slip. They have long realized that we are frequently visited by doubts, especially when we spend large sums of money. The little voice that questions whether 450 euros on a new digital camera was a good idea or trading up to a top of the range Volvo is really affordable. They even have a name for these stirrings of heresy: 'post purchase dissonance' – which they deliberately seek to snuff out. Whole campaigns are run just to quiet these sacrilegious inclinations. It is the consumer facing equivalent of the beverage alcohol industry's efforts to suppress the inconvenient truth of alcopops.

Heaven forbid that the consumer should ever come to doubt the religion of consumption, the power of the high street votive offering. But such doubts do creep in for many, not just on an ad hoc should–I–have–bought–that–Volvo basis, but on a systemic have–I–really–spent–my–whole–life–doing–nothing–more–than–working–to–amass–a–heap–of–consumer–durables basis. Echoing Biff Loman, we wonder if it is worth devoting 'your whole life to keeping stock, or making phone calls, or selling or buying. To suffer fifty weeks a year for the sake of a two week vacation, when all you really desire is to be outdoors, with your shirt off.'[10] This doubt has been precipitated in many by external financial pressures – most dramatically in the recent economic crisis.

But for most of us, and for most of the time, our post purchase dissonance is dissipated and the insidious sense of entitlement remains and grows. It can even begin to invade the rest of our lives – our real relationships, our sense of purpose, our aspirations – the things that really matter. We want our lovers, our children, our parents to deliver immediate gratification and first class service. As Richard Sennett points out, echoing our discussion of politics in the last chapter, this thinking has begun to infiltrate and sap the democratic process:

> user friendly makes a hash of democracy. Democracy requires that citizens be willing to make some effort to find out how the world around them works. Few American proponents of the war in Iraq, wanted to learn about Iraq (most couldn't in fact locate it on a map).[11]

We are trained into a culture of she who pays the price has a right to satisfaction. Like the marketer before us we turn a blind eye to the rights and wrongs of that satisfaction – not just for us, but everyone else. Time and again we forget the real price and who is paying it; and corporate marketers, of course, help us to maintain this mendacious idyll.

The Commonweal

During the Cold War it was argued that the concept of 'Mutually Assured Destruction' – both sides having the capacity to destroy the whole world – was sufficient to keep the peace. Nuclear war did not break out, so maybe this dangerous game of brinkmanship worked; but the policy had built-in nuclear proliferation: both the Soviets and the Americans had to make sure they kept up with each other's missile count and capability. The nuclear armaments market grew continuously.

Marketing has much the same effect. Corporations, like the superpowers of yesteryear, are competing to sell ever more things to us, and we are all frenetically involved in the resulting process of proliferation in every sector of the market. So involved, that we seem barely to notice that the same principle of 'Mutually Assured Destruction' is at play. In a finite world, if marketers keep selling and we keep buying, the result will be just as destructive as nuclear war. As the acronym has it: MAD.

The Victorians recognized consumption as a killer; we have been much slower to catch on and marketing is at the heart of our torpor. Our forebears, of course, were anxious about tuberculosis (TB), which once identified was immediately seen as a scourge: no one needed to be convinced that TB was a bad thing and the task of motivating people to avoid it was relatively straightforward. Responding to TB was also a unified purpose: all sections of society – public, private and voluntary – were involved. The challenge then was not whether to act, but what to do. Initial attempts based on inadequate understanding of the aetiology of the disease were largely unsuccessful. However scientific advances which isolated the cause – the disease vector – and then a means of either preventing it infecting people in the first place, or reducing its rapacity, brought about massive reductions in the illness and its symptoms. The battle is far from over: in developing countries the poor continue to be ravaged by TB, and drug resistant strains of the bacillus saw over 6,000 cases in the UK last year. But the former is largely a function of economics and the latter compares favourably with an estimated one in four deaths from TB in nineteenth-century Britain. The Victorians' dangerous form of consumption may not have been defeated, but it has been successfully and consistently combated.

Our dangerous form of consumption – both of individually harmful products and of all products to excess – is, however, proving more resistant. We have taken the first step and recognized that there is a problem; like the Victorians we have spotted our adversary. Indeed we have the advantage on them in that we have also isolated the bug – an over-enthusiasm for stuff – and the steps to stop it spreading are nice and obvious: we just need to avoid spending our hard earned money on harmful products, and reduce our expenditure on everything. In fact we don't actually have to do anything – just stop doing something: shopping. And yet we are failing.

The explanation lies in marketing: the TB bacillus, nasty though it is, does not have armies of bright, energetic, well-resourced MBAs on its side planning and deploying complex and subtle marketing strategies. It can't marshal massive research budgets to explore the deepest recesses of our psyches or buttress itself with multi-million pound ad campaigns and evocative brands. It can't persuade us to engage in synthetic relationships, sign us up to specious loyalty schemes or adopt the guise of our favourite celebrities. It can't invite our leaders out for games of golf and recruit them to its cause. Compared to the corporate marketer, the humble bacillus is hapless and disempowered.

Marketing doesn't just inure us to climate change; it also blinds us to all the inequities that got us to this point in the first place. The material good fortune of being born into a rich country, of acquiring the money to make yet another purchase, of having all the other stuff that makes this latest bauble a 'must-have'. And the inequities that our purchases perpetuate – the sweat-shops, the fruit from Neruda's 'dictatorship of the flies' and its descendants, the pharmaceuticals tested on cheap third world guinea pigs.

Fairtrade perhaps points up the moral shortfall here. It is a wonderful idea: fairness for all those involved in the marketplace; making sure that everyone's needs are understood and catered for – just as marketers purport to do, but in the case of the Fairtrade Foundation at least, they make sure the reality matches the rhetoric. Except that their impact is miniscule.

The UK is a world leader in this noble cause, but it still has a very limited number of product categories in which Fairtrade is practised. And the biggest penetration, by far, is for bananas and coffee – both at 20 per cent. This is an honourable effort, which undoubtedly makes an immense difference to the quality of life of many majority world farmers. But what about the other 80 per cent of bananas and coffee? and 90 per cent plus of the other categories? and the 100 per cent of everything else? Why are these not fairly traded? Given the world's immense income inequalities, how can the rich north ever justify short-changing the poor south? And given the marketers' avowal of consumer sovereignty, mutually beneficial exchange and long term relationship building, how is this possible?

Birthday cake

At the heart of this manipulation is greed – both the marketers' and our own. Our carefully planted and tended sense of entitlement crowds out feelings of responsibility.

Imagine you went to a children's birthday party and all the five-year-olds were about to enjoy the generously proportioned rocket-themed birthday cake. Then a couple of the bigger boys started pushing the other kids out of the way and grabbing all the cake for themselves. While they fended their fellow guests off with one hand and alternating feet, they stuffed their mouths with their other hand. You would protest, intervene and insist on a fairer distribution of the goodies. You might also explain to the malefactors that their behaviour wasn't even in their own interests – for example that they would end up making themselves sick.

The drip, drip, drip of non-stop marketing has worn away such wisdom from our adult lives. Bankers and CEOs pay themselves ludicrously large sums of money that they cannot even spend without help. The *Financial Times* produces a fortnightly magazine for the over-rich called 'How to Spend It', full of outrageously expensive baubles designed to keep the money flowing out of your bank account just as fast as it flows in. My favourite is a perpetually rotating storage and display cabinet for your collection of self-winding Swiss watches (sorry, chronometers); it rotates in order to keep the ones you aren't wearing wound up. Leaving aside the gross profligacy of owning multiple expensive watches, consider the asinine waste of a machine built to wind up self-winding watches. Was there ever a better illustration of the ecological imbecility[12] that Huxley warned of a full fifty years ago? And it makes the greedy five-year-old bullies seem quite innocuous.

It is easy, however, to condemn the obvious profligacy of the super-rich. The obscenity of luxury yachts lined up in the Thames so that their over-privileged owners can be bussed to seats at the Olympics that we ordinary folk could not possibly afford; or a Smythson handbag priced at £2,500 (it would take an adult on the UK minimum wage over two and half months to earn this sum – and that's assuming zero deductions); or Bob Diamond's £10 million salary. All scandalous.

But in a world of finite resources we ordinary mortals have to look at our own excesses. A Learjet may leave an SUV standing in the carbon stakes, but when millions of us buy the latter and only an elite few the former, we are the ones causing the greater ecological damage. There is a direct link between the gross product ranges in the supermarkets and coffee shops we patronize and the degradation of our planet.

That's a planet on which almost half the population, around three billion people, live on less than two euros a day[13] and to whom owning a car is as distant (and profligate) a prospect as a Smythson handbag or a Learjet. Over 200 coffee options in a North of England Starbucks; one in Cuba, if you are lucky. And they grow coffee in Cuba.

Thus, not satisfied with our bodies and minds, corporate marketing takes our souls, turning us into cut-price merchant bankers who willingly soil our own nests for the sake of a bag of Kettle Chips and a jar of dip.

Willing victims

The Ford Challenger ad begins with a scene from the American War of Independence. A British regular is seen returning from a scouting trip to report that he has seen something (apparently) bewildering. Suddenly a posse of Ford Challengers, each streaming the stars and stripes and one driven by George Washington himself, roar over the hill to save the day. The voice-over intones: 'here's a couple o' things America got right – cars and freedom'.[14] The idea that cars bring us freedom has been a mainstay of the auto industry's advertising for generations, and continues despite its increasing implausibility as fuel prices escalate and roads clog up. Meanwhile Nike reminds us we can 'just do it'; Range Rover invite us to experience 'the power of presence'; Diageo purrs that 'every day, everywhere, [we] can celebrate with [their] brands' and L'Oréal, of course, reassures us that we are worth it.

We just have to buy the $200 trainers; spend anything up to $100,000 on a car, fork out $50 (at least) for some champagne and pay out another $50 for an anti-aging treatment. And we are not going to do this once, but for ever. Trainers go out of fashion, cars depreciate – tendencies which marketers are happy to encourage. Remember we won't buy unless we are dissatisfied. And don't forget that the anti-aging cream needs a daily application, and Diageo wants us to celebrate every day. Richard Sennett takes this a step further and points out, with regret, that our consumption is taking on a more fundamental purpose. A generation ago we defined ourselves by what we produced – even our surnames reflect this: Taylor, Schneider, Sastre, Tailleur; but today we get our identity from what we wear, drive and drink: by shopping. Good evening, Mr Shopper ...

So the consumer choice and the mutually beneficial relationship that marketing extols rapidly change into a treadmill. We have to work to get the money to buy the products to access the good life; and we have to do this perpetually. Thus another paradox emerges: the deep-seated sense of entitlement we are all busily acquiring comes at the price of dependence. We are living in a gilded cage, and paying for its upkeep.

We all know this; yet we go on shopping. We are well aware that we are becoming ever more materialistic, but our happiness is, if anything, reducing. We know we buy at the expense of our own, our fellow human beings' and our planet's wellbeing. And we know it's not worth it. We nod sagely at the quip that no one on their deathbed ever said, 'I wish I had spent more time at the office,' and yet we carry on working to earn the money to buy the stuff that we know we don't need and will not bring us contentment. We are like Sisyphus, the king in Greek mythology who was condemned by the gods to push a huge rock up a hill, only to see it roll down again just before he reached the summit – so his task continues without end. But we haven't been condemned by the all-powerful Olympians, we are just being manipulated by corporate marketers.

Corporate marketers may be less intimidating than temperamental Greek gods – and they are certainly less pleasing on the eye – but the honeyed word and superficial charm of soft power can easily outperform more brutal methods. They know their work and they seem to have us under control. This has fundamental political ramifications, as Aldous Huxley observed: 'a really efficient totalitarian state would be one in which the all-powerful executive of political bosses and their managers control an army of slaves who do not need to be coerced because they love their servitude'. The ultimate success of corporate marketing has been its ability to make us love our servitude. As our waistbands expand and our needs are out-sourced so our critical faculties are dulled.

The next few chapters will help sharpen them up by examining the corporate marketers' methods.

The Corporation

1. *You wear my name upon your breast*
    Your body end to end
    It's plain for all the world to see
    You are my greatest friend
    You are my greatest friend, you are
        my greatest friend
    I am the Corporation and you are my
        greatest friend

2. *You love my Golden Arches*
    You crave my stylish swoosh
    The looks you give my logos
    Would cause a stone to blush
    Cause a stone to blush, cause a stone
        to blush
    I am the Corporation and I'd cause a
        stone to blush

3. *My slogans are your poetry*
    Though they'd make a poet scream
    They give your life its meaning
    And craft your hopes and dreams
    Craft your hopes and dreams, craft
        your hopes and dreams
    I am the Corporation and I craft your
        hopes and dreams

4. *You let me recreate you*
    In my image, by my hand
    Like masochistic cattle
    You queue to get my brand
    Queue to get my brand, queue to get
        my brand
    I am the Corporation and you queue
        to get my brand

5. *Now my work has just begun*
    I have ambitious goals
    I've started with your heart
    But soon I'll have your soul
    Soon I'll have your soul, soon I'll
        have your soul
    I am the Corporation and soon I'll
        have your soul

6. *For I am the new Jehovah*
    You answer to my call
    You kneel before my labels
    And worship in my malls
    Worship in my malls, worship in my
        malls
    I am the Corporation and you
        worship in my malls

7. *You wear my name upon your breast*
    Your body head to toe
    Little do you understood
    I am your greatest foe
    I am your greatest foe, I am your
        greatest foe
    I am the Corporation and I am your
        greatest foe
    For I'll crush you in the end, crush
        you in the end
    I am the Corporation and I'll crush
        you in the end

4

NOT EXACTLY LYING …

When it's right to shoot the messenger

I used to work a lot with advertising agencies, and I never met a single account planner or creative director who thought their commercials had no effect on people. And few would argue that the media more generally is innocuous and can be allowed to get on with its business without regulation or oversight – especially since the *News of the World* hacking scandal. And yet marketing textbooks and practitioners are insistent that advertising has no effect beyond reflecting current mores and confirming existing purchasing habits. We will explore this uncharacteristic humility a little further in this chapter, and how it is contradicted by both common sense and hard evidence.

There is, however, little that is hard about advertising. It employs subtlety and subterfuge and deals in emotions and imagery, which speak to the heart not the head, and time and again get under our critical radar. Doing this successfully depends on knowing us well; so marketers study us as minutely as any psychologist or anthropologist.

It also involves using many channels of communication as well as multimedia advertising: sponsorship, loyalty schemes, merchandising, free samples, brand stretching, point of sale display, direct response (what we used to call junk mail but which is now hydra-headed thanks to digital technology) and any other possible channels are pressed into service. These different elements are combined and aligned, much as individual strands in a rope, to create a much more powerful whole. All to no effect of course, the advertisers assure us, beyond a little reassurance and reflection (unless they happen to be talking to a client).

Despite the 'what me, gov?' stance of corporate marketers, regulators have attempted to control advertising. However, their efforts have been piecemeal and ineffectual, usually restricted to rules on what advertisers can say. Given the ethereal nature of most advertising messages, this works about as well as using a net to catch the wind. What does work is simply to stop advertising (or marcomms) altogether – as many countries are now finding with tobacco. However, marketers resist this at every possible opportunity and in every possible way – fighting, delaying and evading (whilst still maintaining their advertising doesn't have any effect on behaviour, of course).

The result is that the regulation of advertising is largely ineffectual, and advertisers continue unencumbered in their efforts to persuade us to consume, not just individually harmful products, but more of everything. This is doing to the planet what tobacco smoke does to the lungs.

A nation in crisis

On Monday 13 October 2008 the BBC's main nightly news bulletin was devoted to the shock announcement that the UK Government had just agreed to pump £37 billion pounds of taxpayers' money into the country's three main banks. The then Prime Minister, Gordon Brown, said that the circumstances and the injection of money were 'unprecedented', adding ominously, 'but essential for all of us'. Numerous pundits were then brought in to explain that a) we were on the brink of ruin, b) the folly and cupidity of the banks was to blame for this calamitous turn of events and c) we would be picking up the tab for many years to come. This last point came from a former Chancellor, no less, reflecting the fact that the £37 billion actually had to be borrowed from the same financial sector we were bailing out. Adding this insult to the injury presumably underpinned the BBC business correspondent Robert Peston's observation that the banks faced 'absolute humiliation'.

So this was not a good day for the UK banking sector in general, and especially not for the Royal Bank of Scotland, which had swallowed a full 20 of the 37 billion pound hand-out. One would, then, expect at least a tad of humility – if not a public apology and tearing of hair. Far from it.

The fiscal calamity, not surprisingly, dominated the half-hour bulletin, pushing out all other news. The only relief was the usual five minutes of sports coverage, which remained intact. This majored on the Six Nations rugby tournament sponsored by none other than the Royal Bank of Scotland (now *our* Royal Bank of Scotland). The same RBS logo that had so portentously overshadowed the Prime Minister's stark words a few minutes earlier now smiled at us benignly from the centre spot. Surely this must be an unfortunate contractual hangover from the previous decade of financial partying, overlooked in the distractions caused by imminent economic meltdown? The 'unprecedented circumstances' could justify breaking any agreement for such insensitively frivolous expenditure – especially as the contract in question had been signed back in 2006 and had less than a year to run. An embarrassing wee gaffe, then, that would be quickly corrected? Not at all. No apology from the bank, no comment from a pundit at the incongruity – not even an ironic reference from the newsreader. Our national rugby teams playing around the symbol of our fiscal albatross didn't even raise an eyebrow. Indeed, far from expressing regret, RBS, despite its now parlous state, went on to renew its (that is, the UK taxpayers') Six Nations sponsorship just three months later – the new contract to run until the end of 2013 at a cost of £20 million.

How could this be? Why would a hard-nosed – and very hard-pressed – banker choose to squander such a large sum (although only 2 per cent of their taxpayer hand-out, £20 million would still take the average British worker about 750 years to earn) on a game of rugby? The answer is that RBS would not consider the money as squandered, but as a wise investment in marketing communications. As the RBS website proclaimed, 'Our involvement in sponsorship has previously helped us build our brand and deliver specific business objectives across the globe.'[1] Similarly the world of rugby promoted its marketing facility:

> The sponsorship began in 2003 and is currently contracted through to the end of the 2013 Championship. The RBS 6 Nations sponsorship has multiple objectives. In addition to generating positive brand association for RBS, the sponsorship is also used to reward customers and to support community rugby.[2]

This last reference to community support may raise hackles given that the massive bailouts of RBS and the rest of the banking sector have now led directly to massive cuts in public spending: statutory support for local communities determined by a democratic mandate has been replaced by optional support determined by the business interests of the banks.

But all the evidence is that, unlike sub-prime mortgages and collateralized financial instruments, such image management is indeed a very wise investment. It underpins the success of all our major corporations enabling them to put a human face on what are monolithic, technocratic and ruthless organizations. Obscene bonuses, fat-cat salaries and an all too obvious single-minded focus on profit are likely to frighten the horses. The Six Nations rugby, by contrast, is couthie, honest and down to earth. Using the power of association it provides the perfect way of presenting a more acceptable face to the world – and keeping us all on-board. It's not exactly a lie ...

Getting under our radar

Welcome to the world of marcomms.

It all began with the prostitutes of Ancient Greece putting nails in the soles of their sandals to spell out the words 'follow me' in the sand to potential clients, and the core principle of communication to sell one's wares remains. However, over the last hundred or so years the advent of truly mass media – radio, film, television and more recently the internet – has raised concerns about power and influence. Early thinking adopted the fairly crude model of the hypodermic syringe: messages were 'injected' into a passive audience by an active communicator and the impacts on our behaviour were predictable and plain to see. The audience was characterized as powerless – we did what we were told.

The famous events surrounding Orson Welles' radio production of *The War of the Worlds* in 1938 lent verisimilitude to this view. Tens of thousands of Americans actually believed that the story, concerning an invasion of Earth by Martians, was really happening – resulting in panic and even deaths. Such was the furore that the rules of broadcasting were changed as a result. The notoriety of these events, combined with the palpable success of Nazi propaganda in Germany, seemed to confirm the idea that the media were all-powerful and people were easily fooled. As Joseph Goebbels put it: 'nothing is easier than leading the people on a leash; I just hold up a dazzling campaign poster and they jump through it'.

Advertisers soon learnt that this model was too simplistic, however. Just putting an ad out did not guarantee commercial success. Indeed it could have the reverse effect: the 1960s campaign for Strand cigarettes, for instance, is credited with killing the brand. Its image of a trenched-coated man in a dark urban street pulling on one of the eponymous fags under the strap-line 'you're never alone with a Strand', only succeeded in defining the Strand smoker as a terminal Billy-no-mates. The audience, it became clear, plays a big part in the communication process; the meaning of the message, like beauty, lies, at least partly, in the eye of the beholder.

The mistake is then to rush to the other end of the spectrum, and see us the audience as all-powerful, with the ad cowering before our mastery. Again this is too simplistic. Indeed if there is one generalization that can be made about advertising it is that nothing about it is simple, nothing quite as it appears.

The key lesson Orson Welles teaches us is not about the power of the media, but the power of subterfuge, subtlety and shade. First, subterfuge: Welles set out to produce a documentary disguised as theatre; he thought through how a real invasion from Mars would be covered by radio – sudden news flashes interrupting normal programming, comments by a trusted anchor, snatches of expert opinion, vox pops – and then very deliberately set out to replicate it. People who tuned in late, and hence missed the programme's billing as part of the *Mercury Theatre* series, were far more likely to fall for the ruse than those who listened from the start – but not so likely as those friends and neighbours they then telephoned to advise of the unfolding horror, and who tuned in to the programme as a result. A simple, straightforward statement from Orson Welles that the Martians were invading Earth would no doubt have been met with considerable scepticism, but when the revelation comes from the radio news (the key source of reliable current affairs information in 1930s America), accredited experts, significant others, that's quite a different matter – and much more convincing. The power of what marketers call 'source effect', that *who* says something matters as much as *what* is said, had been well demonstrated. As had word of mouth, especially from real people.

Second, subtlety: this was entertainment not persuasion; no overt attempt was being made to win the audience over; no apparent gain was being made by the communicator. The circuitous route, the less obvious approach is actually more powerful than the direct message. Thus subterfuge and subtlety between them deliver up a key benefit for advertisers: that of getting under our guard and by-passing our critical faculties. Madison Avenue, although already practising these methods, was nonetheless paying attention and girding its loins. Getting under our radar has become the stock in trade of advertising.

And so finally to shade: do you not feel that the sun has slipped behind a cloud? Has not the world got a little darker? As for Frodo, when Gandalf first explains the compelling power of his seemingly innocent ring, hasn't the brightness of the day reduced? Advertising's power comes from such dimming of the light; as with conjuring it works better when we can't quite see what's happening. So we need to turn up the light, to keep our wits about us. As your team wins the Six Nations and the RBS logo tucks itself in with that warm glow of triumph, remind yourself just how much loot Fred Goodwin pocketed; as BP trumpet their supposed move 'Beyond Petroleum' and flaunt their green, flowery imagery remember Deepwater Horizon and the pollution of the Mexican Gulf.

Knowing your audience

Welles' genius lay in his ability to see his production through the eyes of his audience. He understood their trust in the radio, their susceptibility to word of mouth, their insecurity caused by the depression and the rise of fascism in Europe and especially Japan (there were serious fears of invasion on America's West Coast at the time of the broadcast).

Marketers, for the most part, do not have Welles' artistic sensibilities or skills, so they compensate with research. They interview, watch and count us before, during and after every campaign. A vast 'advertising research' industry has grown up using focus groups, social surveys, observation and secondary statistics to study what we watch, read and attend. This is married with the vast academic literatures from psychology, sociology and even anthropology which give powerful insights into human behaviour: why we do what we do. But, as we noted in Chapter 2, these aren't social scientists with an enlightened intent to understand the world and thereby help make it better; they are corporate marketers who just want to know how they can get better at selling us things.

Advertising research is actually just a small corner of a burgeoning field called 'consumer behaviour', about which countless courses are taught in our business schools and massive, erudite tomes are written. As I write this I am looking at one such, called *Consumer Psychology for Marketing*, which has distilled all that marketers need to know about the psychology of our behaviour into accessible, bite-sized, practical lessons. And you thought psychologists all work tirelessly for our mental wellbeing? Furthermore, this commercial emphasis in academe is set to grow as public funding for universities decreases across the world thanks (with abiding irony) to the private sector's failings. Academics are inevitably being driven to applied disciplinary areas which pay their way. I know of at least one Scottish university that is closing down its geography and psychology departments and transferring their business teaching and research, which was refreshingly critical, to its more deferential business school.

Marketers, then, do their advertising research to get inside our heads and hearts, to enable them to see the world as we see it. Like Welles, they too want to understand our insecurities – remember Huxley's 'failings and weaknesses' – as well as our physical, emotional and even spiritual needs. Like Welles they also want to know what resonates – the language, images, role models we use and defer to. These insights provide the footholds for their messages, guide their design and deployment, and as a result help make them more persuasive.

They also bridge the gap between the marketer and his or her customers, who typically come from very different backgrounds and life stages. How else is a forty-year-old advertising creative going to be able to sell a new toy to an eight-year-old girl? To tease that whim to a want, to a need and thence to a must-have? Or how else can an affluent non-smoking tobacco executive design a brand that resonates with a poor, blue collar smoker? This latter gulf was brought blinking into the sunlight a few years ago when an RJ Reynolds executive was asked why he and his colleagues did not smoke and he answered, on camera and with no apparent sense of shame: 'We don't smoke this shit, we just sell it. We reserve the right to smoke for the young, the poor, the black and the stupid.'[3]

Advertising research is painstaking and delicate work. Every element that makes up an ad – every slogan, character, role model, word, situation, colour and sound – will be subject to perpetual and very sensitive checking. Does it get – and keep – our attention? Will we understand it? Will it resonate? Above all, how will it make us feel? Remember most advertising is not actually about factual information because the great majority of the products we buy are completely familiar to us.

Hopes and dreams

Perhaps the best evidence of this gulf between corporate advertising and objective truth comes from France and the Loi Evin (from the French word for law; Evin was the minister who brought it in). This is a law that was passed in 1990 to help reduce the country's dangerously high levels of drinking. It doesn't do anything as dramatic as ban alcohol advertising, it just requires advertisers to restrict their marketing communications to verifiable, factual statements about their products – such as alcoholic strength, composition, place of origin, means of production and patterns of consumption. Given that advertising is supposed to be 'legal, decent, honest and truthful', this seems to be a perfectly reasonable injunction for any campaign. Predictably, the beverage alcohol industry hates the Loi Evin. It lambasts it at every opportunity. And when an attempt was made to introduce equivalent legislation into booze-sodden Britain in 2011 it was obediently snuffed out by our dutiful government.

Tobacco provides the most egregious illustration of this race for the ethereal. Box 4.1 presents the creative brief – the core document that guides and justifies the creative development of every campaign – developed by UK ad agency TBWA

BOX 4.1 SELLING FREEDOM – A CREATIVE BRIEF FOR
MARLBORO

Why are we advertising?
To strongly evoke core Marlboro values (individuality, freedom, real and
America) by continuation of 'Marlboro Country' campaign.

Who are we talking to?
Primary: 18–24 males, student and non-student, into making a
                      definite statement (rock, cult, bikes, cars).
Secondary: Older, established smokers (you're doing the right thing).
Consideration: Lights target smokers (Lights is 'Marlboro, not Reds').

How do we want to change what people think, feel or know?
We want to engage their aspirations and fantasies – *'I'd like to be there, do that,
own that'.*

**What is the most powerful thing we can say to achieve this? (The
proposition.)**
Escape to Marlboro Country.

**What is the best way of supporting this proposition (facts, emotions,
values)?**
Strongly conjure up Marlboro core values: individuality and freedom and real
and America.

Simons Palmer Limited for Marlboro cigarettes. Factual copy would need to read
something like: 'Marlboro cigarettes are highly carcinogenic and fiercely addictive;
one in two of those of our customers who don't manage to quit are killed by
them.' I accept it is not catchy – but it is true. It would meet the terms of the Loi
Evin. Instead of this honesty, the brief opts for conjuring tricks: 'We want to
engage their aspirations and fantasies – "I'd like to be there, do that, own that".' ...
'the most powerful thing we can say to achieve this? the advertising "proposition":
escape to Marlboro Country'. The brief continues: 'the best way of supporting this
proposition facts, emotions, values: Strongly conjure up Marlboro core values:
individuality and freedom and real and America.'

The use of the word 'facts' in the last set of brackets would be laughable if it
weren't for the lung cancer patients and heart attack victims that will result from
such mockery of the truth.

So the idea of advertisers sticking to the facts is unthinkable. Facts speak to the
head, not the heart. They are direct and straightforward, flying in the face of
Welles' key lessons of subterfuge, subtlety and shade. Anyway, as we have already

noted, there is really very little new that Mars can tell us about their chocolate bar, or Ford can about the Focus. They have been pushing them so intensively for so long that we know them better than we know our families – as the UNICEF report, discussed in the next chapter, chillingly shows. The problem for the advertiser, indeed, is that their offerings are all too familiar – they need to find ways to intrigue and interest us; to tempt our jaded palates and tantalize our over-loaded inclinations to consume. How then can they trigger a whim, and tease it into a want, to a need and finally to a must-have? So they study us, intensely, perpetually and using all the skills – and professionals – they can buy.

In this sense, the corporate marketer uses advertising research to turn the clock back to the earliest thinking on mass media effects. It is there to put more power into the hands of the communicator, to make his or her message more convincing, to find ways around our scepticism and doubts. The marketers' aim is to repossess the hypodermic syringe: to keep us passively, uncritically consuming – and for many years now they have succeeded.

Business before pleasure

Marketing texts still give great credence to the so called 'Hierarchy of Effects' models of advertising effect, whose origins pre-date even Mr Welles. These models 'describe the steps or stages through which consumers typically pass when they contemplate the purchase of a product … from being unaware to aware, to having knowledge, then to liking and preference, and finally to conviction and purchase'.[4] Thirty years ago such thinking was criticized (by marketers in fact) for portraying the consumer as too passive, but hierarchical models have withstood the attack because they make a great planning tool for advertising agencies. They simply reflect the reality of the advertising world.

Table 4.1 presents the key guiding questions that are used in the creative brief by three leading ad agencies. It forcefully reminds us that creativity is very much the servant of business. The bright ideas, witty one-liners and winning sound tracks are devised for one reason and one reason only: to change what we think, feel and do for the sake of the corporate bottom line. 'What is the advertising intended to achieve?' 'Exactly what do we expect the advertising to do?' 'How do we want to change what people think, feel or know?' There is no doubt about the clear agenda of these ad agencies: to change us in some way – any way – that will boost sales.

And yet the same business text that extolled the virtues of the hierarchical models that underpin this manipulative framing, then goes on to argue that the idea that advertising actually changes things is preposterous:

> both the empirical evidence and logical deduction offer compelling evidence that marketing communication does not create demand: it is a response to demand. People buy things because they want them, not because advertising somehow compels them to purchase. When the influence of primary drivers of demand, like demographic changes, broad societal changes, and the effects

of other marketing actions, such as lower price, are controlled, there are no studies that demonstrate that marketing communication creates demand for established products.[5]

TABLE 4.1 Business not art: how advertisers focus on delivering change

Advertising agency	M&C Saatchi	Collett Dickenson Pearce & Partners	TBWA Simons Palmer Ltd
Standard checks and questions that are included in every creative brief	• Target audience • What is the advertising intended to achieve? • The single minded proposition • Substantiation for this proposition	• Exactly what do we expect the advertising to do? • Who are we talking to? • What is the single most important point we want people to take from the advertising?	• Why are we advertising? • Who are we talking to? • How do we want to change what people think, feel or know? • What is the most powerful thing we can say to achieve this? (The proposition.) • What is the best way of supporting this proposition (facts, emotions, values)?

Source: http://www.tobaccopapers.com

Given the naked change agenda of the practitioner and the assumed audience passivity of the models, this makes Orwell's Newspeak seem positively transparent. And note this isn't some backwater, low-level textbook I'm quoting. It is part of an erudite series of high quality reviews of the business literature targeting leaders in the field.

Advertising works

The writer is also completely wrong when he says there are no studies demonstrating the effect of advertising on demand. There are many such studies, which have demonstrated that advertising is encouraging people to start and continue smoking, drinking alcohol and eating fast foods. That they are focused on public health issues – and often also on children – simply reflects the urgency and concern the tangible downsides of smoking, drinking and dietary behaviours are having. And 'logical deduction' strongly suggests that what is true in these markets is true in every other consumer market.

Such is the strength of the evidence on tobacco advertising, for instance, that dozens of countries across the world, including the UK, Canada, Australia and much of Europe have now introduced primary legislation to ban it altogether. You can be sure that the multinational tobacco corporations would have contested these laws long and hard in the courts if there really were 'no studies that demonstrate that marketing communication creates demand for established products'. As we shall discuss in Chapter 8 the Marlboro Cowboy and his marketing cronies in Madison Avenue are rich, litigious and extremely solicitous of their own interests.

Corporate marketers are bound to have a difficult relationship with evidence. If the truth threatens shareholder value, it is all too likely to be ignored or denied. When E. M. Forster observed a century ago that 'Business men saw life more steadily, though with the steadiness of the half-closed eye'[6] he was just reworking the truism that we all accept – it is not possible to serve God and mammon with any consistency. The corporate marketer has to remain loyal to mammon at all times.

This troubled relationship between corporate marketers and hard evidence was hammered home to me ten years back when we were asked by the UK Food Standards Agency to examine the research evidence on what might or might not be the link between food advertising and childhood obesity. When I say 'examine' I understate the task: we were to conduct a 'systematic review' – an SR – of all the studies done over the previous thirty years. SR is an assiduously rigorous process, involving searching for every study and adjudging its quality. Ben Goldacre expresses it elegantly:

> The science of systematic review that grew from this research is exactly that: a science. It's a series of reproducible methods for searching information, to ensure that your evidence synthesis is as free from bias as your individual experiments. You describe not just what you found, but how you looked, which research databases you used, what search terms you typed, and so on. This apparently obvious manoeuvre has revolutionised the science of medicine.[7]

Amongst other things it obviates disputes because all of the workings-out are revealed – so if you don't like a finding you have to say why; to identify the precise link in the argument you reject. To add to the rigour, our systematic review of food advertising was also subjected to thorough and independent peer review – on six separate occasions.

Unfortunately, no one had explained any of this to the food and advertising industries.

When they learnt that our review[8] had concluded that food advertising did influence children's eating behaviour and was linked to obesity – as all good quality reviews have done since – they went into attack mode. For the most part this involved interminable questioning of the findings, not in a precise 'this–study–was–mistaken' or 'that–specific–link–in–the–chain–doesn't–stand–up' way, but in a blanket 'we–don't–agree' way. Thus the Food and Drink Federation told the *Financial Times* that 'while food advertising plays a role in affecting consumers' choice of brands it does not dictate [the] overall eating habits of children',[9] and the next day an advertising industry spokesman from the Food Advertising Unit (FAU) at the Advertising Association informed *The Times* that: 'the obesity problem hasn't just emerged, it has been around for thirty years; it's ridiculous to suggest that advertising is the cause'.[10] (Incidentally, an Assistant Professor of Marketing from the London Business School is quoted in the same *Times* article as saying 'actually advertising very rarely works, and never has in this area'[11] – which will come as a nasty shock to corporate advertisers such as McDonald's and Coke, as they continue to splurge millions on apparently useless campaigns.)

These denials were repeated each time the review was presented at a long series of public meetings across the UK – and indeed the world. The familiar arguments deployed a generation previously by the tobacco companies in defence of their ads were dusted down and parroted: 'advertising only affects brand choice', 'other non-advertising factors are to blame', 'it's up to parents', 'children understand how advertising works'. No debate; just denial.

However, they also deployed two other ruses used by corporations, from oil to alcohol, wherever a threat to their profits is identified. They went to the business schools and hired their own marketing-friendly academics. The Food Advertising Unit (again) commissioned both a rival review, which argued that the commercial promotion of foods does not influence children,[12] and a critique of our review.[13]

The FSA (Food Standards Agency) assembled a Seminar of leading academics under the chairmanship of an eminent Cambridge professor to discuss the conflicting assessments. The limited coverage of the FAU review was noted, as well as its contradiction of a review conducted by the same author in 1996 and its rejection of virtually all social science research as either too artificial (experimental studies) or having too little control (observational studies).[14] The Seminar concluded: 'it was not felt that further research was necessarily required as, on the balance of evidence, the Hastings review had provided sufficient evidence to indicate a causal link between promotional activity and children's food knowledge, preferences and behaviours'.

The critique of the review was also considered by the Academic Seminar[15] and was not felt to be substantiated. It was concluded that the review was 'honest to the reality of the research landscape' and that the critique 'did not make a sufficiently strong case to warrant re-examination of the conclusions'.

This tooth and nail defence of vested interest is depressingly predictable and extremely time consuming. It also completely undermines the supposed benefits of systematic review methodology which, as Goldacre reminds us, has revolutionized medical science enabling swift, intelligent decisions about immediate matters of life and death – will a particular treatment kill or cure, should this limb be amputated? But with corporate marketers it merely generates attack and obfuscation. Anything to protect the bottom line. And yet these issues are also matters of life and death – not just of individuals, but given the appalling success marketers are having in getting us to consume, the whole planet.

Fortunately there is some sanity – some honesty – out there. Forget the evidence base and the science for a moment, and let's return to 'logical deduction' – better known as common sense. Emerson Foote, former CEO of McCann-Erickson and, therefore, arguably one of the biggest marketers of all time, points out the emperor's nudity with the ruthless precision of a great communicator:

> The cigarette industry has been artfully maintaining that cigarette advertising has nothing to do with total sales. This is complete and utter nonsense. The industry knows it is nonsense. I am always amused by the suggestion that advertising, a function that has been shown to increase consumption of virtually every other product, somehow miraculously fails to work for tobacco products.[16]

For 'cigarette industry' insert food, pharma, oil, automotive or indeed any corporation you care to think of. Better still, just substitute 'corporate marketer'.

So the threat of even the slightest constraint on what, as we have noted and shall go on to explore in detail, is just a fragment of the marketers' armoury has been the cause of a massive and sustained defensive campaign. Every inch of territory, every iota of evidence is fought over to deny culpability, and when that fails, to maintain doubt; and when that fails, to resist action. All to buy time to continue using a tool that 'very rarely works, and never has in this area'. Such determination and self-obsessed single-mindedness over advertising bodes ill for any efforts to control marketing more generally. But control it we must if we are to save the planet.

Gang warfare

Advertising is just one member of the large and powerful marketing communications gang. Marketers call this the 'marketing communications mix' and it takes in every conceivable channel that you could possibly dream up for getting across a sales pitch. One ad agency even toyed with the idea of casting an image of its client's brand on the face of the moon. Mostly though, the marketing communications mix is a much more down to earth affair: marketers just want to take every opportunity to gain access to our senses – and thereby our hearts and minds. We've already noted sponsorship at the outset of this chapter, but there are numerous other favourites, as the second circle of Figure 4.1 shows.

I don't think many of these need any introduction; they are mostly tediously familiar. But maybe a word is needed about two: brand stretching and product placement. The first is the habit that marketers are increasingly developing, of taking their brands beyond their core products. Virgin is an obvious example – it started in music but has now migrated all over the place, including even to running railways.

FIGURE 4.1 The marketing communications mix

Source: Based on National Cancer Institute (NCI)

Product placement is another less obvious channel. It involves paying to have your product inserted into an existing artistic space such as a television programme or film. It is worth spending a little time on because it illustrates again those core marketing ruses of subterfuge, subtlety and shade – and where these inevitably lead.

Escort service

Product placement is the escort service of marketing, but without the saving graces.

Escort girls pretend to be genuine partners for a succession of lonely guys, and in return receive cash. Both parties know the rules of the game; neither is deceived. Those around them, who are fooled into thinking they are witnessing true romance, are unharmed by the deception. And the masquerading couple won't try to persuade the rest of us to succumb to the dubious joys of commercial love. Perhaps not saving graces, but at least the collateral is ring-fenced.

Not so with the product placers who slip their cars and coffee brands into our favourite soaps and Hollywood blockbusters. We have already noted that advertising works, and product placement is just a variation on the theme. Indeed all the marcomms techniques listed in Figure 4.1 have been shown to work – that is to influence our consumption behaviour.[17] And product placement isn't just any advertising; it is the apotheosis of under the radar advertising – kitted out with smart ordnance and camouflage gear. With an old fashioned ad you know where you stand: it has an overt sales pitch and you can boot up your Mandy Rice-Davies antennae and remind yourself that the adman 'would say that, wouldn't he?'.

Product placement – or 'branded entertainment' as the corporate marketers call it – gets under the radar and it is this very deception that gives it its power. By comparison the pretence of the escort girl is Sunday school stuff.

The bedrock of good business practice is the consumer sovereignty which corporate marketers are here again treating with disdain. It enables ordinary people to keep the market in check by punishing bad practice and rewarding good: a kind of pocket-book democracy. But this depends on transparency and a well-informed public; *caveat emptor* turns to cant if the buyer is kept in the dark – like telling flies to beware spiders without warning them about cobwebs. More specifically, as we have already noted, all advertising is supposed to be 'legal, decent, honest and truthful'. Product placement can never be any of these because it is founded on a lie.

This lie, as so many before it, sets ripples in motion which cause wider and more insidious problems. Product placement is in fact just one of several sorts of stealth marketing – commercial pitches being dressed up to avoid detection and regulation – and the sort of complex emotional messages favoured in conventional advertising achieve the same ends. And so we have come to accept duplicity as a norm and foisted the responsibility on the consumer to beware. More power to the corporate marketer; hand me that syringe, Mr Saatchi.

And still the ripples spread: where marketers have led, programme makers follow. If producers can make money by featuring certain products the temptation to create situations – or indeed whole programmes – that provide better promotional possibilities is plain. In the US, where branded entertainment is commonplace, the market is booming, driven by agencies such as '1st Approach', which help 'brands generate competitive value by leveraging the power of entertainment and technology'.[18] No longer satisfied with placing products in programmes, marketers create programmes to serve the interests of the products. So art comes to imitate not life, but commerce. Our airwaves will become a virtual mall and a vital cultural space will become just one more avenue for the ceaseless drive to keep us consuming.

Luckily we in the UK have a government that is alert to these dangers. They have rules in place to stop product placement for all the reasons we have just discussed. Except that, thanks to successful lobbying by corporate marketers, these rules have just been relaxed. Branded entertainment here we come.

Catching the wind

With one or two noble exceptions, such as the Loi Evin and tobacco adbans, the regulators are depressingly behind the curve. For the most part advertising controls, where they exist at all, concentrate on defining the content of advertising, not restricting the amount: limiting *what* rather than *how much* advertisers can say. This might be a feasible idea if we really understood what advertisers are saying, but the subterfuge, subtlety and shade we have been examining makes this quite impossible. If Marlboro were to say in black and white that smoking their cigarettes makes you independent, real, free and American, then they would easily be snagged by the regulator. But they don't. They just sit a cowboy on a horse, put him against a backdrop of Monument Valley and call it Marlboro Country. You can't control the content because the audience does the joining of the dots; the message is in their heads and hearts – and all the more powerful as a result.

Think of almost any glossy ad you have seen recently and then try and write down the message. In black and white it will look facile and ridiculous: I'm going to look rugged and intrepid if I drive this SUV, or look like a supermodel if I use this eyeliner. As I say ridiculous – which is why advertisers much prefer the circuitous route to our pockets: hints, associations and oblique references are much more effective than overt claims. Under the radar again.

And oblique is not only much more effective, but much more difficult to regulate. That which fools the consumer, also fools the regulator. In this way content regulation just plays the advertisers' game, reminding them of the need for subterfuge, subtlety and shade. This is how the UK used to regulate tobacco advertising and it was a pathetic game of cat and mouse which only resulted in more creative and cunning campaigns. Remember the Benson & Hedges modern art ads? My favourite was a picture of the pyramids of Giza with cigarettes raining down on them: tombs being peppered with lethal carcinogens – but there was no denying its beauty. Remember the Silk Cut dash of purple campaign? This provided the perfect preparation for tighter restrictions; the brand took possession of the colour and to this day just a hint of it can conjure up the brand for aficionados.

David Abbot, like Emerson Foote an honourable advertiser, argued cogently that the restrictions actually helped tobacco advertisers, by pushing them to be ever more creative. The clear and present harm being done by tobacco forced the UK Government – and many others around the world – to stop foutering with content, and address the core problem of the sheer amount of advertising.

It was clear that tobacco advertising was pulling children into the market, and that content regulation was probably making things worse, so the government implemented a complete ban. This has been a great success and children's inclination to smoke has reduced as a result. But even here the tobacco industry has fought every step of the way. The adban took out most of the marketing communications mix, but left the pack and the display at point of sale in place. The result is, once again, entirely predictable: the tobacco industry has put inordinate marketing investment into increasingly elaborate shop displays and innovative new packs – thereby turning these into advertising platforms.

The trade press, where marketers are much less guarded than in public or when talking to politicians, makes interesting reading. These comments were garnered from magazines such as *The Grocer*, *Off Licence News* and *Forecourt Trader*; you can almost hear the licking of lips at the prospect of the increased sales their marketing cleverness will bring them:

Imperial Tobacco has introduced a new pack design across its Richmond cigarette range. Available from July, the new look is designed to give the brand a modern, contemporary appearance.

The limited edition 'Celebration' Lambert & Butler packs increased sales by £60 million. Imperial Global Brand Director said that 'the pack design was the only part of the mix that was changed, and therefore we knew the cause and effect'.

The B&H Silver slide pack increased market share by 57.5% (c.£120million) within 18 months.

Slide is all about the packaging … [it] appeals to young adult smokers and research shows they will buy into innovations such as unique packs.

The 'perfume pack' Silk Cut Superslims in October 2008 added a new dimension to creative pack change, one which Blackburn [Gallaher trade communications manager] explains 'is sure to make Silk Cut Superslims a popular choice, especially among female smokers between 20 and 44 years old'.[19]

The futility of expecting anything from corporate marketers but a ruthless determination to carry on marketing – despite the clear will of Parliament to contain them, despite the harm done to their customers – was well demonstrated by the Gallaher spokesperson who gleefully pointed out that 'marketing restrictions make the pack the hero'. Just another opportunity for disguise; just another obstacle to be side-stepped in the remorseless quest to service the bottom line.

Their arrogance may be cringe-making, but it is justified. My colleague Allison Ford interviewed fifteen-year-olds to see what they thought of the new packs. The responses are as predictable as the tobacco companies' callous avarice. Here are some girls talking about that beautifully redesigned Silk Cut 'perfume pack':

It's as if you are not like smoking … .

If you went home and if you were smoking and you were trying to like hide it from your mum and dad and that like fell out your pocket or something it wouldn't be cigarettes …

Like if you were carrying perfume …

You feel like a lady with this one.[20]

Once again we have to pinch ourselves and ask how anyone can seriously maintain that advertising does not affect our consumption behaviour; can say, 'actually advertising very rarely works, and never has in this area' – whatever the area of consumption involved. Once again we can see the remorseless fight to continue marketing; when the long defence of advertising had finally failed, the industry simply side-stepped the overt will of Parliament and poured its adspend into 'making the pack the hero' – though rarely can there have been a more villainous hero. Once again we get a glimpse of the unflagging fight the corporate marketer will put up to defend his or her profits.

If asked, of course, the tobacco marketer would deny that there is any attempt to appeal to children with this packaging. I know because I saw and heard them do the same for all their advertising in front of a UK Government Select Committee a decade ago. One after another they maintained that advertising did not recruit new smokers, only encouraged brand switching between existing smokers; that they had no interest in marketing to children, despite the fact that 85 per cent of their new customers were and are children.

Thinking big

Tobacco is a vital issue, and the harm it is doing is unconscionable, but we have to think bigger. This is not just about the consumption of individually damaging products, it is about consumption per se. Unless we can begin to reduce the amount of stuff we are collectively buying, using – and often simply throwing away – day in, day out, our planet is doomed. If the tobacco industry can fight such a powerful rear-guard action so successfully for so long in defence of such a noxious and superfluous product, how big is the broader battle to contain marketing as a whole going to be? Yet this is what we have to do. The army of diehard marketers who spend their days endlessly persuading us to carry on blithely consuming has to be decommissioned.

Some hope must lie with the younger generation, who are going to have to live with the repercussions of our laxity. But as we have just seen – and will go on in the next chapter to explore in more detail – they are also very much in the corporate marketers' sights.

Give Me the Child

all through our youth and adolescence, before the conscious and critical mind begins to act as a sort of censor and guardian at the threshold, ideas seep into our mind, vast hosts and multitudes of them. These years are, one might say, our dark ages during which we are nothing but inheritors; it is only in later years that we begin to sort out our inheritance.

Fritz Schumacher[1]

not so much like drops of water, though water, it is true, can wear holes in the hardest granite; rather drops of liquid sealing-wax, drops that adhere, incrust, incorporate themselves with what they fall on, till finally the rock is all one scarlet blob.

Till at last the child's mind is these suggestions and the sum of these suggestions is the child's mind. And not the child's mind only. The adult's mind too — all his life long. The mind that judges and desires and decides — made up of these suggestions. But these suggestions are our *suggestions.*

Aldous Huxley[2]

Children are important to marketers for three fundamental reasons:

1. *They represent a large market in themselves because they have their own money to spend.*
2. *They influence their parents' selection of products and brands.*
3. *They will grow up to be consumers of everything; hence marketers need to start building up their brand consciousness and loyalty as early as possible.*

Consumer Psychology for Marketing[3]

5

SUFFER THE LITTLE CHILDREN

Consumers of everything

Children are being harmed by marketing. Not just specifically by the marketing of damaging products such as tobacco, alcohol and fast food, but by marketing as a whole. The materialism and consumption it drives is not wanted by young people, but is being foisted on them by disempowered parents and an increasingly commercialized social environment. It is very difficult to stand out against the latest gizmo when everyone has one, and not joining in attracts opprobrium.

To corporate marketers, though, children are no more and no less than consumption opportunities. Indeed they represent a triumvirate of opportunities: now in their own right; as a conduit to their parents' pockets; and as future adult consumers. So they need to be sold to directly, encouraged to leverage their pester power and be inculcated into the market to ensure their devout and life-long attendance at the mall.

To put some unwarranted respectability on this exploitation, marketers argue that children are capable of understanding advertising and therefore of negotiating its ploys successfully – and doing this provides them with a bit of healthy consumer socialization (otherwise known as inculcation into the market). At the same time marketers are fully aware that influence operates way beyond the individual, and they actively exploit powerful collective drivers like social norms and modelling.

This influence expands from the group to the generation as advertisers co-opt culture to the cause of consumption. Thus a beat poet who spent his life fighting the system and rebelling against conformity, has in death been exploited to sell jeans – as has Walt Whitman, despite his warning in a separate poem that we are becoming 'demented with the mania of owning things'.

All this influence is distilled into the brand, which has taken on a significance once reserved for religious icons. It is becoming a way in which people express themselves both as individuals and as members of the group – and it cuts to the core of how marketing communications inveigle the young.

Report Card 7

In 2007 the UK got a wake-up call when UNICEF[4] put it bottom among twenty-one developed countries for child wellbeing. It was a shocking judgement, which triggered some xenophobic muttering about being able to understand the Netherlands and Sweden (who came top), but Spain (5th) and Italy (8th) – surely we are doing better than them? It is worth remembering that Report Card 7 emerged at the height of the UK's Blair/Brown boom. In material terms at least, things had never been better. Also, that Sweden deliberately and robustly protects young people from marketing: for example, it does not allow any advertising to children up to the age of twelve. And that Spain and Italy are considered to be sickly economies.

UNICEF[5] didn't leave matters there – they commissioned a follow-up study looking behind the statistics to understand why British kids are so badly off. This was an extremely thorough, in-depth exercise, which involved talking to and observing around 250 children and parents in the UK, as well as Sweden and Spain.

The conclusions tell us much about the impact of marketing on British children:

- They are actually more leery of marketing than we parents. The study notes that 'many UK children do not refer to material goods when talking about what makes them happy, and also understand the principles of moderation in consumption, but may have parents who feel compelled to purchase, often against their better judgement'.[6]
- However, as they grow older they gain an increasing 'awareness of inequality as they approach secondary school and the role of consumer goods in identifying and creating status groups within peer groups'.[7]
- Nonetheless they retain a 'very ambivalent attitude to those who appear to be able to afford all the latest status goods. Whilst many UK parents are complicit in purchasing status goods to hide social insecurities this behaviour is almost totally absent in Spain and Sweden'.[8]
- Finally the report 'found British families struggling, pushed to find the time their children want, something exacerbated by the uncertainty about the rules and roles operating within the family household'.[9]

British kids are, then, beset by insecurity, misplaced materialism and time-poverty – which we parents both recognize and inadvertently exacerbate.

Now let's return to *Consumer Psychology for Marketing*, which we briefly consulted in Chapter 4 and which helpfully reminds us that

Children are important to marketers for three fundamental reasons:

1. They represent a large market in themselves because they have their own money to spend.
2. They influence their parents' selection of products and brands.
3. They will grow up to be consumers of everything; hence marketers need to start building up their brand consciousness and loyalty as early as possible.

No mention of wellbeing here. Just their money, the conduit they provide to parents and, our old friend, 'the economic advantage which endures', expressed in positively Jesuitical terms (except the Jesuits were trying to save our eternal souls, not turn a coin with them). The UNICEF report reveals deeply disturbing problems with all three of these levels of 'importance'. First, children are wise enough to be deeply ambivalent about material possessions. As the report cogently points out, having met with and interviewed 250 children from a range of backgrounds in all three countries: 'the message from them all was simple, clear and unanimous: their wellbeing centres on time with a happy, stable family, having good friends and plenty of things to do, especially outdoors'.[10] But there is not much profit in that, so marketing will have to go to work on them and start digging out some whims to tease into wants, needs and must-haves. Worse still it seems children don't even have a sense of entitlement – they are disparaging about what they see as 'spoiled kids', who don't have to wait, save up for and earn their rewards. Time to sound the because-we're-worth-it drum. A sensible reticence about the real potential benefits of consumption will need to be overcome to access the child pound.

This brings us to the second level of marketing importance. Conduits work in two directions: if children give you access to parents, parents (especially insecure and vulnerable ones) give you access to children. This undermines family relationships. In particular, UK parents almost compulsively resorted to products in a failing attempt to compensate for the absence of quality time with their kids. The report speaks evocatively of 'boxes and boxes of toys, broken presents and unused electronics' being 'witness to this drive to acquire new possessions, which in reality were not really wanted or treasured'.[11] The irony that the need to earn the money to buy this stuff costs us parents the very time that our children crave, seems to have escaped us (or been neutralized by relentless marketing).

Trying to pull something cheerful out of this morass, one might see the children's wisdom relative to their parents as boding well for the future – they are, after all, the next generation of parents and they will get the priorities right. Not if the marketers have their way. Remember, to Madison Avenue their third level of importance is that 'they will grow up to be consumers of everything; hence marketers need to start building up their brand consciousness and loyalty as early as possible.' That awful phrase 'consumers of everything' is a chilling distillation of the impact of over-consumption on our planet. Nonetheless the marketer eyes not threats to the planet, but opportunities for long term sales – 'the economic advantage which endures'. It is vital to get the next generation trooping into the malls.

So marketers do what they do. They assiduously seek out and stimulate opportunities to sell their products. Perhaps not surprisingly they do not have much sympathy with the notion of child vulnerability. It just leads to debates about the need to protect young people, and when their exhaustive advocacy occasionally fails, restrictions on their activities. Linking childhood with innocence and helplessness threatens the bottom line and cannot, therefore, be countenanced.

Children, what children?

The first line of defence, then, is to argue that children are actually nowhere near as naïve and malleable as social scientists suggest. They often rely on observational data here, because talking to children doesn't bring this out; it is wrong, the argument runs, to let children's inarticulacy mask their sophistication. Thus a paper in the *Journal of Marketing Management* argues:

> In the past an over-reliance on children's verbal responses may have led to an underestimation of what children really know. In this paper we argue that children can have knowledge that they are unable to articulate .... The findings suggest that, although young children may show a lack of understanding in their verbal responses, the use of non-verbal measures can reveal some implicit understanding in children from 4 years of age.[12]

There is no hint of irony here; the fact that this lack of fluency might itself be a sign of immaturity is overlooked. Just a blithe acceptance that these subtle research techniques show that children as young as four can distinguish ads from TV programmes, and by the age of eight know these are partial pitches on behalf of the advertiser. By ten and eleven they are rejoicing in their capacity to cynically deconstruct ads.

The strategy seems to be one of minimizing childhood. We are all just trainee adults, serving an apprenticeship in consumption. The chilling warning provided by smoking, the uptake of which, as we noted in Chapter 1, is limited almost exclusively to children, cuts no ice. The fact that virtually no one over the age of twenty-five takes up the habit because they acquired a proper understanding of the repercussions of addiction and death, and the self-evident implications this has about the competence of teen consumption decisions, is just ignored. And the obvious evidence it provides about the relative power of the marketer, who can con kids into smoking but struggles when he meets someone his own size, might as well not exist.

The corporate marketer just blusters on. The idea of consumer socialization is then invoked to provide a measure of respectability. This isn't about the ruthless pursuit of sales and profit, it's about education. Young people need to learn about advertising and marketing if they are to cope as adults in a consumer society (and 'grow up to be consumers of everything').

Schumacher reminds us of the hazards this laissez-faire approach exposes our young people to:

all through our youth and adolescence, before the conscious and critical mind begins to act as a sort of censor and guardian at the threshold, ideas seep into our mind, vast hosts and multitudes of them. These years are, one might say, our dark ages during which we are nothing but inheritors; it is only in later years that we begin to sort out our inheritance.[13]

But to the corporate marketer children are just blotting paper to be soaked in the mantra of consumption. If the bleeding hearts bang on too much about child protection 'media literacy' is then held up as the solution: make sure that children understand fully what the marketer is up to by constructing a curriculum and teaching it in school.

This is like teaching people how to boil their drinking water, rather than intervening upstream and providing potable drinking water in the first place; or tackling malaria by educating vulnerable populations about the mosquito, but not taking the obvious next step of providing protection through mosquito nets and insecticides. And as Steinbeck pointed out, the dangers from marketing are surely much easier to control than contaminated water supplies and insect-driven diseases, because they are man-made.

Remember Wallace's fish

The metaphor of water provides an appropriate reminder that individual cognitive development and personal skills are only a part of the picture. Social norms are also a big influence on our behaviour, as the story of Wallace's fish we discussed in Chapter 3 illustrates. We do things because those around us do them, because they exist as obvious options in particular circumstances or because our culture approves of them – and these influences are the more powerful because they are often imperceptible. Under the radar again.

Well-established theories of behaviour change, such as the Theory of Reasoned Action (TRA) and the Theory of Planned Behaviour (TPB), recognize this social dimension to what we do by acknowledging the importance of other people's actions and opinions in our decision making. And Pavlov's experiments with dogs have spawned many insights about how we can be conditioned or trained into certain behaviours.

Marketers are well aware of this; *Consumer Psychology for Marketing*, for example, discusses both TRA and conditioning at some length, and then unpicks the practical implications for marketers. It discusses 'a variety of strategies for changing consumer behaviour by modifying attitudes or subjective norms'.[14] The suggestions include 'change normative beliefs by suggesting that important others believe that the consumer should buy the brand': 'your friends will think that Fox brands are the ones to buy' and 'add a new belief combination to the brand. Thus products are constantly "new and improved" …'

Over the page the book discusses the 'Influencing of Personal Communication', explaining how advertisers and marketers frequently make use of reference group appeals in advertisements ... such ads may feature either 'typical consumers' or ordinary people as well as celebrities ... because word-of-mouth information about a product is seen by other consumers as high in credibility and trustworthiness. Their credibility is, in fact, likely to be higher than the sales pitch or impersonal paid advertising because ... they have no apparent vested interest in the product's success.

Except this will invariably be carefully scripted or selected word-of-mouth, and the person speaking it will be getting paid to say what they are saying. It is a sales pitch – just a well-disguised, and thereby more powerful, one.

Given these social determinants of our behaviour, and that marketers exploit them with such enthusiasm, it is simply blinkered to analyse advertising to children on the narrow basis of cognitive development. An insight into Pavlovian responses doesn't stop you salivating, nor does an understanding of peer pressure make you immune from the sales pitch that harnesses the need to belong.

Subterfuge again

Marketing communications in the UK booze market epitomize this proclivity to use reference groups, modelling and group think to get through to potential new customers. In Chapter 1 we touched on a recent UK Health Select Committee (HSC)[15] enquiry into the alcohol industry and its marketing practices. The investigation gained access to a large quantity of internal marketing documents from beverage alcohol companies and their advertising agencies. These comprised such things as contact reports between client and agency, client briefs, creative briefs, media briefs, media schedules and market research reports.

The sheer number of the documents that emerged speaks volumes for the scale of the alcohol marketing effort in the UK. The exercise replicated one conducted in 2000 during an equivalent inquiry into the tobacco industry, when all the major ad agencies with tobacco accounts were required to submit a similar range of documents. However, alcohol promotion is far more extensive than that for tobacco ever was; so the search had to be more circumspect. Requests were therefore sent to only four producers and their respective communications agencies; and they were asked to send documents relating to just five brands out of the dozens on their books (Table 5.1).

Despite the limited nature of the request it resulted in thousands of pages of paper documents and nearly three gigabytes of electronic ones. And one producer felt it to be impractically big, arguing that the documentation for just one brand would run to over a million pages. In this instance the request was therefore reduced to documentation for the 2005 and 2008 financial years for this producer. Perhaps it is not surprising that research with UK youngsters funded by the Medical Research Council shows their lives to be suffused with alcohol promotion. For example, 96 per cent of thirteen-year-olds – that's a full five years below the legal

TABLE 5.1 The sources of the documents

Producers	Brands	Communications agencies
Beverage Brands	WKD (an alcopop)	Big Communications Bray Leino PR Five by Five (digital)
Diageo	Smirnoff Vodka	AKQA JWT
Halewood International	Lambrini (a perry) Sidekick shots	BJL CheethamBell JWT
Molson Coors Brewing Company	Carling	Beattie McGuinness Bungay (BMB)

drink age or LDA) – could, on average, recall having seen drink advertising in more than five different channels.[16]

The stealthy, indirect power of the sponsorship of music and sport stands out in the documents, particularly as a means of reaching the young. For example, sponsoring a major UK football tournament (see Box 5.1) provides powerful opportunities for a leading UK brewer to 'give LDA-21 males a reason to believe in the product whilst building an emotional connection to the "Vivid me" state', 'create emotional experiences for young male drinkers' and 'maintain a level of awareness that allows us to leverage key tournaments'.

The sponsorship strategy seeks to ensure that the emotions, enthusiasm and drama experienced by cup final spectators transfer to the product, creating a connection in their minds between the two which will 'recruit young male (LDA-21) drinkers into the brand'.

Incidentally, the ad agency's assiduous reference to target groups beginning at the legal drinking age may seem admirable, but it fails to explain how it avoids younger age groups being affected by this marketing activity. Seventeen-, sixteen- and fifteen-year-olds are also engrossed by 'key tournaments', and will see and experience the sponsorship – so what is to stop the campaign (even if inadvertently) 'building an emotional connection to the "Vivid me" state' with them? And they are, after all, tomorrow's 'consumers of everything'.

Similarly, the makers of the alcopops WKD (pronounced wicked) teamed up with *Nuts* lads' magazine ('heaps of extra-sexy girls, hilarious gags and awesome features'[17]) by sponsoring the '*Nuts* football awards'. The magazine provided access to a high proportion of young men in the WKD target group and linked perfectly with their interests and values. As a representative of WKD's PR agency explained when giving evidence to the Health Select Committee:

> WKD are partnered with Nuts; Nuts has an average age range of 24 years in terms of readership. 92% are over 18 in terms of the readership again, so it is

absolutely targeted to our target audience. It is very football focused in terms of content. Football in terms of an aside, in terms of the award itself, about 35% is the current figure of 18 to 25-year-olds play regularly and 54% watch sport in a social environment, so maybe with their friends at home or in a pub, for example. So it is an appropriate link for us as a brand.[18]

BOX 5.1 FOOTBALL, YOUNG MEN AND BOOZE – THE PERFECT MATCH

BRIEF FOR CARLING CUP FINAL – 2005

Brand	Carling
Coors Contact	Richard Smith
Agency Contact	

Carling Brand Strategy
Recruit young male (LDA-21) drinkers into the brand, giving them real reasons to believe in our product superiority and through our distinctive British attitude.

Carling Brand Promise
Carling's balance of taste & refreshment and its grounded & sharp witted British attitude guarantees it will put you on the front foot with your mates.

Carling Advertising Strategy
Give LDA-21 males a reason to believe in the product whilst building an emotional connection to the "Vivid me" state, to cut through in what is seen as an undifferentiated market.

Carling Sponsorship Strategy
Create emotional experiences for young male drinkers & amplify the uniqueness of these experiences in a grounded & sharp witted way.

Carling and Football:
What we need to achieve in Football:
Maintain a level of awareness that allows us to leverage key tournaments.
Providing the things that real fans really want.
Our history, our actions, we're a real fan, like you.
Headline activity: Carling Cup, Old Firm, FAW, Club Deals.

Source: Hastings, G., Brooks, O., Stead, M., Angus, K., Anker, T. and Farrell, T. (2010) 'Alcohol Advertising: The Last Chance Saloon' in *British Medical Journal*, 340, 20 January 2010.

And again Diageo, the producers of leading vodka brand Smirnoff, built a partnership with *FHM* lads' magazine (a slightly upmarket version of *Nuts*) which involved running monthly editorials and promotions themed on 'Original Nights Out'. Through ongoing market research, *FHM* readers could then be followed up to assess whether there was any heightened awareness of other Smirnoff-sponsored events 'and whether this has generated impact at the brand level'.[19] The same analysis goes on to note that, although overall penetration of the *FHM* readership is quite low, 'the profile suggests it's an ideal way of reaching a younger consumer'.

The brand is, then, the key to connecting with the consumer.

Branding

If advertising started with Spartan prostitutes, branding began with cattle. And again the core principle – this time of identifying ownership – seems to have remained intact. In the words of the American Marketing Association a brand is 'a name, term, symbol, or combination of them that is designed to identify the goods or services of one seller or group of sellers and to differentiate them from those of competitors'.[20] However, the brand has grown into much more than a simple identifier. Indeed in many ways it has become the antithesis of an identifier, in that its principal role is, if not to deceive, then to lull us into a false sense of security. Bakan points out that the first brand was developed by the giant US corporation General Electric, to try and give a human face to what was in reality a monolithic conglomerate focused on delivering maximum returns to its shareholders and management. Since General Electric's first foray into this field, the brand has developed from being a simple mask into the crucible of corporate attempts to win our hearts and minds. In fact, rather than identifying and clarifying, it blurs. In the process it has become a massively successful driver of corporate power.

As a leading thinker concludes after reviewing the field: 'Branding effects are pervasive and the effects of virtually any marketing activity seem to be conditioned or qualified by the nature of the brands involved'.[21] So everything the corporate marketer does can be magnified through the lens of the brand. Furthermore the many facets of the brand, 'names, logos, symbols, slogans etc. all have multiple dimensions, which each can produce differential effects on consumer behaviour'.[22] Not surprisingly, the commentator also confirms that brand equity (the value that is attributed to a particular marque) has been shown to link directly to shareholder value.

A minor altercation on the number 42 bus to Crieff, a small Scottish market town, brings out the human side of this emotional quest for wealth. The fourteen-year-old boy on the back seat clearly had an atavistic love of black; he was decked out in it from his workman-like boots to his charcoal beanie. This caught the eye of another teenager, who, as teens will, began to mock him: 'you're wearing a flipping uniform' he laughed 'what sort of person does that?' (I have cleaned up the language a little.) The black-clad boy responded in kind, mocking what he felt was the regulation outfit of his attacker – trainers, trackies, hoody and (back to front) baseball cap. 'What do you mean?' came the indignant riposte, as the second teenager's finger pointed first to his shoes, then his trousers and finally his top: Nike; Adidas; Converse. In the young teen's eyes the brands repelled all criticism.

And these effects become manifest long before children reach their teens. Two decades ago research with US youngsters found six-year-olds were as familiar with RJ Reynolds' Jo Camel as Disney characters[23] – with the same study demonstrating that the tobacco campaign worked on children better than it did on adults. Similarly, in 2007 a study in California among three- to five-year-olds showed that children's food preferences are being moulded by branding even before they have learnt to tie their shoelaces.[24] The little children were served food in both branded and unbranded packaging. Items that came in McDonald's wrappers were thought to taste better, even if they were foods like carrots, which McDonald's didn't sell. On the other hand McDonald's products didn't taste as good without the liveried packaging. These effects were apparent across the group, but most marked amongst those who had been most exposed to McDonald's and its advertising. Remember *Consumer Psychology for Marketing* and the third level of corporate interest in children, who 'will grow up to be consumers of everything' and consequently that 'marketers need to start building up their brand consciousness and loyalty as early as possible'. They are succeeding.

It all works, as Huxley puts it in *Brave New World*,

> not so much like drops of water, though water, it is true, can wear holes in the hardest granite; rather drops of liquid sealing-wax, drops that adhere, incrust, incorporate themselves with what they fall on, till finally the rock is all one scarlet blob.
>
> Till at last the child's mind is these suggestions and the sum of these suggestions is the child's mind. And not the child's mind only. The adult's mind too – all his life long. The mind that judges and desires and decides – made up of these suggestions.[25]

Building an identity

Given branding's obvious power, and the urgent need to exploit it at the first opportunity – and incessantly thereafter – it is unsurprising that corporate marketers put enormous thought, resource and skill into their brand-building strategies. This strategizing takes us way beyond marcomms; as we will discuss in the next chapter the rest of the marketing mix (product, price and place) is also brought to bear. Nonetheless branding is first and foremost about communication and the starting point is the creation of an enticing identity – albeit a synthetic one. It is all about authenticity, and so, as the quip goes, once you can fake that you've cracked it.

This calculated and carefully choreographed process is beautifully illustrated by the Carling beer brand team in their strategizing about music sponsorship. Internal documents refer to the need to build credibility and 'emotional connections'. With music and sport, where having a real knowledge and being a 'true fan' are critically important, brands need to demonstrate that they have a genuine 'right' to be associated with the event in question. Carling, for example, speaks about 'earning the right to "play" in key tournament years'[26] in its football sponsorship strategy. This 'right' to be associated with the event is even more important in music, where, because it is not one of the leading sponsoring brands, Carling recognizes it needs to work hard to demonstrate to consumers that it has a genuine interest and a legitimate presence. This involves moving away from obvious forms of sponsorship – covering a music venue with Carling logos, for instance – to more subtle and involving messages and activities. After all one of the key strengths of sponsorship is its subtlety; its capacity to hide the sales pitch:

> [We need to] ensure that Carling do not simply 'badge' the venues and install 'Venue Logos' for no reason other than to brand. This would create logo blindness and not generate any emotional connections with the consumer.[27]

Similarly there is a need to 'demonstrate Carling's grounded sense of humour and that they "get" music'.[28] 'Ultimately, the band are the heroes at the venue and Carling should use them to "piggy back" and engage customers [sic] emotions.'[29]

You have to pinch yourself and remember that a brand is not a person, it cannot 'earn a right', 'have a sense of humour' or 'engage emotions' in any meaningful way. It is an artificial construct developed by a corporation to sell us stuff. In this case it is being used to sell booze to young men. It does this indirectly, using the learning social scientists have gained about how susceptible we are to human qualities and the honest opinion of others – especially of others who hold some special significance for us.

Only belong

This brand identity with its sense of humour, rights and authenticity also needs to link to the collective. The Select Committee enquiry revealed how advertising was used to do this for the same beer brand. The campaign built on research with the customer (of course) which suggested that young men are very anxious to gel with their peer group, or in the ad agency's words, the 'Consumer Insight' was that 'Young drinkers live, think and drink together in packs' (the PowerPoint presentation illustrated this with a picture of a pack of wolves). This led them, in the same presentation, to what they termed the 'Category Insight' that 'to own sociability is to dominate the beer market'. Figure 5.1a explains the reasoning behind this.

A related strategy document reveals the marketers' full ambitions:

> currently Carling has two very specific routes to sociability, through the brand's association with football and music. A dominant brand goes further. Carling can own all routes to sociability: football, music and everything else that brings the lads together. In short, Carling can position itself as social glue. (See Figure 5.1b.)[30]

Achieving Dominance

- Dominance is achieved by owning the most important benefit to consumers.

- In alcohol, sociability is the king of all emotional benefits for young consumers. To own sociability is to dominate the beer market.

FIGURE 5.1a Owning sociability

Owning Sociability

- Currently Carling has two very specific routes to sociability, through the brand's association with football and music.

- A dominant brand goes further. Carling can own all routes to sociability: football, music and everything else that brings the lads together.

- In short, Carling can position itself as social glue.

FIGURE 5.1b Positioning Carling as social glue

Source: Mobious (2009) *Carling Objective: Evolve Passive Respect to Active Preference*. Slide 3 of 11. Document S10, Folder 3 Sport Strategy Documents 2006. Molson Coors Brewing Company (UK) Limited, 14 May.

Meanwhile the brief for the resulting ad states that: 'Carling celebrates, initiates and promotes the togetherness of the pack, their passions and their pint because Carling understands that things are better together.'[31] This splits into

3 Aspects of Belonging:

- Initiation: Expressions of the moment when an individual joins a group and finds a happy home in the pack—the moment of belonging
- Celebration: An expression of the sheer joy of belonging
- Contagion: An expression of the magnetic power of the group—the power of belonging.[32]

'Broadly speaking' the document continues 'each piece of communication will either celebrate "Join Us" by championing the benefit of togetherness or facilitate "Join Us" by providing and enhancing experiences where togetherness is key.'

The finished commercial, for use in cinemas, features a flock of starlings that gradually come together to reveal the word 'belong' in a design identical to that of the Carling brand logo. The soundtrack is English indie rock band Hard–Fi playing their powerful anthem 'Living for the Weekend' (the lyrics include: 'When it gets too much; I live for the rush; Got some money to spend; Living for the weekend' – with the lyrics featured in the ad a repetitive 'Going out tonight; Going out tonight'). The result is an impressive and powerful film – I know, I have shown it at numerous conferences and witnessed its impact.

All in all, this reveals an extremely adept understanding of consumer behaviour; the team in question must have studied *Consumer Psychology for Marketers* very well. It also provides an evocative glimpse of brand-building in action. An additional insight from that slide presentation is the 'brand insight' which is that 'Carling is Britain's most sociable, most sessionable pint.' The strategy personified.

Incidentally, the campaign also provides a stunning illustration of the failure of advertising regulation, which we discussed in the previous chapter. There are clear 'content' rules saying that UK alcohol advertisers cannot link alcohol to social acceptance or the social success of individuals, events or occasions. Formal complaints to the ASA by Alcohol Concern, a leading alcohol NGO, and members of the general public argued that the ad suggested that drinking could lead to social success and overcome loneliness.[33] Carling executives responded by saying that 'their research indicated that consumers thought the ad referred to sociability and social norms, but not conformity'.[34] The complaint was rejected by the ASA because 'the ad did not imply alcohol contributed to the popularity of an individual or the success of a social event'.[35] This seemed perverse at the time, but given the planning documents that the HSC enquiry uncovered, and Carling's triumphant pitch to 'own sociability' and thereby 'dominate the booze market' it now looks farcical.

A culture of consumption

Brand managers don't stop at the peer group, they have whole generations in their sights. Thus corporate marketers begin to exploit not just groups and social phenomena, but culture itself. Carling goes for an indie rock band, Levi's uses beat poet Charles Bukowski's work to add power to its marketing.[36] 'The Laughing Heart',[37] the poem the company purloins, is indeed a potent piece of writing, with particular appeal to the young and rebellious. It starts by reminding us that our life is our own and we shouldn't 'let it be clubbed into dank submission'. It goes on to offer immense hope: 'there are ways out, there is a light somewhere.... the gods will offer you chances'. It urges us to take these chances and reminds us that the more 'often you learn to do it, the more light there will be'. Finally Bukowski tells us that we are 'marvellous' and that 'the gods wait to delight' in us.

Bukowski died in 1994, so can't be consulted, but I would be prepared to hazard a large wager that the poem was not written to push jeans. Interpreting poetry is a fraught business, but to me this one talks of self-assertion, independence and even rebellion. How does buying a brand make you rebellious? A decade ago Joseph Heath and Andrew Potter, in their book *The Rebel Sell*, described how, within hours of the Sex Pistols and punk hitting the scene, shops were selling designer ripped jeans and safety pins. This illustrates the phenomenon that corporate marketing is everywhere, continuously exploiting every possible opportunity. They conclude that there is only one way you can rebel against the market; and that is to stop shopping.

Indeed in reality the Bukowski poem says as much, and turns the Levi's campaign on its head: incessant marketing is 'clubbing' us all into 'dank submission'; 'the ways out' and the 'light somewhere' will not be found near any shopping mall, and the gods are not waiting to delight in us because we have bought a new pair of trousers. Bukowski is urging us to find our own way, to do our own thing. But there is no profit in that.

Resorting yet again to subterfuge, the Levi's campaign is, predictably, presented as anything but a sales pitch. As Becca Van Dyck, global chief marketing officer of the Levi's brand, puts it:

> Now, more than ever, the world needs inspiration. The world needs people with a pioneering spirit who still believe that anything is possible. Our 60-second 'Go Forth' film and digital engagement program recognize people around the globe who are stepping forward to transform the world ...[38]

The campaign is linked to a water aid programme, and the audience 'are invited to join the Levi's brand in supporting the efforts of Water.org by making an online pledge'. We will return to Corporate Social Responsibility in Chapter 8; suffice it to say for now that, given the fiduciary duty of corporations to prioritize the bottom line at all times, CSR is the definitive oxymoron.

The Levi's campaign also exploits Walt Whitman's poetry, using his evocative poem 'Pioneers! O Pioneers!', which begins:

> Come, my tan-faced children
> Follow well in order, get your weapons ready;
> Have you your pistols? have you your sharp edged axes? Pioneers! O pioneers!
>
> For we cannot tarry here,
> We must march my darlings, we must bear the brunt of danger,
> We, the youthful sinewy races, all the rest on us depend,
> Pioneers! O pioneers!
>
> O you youths, western youths,
> So impatient, full of action, full of manly pride and friendship,
> Plain I see you, western youths, see you tramping with the foremost,
> Pioneers! O pioneers![39]

Like the Ford Challenger ad we encountered in Chapter 3, it invokes an iconic point in modern US history, linking the jeans not just with a great poet, but quintessential American culture. Again the poet is dead so we cannot ask his view, but it is interesting to note that Levi's have not made use of the powerful lines from Whitman's 'Song of Myself', quoted at the start of Chapter 3, when he compares our lot with that of animals:

> I think I could turn and live with animals, they are so placid and self-contain'd,
> I stand and look at them long and long
>
> They do not sweat and whine about their condition,
> They do not lie awake in the dark and weep for their sins,
> They do not make me sick discussing their duty to God,
> Not one is dissatisfied, not one is demented with the mania of owning things.[40]

Perhaps it was rejected because 'dissatisfaction' and 'the mania of owning things' are the lifeblood of corporate marketing.

Ubiquity

Branding, then, is about an 'authentic' identity, with which the corporate marketer can harness group motivations and co-opt our cultural icons. The final essential ingredient is ubiquity; the power of being there. So brands are now being planted in every corner of our lives. Have you noticed how difficult it has become to buy a garment – even underwear – without a brand name? The young lad on the bus with his all-black outfit had done pretty well to avoid the marque – even if he suffered for his initiative. These logos are now integral to the garment, so anonymizing our clothes is impossible; we are all being drafted as mobile billboards. Remember, also, the importance of source credibility: if we are parents our children will see and make judgements about our values and brand loyalty; if we are teachers our pupils will; our patients, clients, constituents and customers will. Our friends and colleagues will. That child in the street will. Furthermore, this is advertising with 'no apparent vested interest' – no obvious sales pitch, no obvious gain. So it's all the more powerful. That child in the street will absorb it; will be inculcated – just a little bit more – into the creed of consumption.

In this way we are all working as models on the corporate catwalk. We have become Fred Goodwin's handmaidens.

The depth and breadth of corporate marketing's reach is powerfully illustrated by the Olympic Games. This is the ultimate global celebration of the power of amateurism, of humankind coming together to share our sporting accomplishments. As the International Olympic Committee's (IOC's) first Fundamental Principle puts it:

> Olympism is a philosophy of life, exalting and combining in a balanced whole the qualities of body, will and mind. Blending sport with culture and education, Olympism seeks to create a way of life based on the joy of effort, the educational value of good example, social responsibility and respect for universal fundamental ethical principles.[41]

But, if you click on the IOC sponsorship site[42] you discover that actually 'The Olympic Games are one of the most effective international marketing platforms in the world, reaching billions of people in over 200 countries and territories throughout the world.' You will also learn that Coke has been a major sponsor since 1928, and it has been joined by McDonald's for the last three and half decades – though sugar and fat are hardly at the core of a successful athlete's diet. Dow Chemicals is another member of the elite band of key or 'TOP' sponsors. Dow is the corporation we touched on in Chapter 1, which took over Union Carbide, of Bhopal infamy – though its website points out, perhaps protesting a little too much, that 'it is important to note that Dow never owned or operated the plant, which today is under the control of the Madhya Pradesh state government'. Nonetheless, the local people might struggle to equate the corporation with IOC's commitment to 'social responsibility and respect for universal fundamental ethical principles'. Interestingly, General Electric, the corporation Bakan credits with inventing branding, is also a TOP.

The IOC site explains that the TOP, or 'Olympic Partners' 'worldwide sponsorship programme' was instigated in 1985 'to develop a diversified revenue base for the Olympic Games and to establish long-term corporate partnerships that would benefit the Olympic Movement as a whole'. In cash terms at least it has paid off: IOC's Olympic Marketing File, available on the same site, boasts how revenues have increased from US$96 million in 1985/8 to US$866 million in 2005/8. In return, 'the TOP programme provides each Worldwide Olympic Partner with exclusive global marketing rights and opportunities within a designated product or service category'. 'The TOP Partners may exercise these rights worldwide and may activate marketing initiatives with all the members of the Olympic Movement that participate in the TOP programme.'

So, at the risk of stating the obvious, sponsorship is about business, not philanthropy. Corporations become TOPs, for the same reason that they engage in all their other marketing activity, because it will enhance their bottom lines in a number of ways. One leading marketing text lists five of these: 'gaining publicity', 'creating entertainment opportunities', 'fostering favourable brand and company associations', 'improving community relations', and 'creating promotional opportunities'. Specifically, it notes, sports sponsorship provides the 'transferred values to the sponsor' of 'healthy', 'young', 'energetic', 'fast', 'vibrant' and 'masculine'.[43] As the text observes: 'the audience, finding the sponsor's name, logo and other symbols threaded through the event, learn to associate sponsor and activity with one another'.

So the IOC takes money from Coke and McDonald's in return for their association with its core Olympic values and imbuing them with a wholly undeserved healthy image. How does this fit with 'the educational value of good example' in its first Fundamental Principle? (I suppose, in the IOC's defence, the burger is at least a fast food, so it fits with the fourth 'transferred value'.)

More widely, how does the strategy of selling the Olympic Games to corporate brand-building fit with the IOC's fifth Fundamental Principle that 'the Olympic Movement shall have the rights and obligations of autonomy'?[44] Freedom ceases to be freedom when it has a price tag.

No escape

So from our most personal garments to our treasured global icons, branding is omnipresent. It colours the very water we swim in. This combined with the evocative, if phoney, identities, group think and cultural imperialism stacks the deck against the hapless consumer, especially if they are vulnerable. As *Consumer Psychology for Marketing* concludes, talking about the much simpler dissembling of ads which orchestrate consumer eavesdropping:

> finally ... one of the principal types of advertisement features consumers talking to other consumers about the product while the audience listens in; such vicarious substitutes work well when consumers are socially isolated and give an impression of community.[45]

Like insecure teens for instance. Or RJ Reynolds' preferred customers: 'the young, the poor, the black and the stupid'.

The rights of the matter

For UNICEF it is this vulnerability which brings us to the crux of the issue. Children have rights, and one of these is to swim in clean water – to be protected from the unwarranted attentions of corporate marketers. The International Association for the Study of Obesity (IASO), a not-for-profit organization representing 56 countries with over 10,000 professional members, argues the same for the specific case of food marketing. IASO's Sydney Principles (Box 5.2) invoke the UN Convention on Human Rights that guarantees the rights of children to adequate, safe and nutritious food – rights that they maintain are threatened by food marketers.

BOX 5.2 THE SYDNEY PRINCIPLES – CHILDREN HAVE A RIGHT TO BE PROTECTED FROM MARKETING

Actions to reduce commercial promotions to children should:

1. SUPPORT THE RIGHTS OF CHILDREN Regulations need to align with and support the United Nations Convention on the Rights of the Child and the Rome Declaration on World Food Security which endorse the rights of children to adequate, safe and nutritious food.

2. AFFORD SUBSTANTIAL PROTECTION TO CHILDREN Children are particularly vulnerable to commercial exploitation, and regulations need to be sufficiently powerful to provide them with a high level of protection. Child protection is the responsibility of every section of society – parents, governments, civil society, and the private sector.

3. BE STATUTORY IN NATURE Only legally-enforceable regulations have sufficient authority to ensure a high level of protection for children from targeted marketing and the negative impact that this has on their diets. Industry self-regulation is not designed to achieve this goal.

4. TAKE A WIDE DEFINITION OF COMMERCIAL PROMOTIONS Regulations need to encompass all types of commercial targeting of children (e.g. television advertising, print, sponsorships, competitions, loyalty schemes, product placements, relationship marketing, Internet) and be sufficiently flexible to include new marketing methods as they develop.

5. GUARANTEE COMMERCIAL-FREE CHILDHOOD SETTINGS Regulations need to ensure that childhood settings such as schools, child care, and early childhood education facilities are free from commercial promotions that specifically target children.

6. INCLUDE CROSS-BORDER MEDIA International agreements need to regulate cross-border media such as Internet, satellite and cable television, and free-to-air television broadcast from neighbouring countries.

7. BE EVALUATED, MONITORED AND ENFORCED The regulations need to be evaluated to ensure the expected effects are achieved, independently monitored to ensure compliance', and fully enforced.

Source: Swinburn, B. et al. (2008) 'The "Sydney Principles"
for Reducing the Commercial Promotion of Foods and
Beverages to Children' in *Public Health Nuitrition*, 11(9), pp.881–6.

Compensatory protections should be statutory, wide-ranging enough to cover all sorts of marketing and rigorously enforced.

It is difficult to argue with this given the link between poor diet and obesity. In any other circumstance – asbestos ceiling tiles in the workplace; child labour; a dangerous pedestrian crossing – we would be shouting from the housetops for protection. So why not here?

And what about the planet's rights? Our children also need a clean planet to live on. The corporate marketing view of each new generation being a market in themselves, a conduit to their parents and the putative 'consumers of everything' is patently unsustainable.

With thanks to Oliver Widder for permission to reproduce this cartoon.

6

DIGITAL REDEMPTION?

Brave new (digital) world

I deliberately ignored the development of the internet in the last two chapters. The digital revolution is often presented as a solution to many of the problems I raised in them. At last us consumers are being given genuine power, the optimists suggest – we can organize into grassroots movements and take on that corporate might. Alternatively, we can join 'brand communities' and partner with them and so help in the great, almost holy, project of 'creating value' for all. There is now balance in the system.

This, however, is just one more comforting myth. Digital marketing, as with all corporate marketing, is just about getting and keeping us consuming. It provides multiple new channels for reaching us, so that our virtual world is as commercialized as the real one – if not more so. These digital channels are typically interactive, giving us an illusion of control, but in reality merely enabling communication to be turned into 'engagement'; that is, our deeper and longer involvement in the consumption process. Brand communities are nurtured and groomed by corporate marketers, and grassroots websites are just another hunting ground and source of spurious authenticity.

In this way we are pulled into the task of marketing, providing data, ideas and couthie community engagement – contributions for which we are (except with rare exceptions) not paid, and from which the financial benefits go to our corporate 'partners'. But we consumers in our fledgling brand communities needn't worry our little heads about that; after all we are helping to build brand equity – or as the corporate marketing patois has it, creating value.

So history is simply repeating itself. In our grandparents' time, corporate marketers took lessons from Orson Welles about the power of subterfuge, subtlety and shade, and combined them with detailed consumer insight to tame the inconveniently active audience of conventional media. They are now repeating the trick with digital media, and this time around they have infinitely better data and far more sophisticated communication tools. So their soft power wins again.

But remember, soft doesn't mean pleasant or harmless; while their marketing teams are keeping us consumers entertained, the corporations are eyeing up the internet acquisitively, and greedily kicking its tyres. History again: all previous 'new' information technologies – telephony, radio, television and film – each of which had a brief flurry of freedom in their formative years, were rapidly taken into corporate ownership. The indications are that the web is going the same way.

From serf to surf?

It does seem like the digital world offers a bracing new dawn of consumer empowerment. We consumers can now communicate with each other across the globe, and form into caucuses that have real power. So we can come together to help snag badly performing products and defy poor service. The electric windows in my friend Paddy's Ford Galaxy ceased to function and the Ford garage told him it would cost hundreds to fix. In the bad old pre-internet days he would have been over a barrel; but a quick visit to an owners' site provided a work-around from a fellow Galaxy driver, all fixed for twenty quid – and sucks to you Mr Ford. How's that for consumers' lib?

Such consumer forums have even developed into a new phenomenon: the brand community. People coming together to discuss how they can get more out of a product, keep one going when the parent company has abandoned it or just share their love of it. For example Apple devised an unsuccessful palm pilot in the 1990s which they then withdrew from the market; a group of customers have kept it going since with self-help and their own software fixes. Grassroots rebellion combined with a noble fight against obsolescence. What's not to like?

The internet also gives us muscle. We can force corporations to bring back discontinued products. An online campaign compelled UK confectioner Cadbury to reintroduce the Wispa chocolate bar that it had insensitively discontinued. Who's in charge now, eh?

We consumers can even make our wishes known before a product has so much as been conceived, and get involved in the process of satisfying our own desires from the very start. Lego have been practising such co-production for a number of years now. Coke did it for a new bottle, RJ Reynolds for a new cigarette pack design. How much more responsive can a corporation be than to work in partnership with its customers to 'co-create value'?

Widening the net

Unsurprisingly these developments in the virtual world have not gone unnoticed by commerce. In fact they are being assiduously pored over, researched and tried out by corporate marketers. Digital or 'Emarketing' is the new black in business studies; courses have been developed and taught, textbooks written and incisive seminars organized. Outside academe, countless specialist agencies have been launched, and every corporation worth its salt is honing its online presence. The virtual matrix is rapidly outstripping the real world one. The result is a tsunami of digital marketing by the corporate sector; and we are standing on the beach.

As an example, a recent study published by Yale University Rudd Center provides a forensic analysis of how the soft drinks industry is using the four key digital marketing arenas of websites, banner advertising on third party sites, social networking and mobile communications.[1] It reveals that 'children and teens frequently visited sugary drink and energy drink websites'; the top-ranking website, MyCokeRewards.com, averaged more than 170,000 unique young visitors per month, each spending more than nine minutes on the site'.[2] And what sort of things do they encounter on these sites? Well on MyCokeRewards they can 'Reward' themselves 'just for having pleasure'. The folksy text continues: 'Here's how it works (it's fun and easy): grab your favourite Coca–Cola beverages and get My Coke Rewards codes.' The surfing youngster can then spend these on competitions, special offers, a special 'Reward Catalog' – or even to help their school, all nicely illustrating the interactive potential of the web. More generally, the Rudd research shows that sugary beverage websites give young people access to 'Inspirational messages, fun', and, 'on more than 40% of all pages', 'messages about soda companies' honesty and trustworthiness'. Nine minutes is a long time for a ten-year-old to spend doing Coke branded sweepstakes and reading about how wonderful the Coca–Cola Corporation is.

The report shows that MyCokeRewards.com is also the front-runner in banner advertising, and the corporation 'frequently advertised Coca–Cola Classic and other sugary drinks on youth websites'. It goes on to explain that 'the main point of the majority of banner ads was to advertise a promotion … in the form of a sweepstake or giveaway and encourage viewers to enter a competition to win prizes and money' – again the all-important interaction and 'engagement'.

However, the really rich territory for engagement is in social media. This is an opportunity to get up close and personal with us, so all the stops are pulled out. We touched on corporate marketing in this sphere in Chapter 1, and noted that social networks are supposed to be social rather than commercial. Just to reinforce the point that the word 'social' is not just an accident of nomenclature, Wikipedia defines 'a social networking service' as

> an online service platform, or site that focuses on building and reflecting of social networks or social relations among people, who, for example, share interests and/or activities. A social network service consists of a representation of each user (often a profile), his/her social links, and a variety of additional services.

Nothing about being 'a useful channel for corporate marketing' or a 'handy new marketing ploy with which brands can stalk us'. But they can and do.

The Rudd report tells us that Coke is again leading the field: 'it is the most popular of any brand on Facebook [itself the biggest social networking site], with more than 30 million fans'.[3] It explains the intricacies of 'engagement devices' which are used to 'encourage interaction', including photos, videos, links and tabs. A marketing friend pointed out that this is all voluntary; people are signing up because they freely choose to do so. I just don't find the idea that 30 million people want to be friends with a bottle of brown sugar water at all reassuring.

> Coca-Cola had, by far, the most extensive Facebook page, with 30 separate pages of content. These customized tabs included downloads (e.g., wallpapers, screensavers, emoticons); greetings and virtual gifts to post on friends' walls; and a calendar desktop application. A 'Where Will Happiness Strike Next?' tab encouraged fans to follow the Coca-Cola 'Happiness Truck' around the globe and view heart-warming videos of its deliveries.

Its Facebook page links to YouTube[4] where you can watch 'The Coca-Cola Company's newest instalment of the Happiness Factory series – The Great Happyfication. A rollicking six-minute anthem that distils the secrets of happiness into five toe-tapping lessons.' 'Eyes shone, cheeks were flushed, the inner light of universal benevolence broke out on every face in happy, friendly smiles.' (Actually this last sentence is not from the Coke site, but Huxley's *Brave New World*, describing the effects of the drug Soma which was prescribed to everyone to keep them nicely quiescent – thank the Ford.)

If you find this a bit cloying, try the Innocent website:

> We were wondering if you'd like to join the innocent family. Don't worry – it's not some weird cult. It's just our way of staying in touch with the people who drink our drinks i.e. you. We'll email you our news as often as you like and give you the chance to win lots of drinks. We'll also invite you to any nice events we might hold and maybe send you the odd present if you're lucky. Finally, we'll ask you what you reckon we should do next now and again, as we sometimes get confused.
>
> So this is the bit where we get a few more details. You know, inside leg, favourite chewing gum flavour, whether you like your fish steamed or grilled.
>
> By the way, we will never, ever pass your details on to anyone else, but you knew that anyway, didn't you. Your information will only ever be used to send you what you ask us to send you. If you would like to leave the family, use the unsubscribe button when you next receive an email from us.[5]

[Translation: we want to get as much information about you as possible so that we can sell more of our products than ever, but we are going to be all cutesy and hick because that way you might forget we are a rapacious corporation. Indeed that we are part of the Coca-Cola Corporation.]

Coke's Facebook page also has a connection to the Corporation's Twitter account, where we can 'Stay in touch with Coca-Cola', and to its Flickr page (photo-posting site) which has the cheery injunction: 'wherever you find refreshment in the world, please take a photo and share it with us'. You will be amazed (or maybe not) by how many such photos include Coke iconography of some sort.

On top of all this there are mobile applications. Innocent Kids, for instance, recently

> launched an iPhone and iPad app featuring a banana-themed game, specifically for its young customers. The app, created by Public Creative, aims to entertain four- to nine-year-olds with Innocent's The Dude's Banana Plane Game, which is available via portable smart-devices.[6]

We – and our kids – have no hiding place.

So the Rudd report details just how successful Coke is in exploiting the web to immerse us in its digital marcomms. And it is far from being the only sugary drinks corporation doing so; it is simply the biggest:

> Coca-Cola had 142 products and 17 brands, the most of any company in our analysis. PepsiCo had 115 products and 12 brands, followed by Dr Pepper Snapple Group with 104 products and 12 brands, and Kraft Foods with 82 products and 6 brands. These four companies produced two-thirds of the products and 79% of the brands in our analysis[7] [which covered around 90 per cent of the US market].

All are actively involved in exploiting the web, as are corporations in every sphere of consumption. The virtual world is populated not just by Coke and Pepsi, but every conceivable consumer brand – from trainers to baseball caps and music to booze.

Furthermore, this virtual promotion isn't happening instead of conventional media, but as well. The Rudd report reminds us that 'three quarters of 2010 media budgets were spent on TV advertising'. (Coke was again 'the highest spending company overall with almost $300 million for its sugary drinks'.) So the digital activity, massive though it is, is actually just a tiny part of the corporate marketers' communications effort. And all of this virtual and real activity, as we noted in the last two chapters, is carefully designed to fit together as a coherent, overlapping and self-reinforcing 'marketing communications mix'.

Pity the poor six-year-old trying to make intelligent objective decisions about her life and the world. What, for example, does the Innocent website do for her conception of family? And what about the entry on another page:

> When we're not busy making nice drinks, there's nothing we like better than doing up our vans and making them look sort of innocent. Naturally, this means that we now have a herd of cow vans and a couple of DGVs

(dancing grass vans to the man on the street). Find out more about the different breeds below, and please make sure you give us a wave when you see us driving around.[8]

Does that sound like a realistic and honest introduction to the remorseless process of getting us to consume?

Indeed pity any of us. As Tim Wu points out in his book *The Master Switch*,[9] which is all about the communications industry:

> It is an under acknowledged truism that, just as you are what you eat, how and what you think depends on what information you are exposed to. How do you hear the voice of political leaders? Whose pain do you feel? And where do your aspirations, your dreams of good living, come from? All of these are products of the information environment.

And this information environment is increasingly orchestrated and choreographed by corporate marketers.

Far from being a free, open space where information (however crazy and anarchic) can be accessed and shared, a sort of people's republic of ideas, our digital environment, and that of our children, is becoming just as commercialized as the real one. Indeed more so, because on a digital platform there are few logistical barriers. The pop-up doesn't need a team of bill posters, an available hoarding or planning permission. It combines the functionality of TV commercials, posters and product placement. It can lead people to other promotional locations, sell to them directly and keep in perpetual touch.

It is the corporate marketers' wet dream.

The day of the RFIDs

The virtual and real worlds are being brought together by a gadget called the RFID. This stands for 'radio-frequency identification' and combines digital and radio technology to produce a microscopic transmitter/receiver which is so small it can be printed. It has proved invaluable in inventory control, prisoner tagging and keeping a track on wandering sheep (look for the plastic label on the ear). It is now being adopted by corporate marketers because it can be used to monitor everything we do, reward us for good behaviour (i.e. consuming) and tell us yet more things about future consumption opportunities. Coke is again in the vanguard. For example, it has for a few years been organizing real world 'Coke village' events or mini-festivals which last 'three days and two nights, during which teens can play in an environment with no alcohol, but plenty of Coke products'.[10]

The company used the RFID to take this to a new level in Israel last year (see Box 6.1). The fifteen- to eighteen-year-old participants were all recruited through Facebook and to qualify they had 'to complete three requirements—obtaining 10 Coca-Cola can codes (which required consuming 10 cans of Coke), getting signed

---

BOX 6.1 COKE'S CUSTOMER TAGGING

Putting the FUN into RFID from Facebook and Coca-Cola

Bringing the virtual world of Facebook into the real world of the Village. Every Village guest received a wristband holding an RFID microchip that contained their Facebook username and password. On each Village attraction we attached an RFID microchip capable of collecting the users' data and sending it directly back to Facebook, creating a real time sharing experience for the guests with their Facebook friends. The teenagers, full of excitement, used the wristband non-stop. In addition, the wristband was also used to auto-tag the teenagers and pictures that were uploaded to Facebook online. The experience moved from the world of Facebook into the real world, and returned to the virtual world in full capacity.

Source: http://www.youtube.com/watch?v=LqwDqN7LNsc
&feature=youtube_gdata_player

---

permission from parents and gathering a group of eight friends'.[11] They also had to pay $50 per person. When they arrived at the event

> each attendee was provided with a wristband containing a passive RFID tag (embedded within a replica of a Coca-Cola bottle cap) that could be read at various attractions, as well as by staff members with portable readers, and the resulting information or pictures would then automatically be posted on that user's Facebook page.[12]

As it says, these postings took place automatically (the attendees had provided their passwords when they arrived), they took place on multiple occasions and could involve up to fifteen people simultaneously: group photos were encouraged. New possibilities are legion; next year apparently the event will include a booth shaped like a Coke can and if a couple goes in their Facebook pages will automatically be updated to show they are now friends.

But what about confidentiality and privacy? This has, according to a more conservative industry pundit, slowed RFID 'adoption into more novel applications such as marketing campaigns or new product development';[13] but not for long.

> A younger generation, firmly grounded in a world based on Twitter, will be the first generation to continuously share personal information on a real time basis. These young consumers will willingly make this trade of personal information in exchange for the perceived added value of products and

services that will be brought to them according to their preferences and their variable location(s).[14]

This helps us understand Coke's targeting of fifteen- to eighteen-year-olds; adults would be much more circumspect. And just to make sure everyone cooperated, incentives were built in: 'those who had their wristbands read the most often on a particular day won prizes, and were invited onstage with performers in the evening'.[15]

For Coke the rewards are obvious: sales, data, ongoing loyalty, and massive awareness: 'Coca-Cola Village and its RFID-enabled Facebook system have been a hit with Israeli teenagers. "We've reached 100 per cent—every teenager knows about it".'[16] The kids though have lost their privacy and consumed massive quantities of sugar. Meanwhile the rest of us have had a disturbing view into the future.

Data to die for

RFIDs point up another great digital advantage for our corporate handlers: an endless stream of invaluable data about our interests, preferences and behaviour. Every keystroke, every click of the mouse, every RFID transmission we wittingly (or unwittingly) make is recorded and available for potential analysis. With each of those sweepstakes, those 'this is the bit where we get a few more details', those photo posts – in pours the data. The witty clip to pass along to a colleague, or 'greetings and virtual gifts to post on friends' walls' will conveniently transmit our digital fingerprints. No need to commission costly focus groups, no expensive surveys required – indeed no need to pay us potential respondents at all. I am exaggerating here; focus groups and surveys will in fact be done as well; the corporate marketer simply can't get to know us well enough. We all donate the information; indeed given that we have to buy the digital devices, pay for their maintenance and contract for broadband we pay handsomely for the privilege of revealing our innermost secrets.

Furthermore this data has become even richer with the explosion in mobile technology. I recently passed a parked Mini in my home town, with four teenage lads squeezed into it so tightly their knees came up to their chins. All had their smart phones out and all were busy texting. Instead of talking to each other, they were paying to talk to other people. It seems the smart phone got its name because it is such a smart move by corporate marketers. As my colleague Mark Grindle points out, the iPhone makes us the first generation to pay for the means of our own surveillance. Arguably the Spanish Inquisition got there first, funded as it was by collections from the faithful, but it didn't fit in your pocket.

Nor are we grudging about any of this; we do it with enthusiasm, glee – even devotion. The near beatification of Steve Jobs shows how far our dedication has taken us. In one of the few critical analyses of the phenomenon of his death – it was almost as if his mortality took us by surprise – Tanya Gold pointed out that the 'eulogies for Steve Jobs' making him 'one pixel short of a saviour' were 'Apple's greatest marketing triumph to date'.[17]

Brand communities

Indeed such is our enthusiasm for sharing our lives with the corporate marketer, we are willingly forming ourselves into 'brand communities', which, the *Harvard Business Review*[18] (*HBR*) explains are groups 'of ardent consumers organized around the lifestyle, activities, and ethos of the brand'. Did I say form ourselves into brand communities? The *HBR* paper dispels any such utopian notion:

> Inspired by Harley's results [Harley Davidson has entered marketing lore through its magical success with brand communities] and enabled by Web 2.0 technologies, marketers in industries from packaged goods to industrial equipment are busy trying to build communities around their own brands. Their timing is right. In today's turbulent world, people are hungry for a sense of connection; and in lean economic times, every company needs new ways to do more with what it already has. Unfortunately, although many firms aspire to the customer loyalty, marketing efficiency, and brand authenticity that strong communities deliver, few understand what it takes to achieve such benefits.

That word authenticity again; and yet the whole thrust of the *HBR* piece is how companies can set about 'researching, building, and leveraging brand communities', 'maximizing their value for a firm', and 'increasing their impact'. The key lesson for the corporate marketer, the authors conclude, is that: 'your decision is not whether a community is right for your brand. It's whether you're willing to do what's needed to get a brand community right.' Maybe I'm over-sensitive or behind the times, but none of this sounds authentic to me.

As with all corporate marketing the key concern is the bottom line: 'brand-community members buy more, remain loyal, and reduce marketing costs through grassroots evangelism'.[19] The now famous Dove soap Campaign for Real Beauty is cited by the *HBR* as a great example of a brand community in beneficent action; in reality it just illustrates the well-tested corporate marketers' strategy of simulating authenticity and so making more money.

Dove's Campaign 'brought "real women" (less-than-pretty, older, large, skinny) together worldwide to fight industry-imposed beauty ideals. The women formed in camaraderie around this mission.'[20] A deeper analysis of the campaign by Danish academics, however, reminds us that

> the corporate pay-off is likely to emerge from the *perception* of the corporation as an active socially responsible agent ... whether the problem is perceived to be actually solved or not. Again, consider Dove; they surely have not solved the problem of distorted beauty ideals in contemporary Western society, but they are *perceived* as addressing the problem and, indeed, they

have gotten their corporate pay-off: the campaign is reported to have led to a 700% increase in product sales, and increased Dove's share of firming lotions in the UK from 1% to 6%.[21]

Firming lotions, incidentally, are antiaging creams; how's that for Real Beauty?

Surely I am exaggerating for effect. Some brand communities are authentic; some of us do spontaneously come together to celebrate and share our interest in a particular motorbike or computer console. Anyway we can choose to join and to leave – and those of us who join and stay presumably do so because we like it, we get some benefit from it. And my friend Paddy did get his car fixed really cheaply. The *HBR* is one step ahead. Once again, corporate marketers deploy the alchemy of artificial authenticity: 'In truth, brand communities generate more value when members control them—and when companies create conditions in which communities can thrive.' The more academic *Journal of Marketing* confirms this thinking: 'ceding control to customers enhances consumer engagement and builds brand equity'.[22] This isn't autonomy; it's just a matter of the corporate marketer being 'willing to do what's needed to get a brand community right'. A puppet is still a puppet, even though the strings are long, and delicate to the point of transparency.

No wonder the *HBR* says a resounding 'hooray for brand communities'.[23]

The price of freedom

But what about Paddy and his car repair? What about the near death experience of Apple's palm pilot and the resurrection from the dead of the Wispa? What, indeed, about sites like http://www.mumsnet, which has given hundreds and thousands of parents access to good advice, pressurized the UK's National Health Service into raising its game and received plaudits from at least one prime minister? It also does some corporation bashing, supporting Baby Milk Action in its fight against Nestlé.

I am not going to be churlish. These are good outcomes. But they will always be small beer compared to the digital machinations of corporate marketing. This is partly a matter of money. The internet is not a free space. It costs a lot to establish and maintain a website, and the skills needed for doing this increase with each technological innovation. So websites need cash. As we have already noted it also costs to access the internet – you need the smart phone, the internet provider, the Wi-Fi access.

At the same time, as we have seen, corporate marketers are hungry for opportunities to reach us, and they will pay well for the opportunity to do so. This means that as successful sites develop they will inevitably be stalked and either bought outright, or seduced with advertising revenue. Radox (once part of the giant US Sara Lee Corporation, now owned by Unilever) signed up as the first sponsor of Mumsnet's book club[24] for instance. P&G are the winners of the Mumsnet Family Friendly Programme Gold Award and its site is peppered with corporate ads. Carrie Longton, co-founder of Mumsnet, in an interview with *Marketing Magazine*, explains why the site is so popular with corporate marketers:

Consumers are much more likely to listen to a message from each other in social media terms than they are from a brand. We have a Mumsnet panel of 2,500 members. We recently helped Innocent drinks [the Coca-Cola Corporation] with the product and packaging of their Kids Juicy Drink. You're so much more likely to tell people about it and buy it if you've been involved with the creation and the marketing too.[25]

It is about association and fabulous source credibility – authenticity for hire.

But if you find this disconcerting, don't alarm yourself: remember, Innocent speaks with a really cutesy voice, and disguises its vans as cows.

The Facebook revolutionaries

Again, am I understating the potential power of social media? What about Tahrir Square? Didn't Facebook, YouTube and Twitter do for Mubarak? This shows they can be a force for major progress. They can empower the people, give them a voice and bring power to its knees. Social media are the people's champions. What worked in Tahrir Square can work in Tesco.

Except this isn't the Arab Spring; it's shopping. And corporate marketers don't usually resort to torture or snatch squads to get our custom. For us customers at least, sweet-talk, bribery and charm are the order of the day, rather than brute force; the soft power of the matrix. Full frontal challenges do happen to the likes of Tesco, as recently happened in the South of England,[26] and digital media no doubt helped the protesters to organize – but they are much less likely to gain traction on ground that has been well-greased with corporate marketing. If Mubarak had spent the last couple of decades intoning 'every little helps' to the Egyptian people, and recruiting well-loved icons like Prunella Scales or Alan Titchmarsh to his cause, maybe he wouldn't have faced a revolt at all – just a patchwork of brand communities 'organized around the lifestyle, activities, and ethos of the brand'.[27]

Off colour hyperbole? Remember Neruda and the United Fruit Company; remember RJ Reynolds' ministrations to 'the young, the poor, the black and the stupid'; remember that our planet is heating up and corporate marketers are still pushing unsustainable consumption with every bit and byte of their massive capability. Above all remember that money is power; as Arundhati Roy (2011) reminds us:

Corporations that are turning over these huge profits can own everything: the media, the universities, the mines, the weapons industry, insurance hospitals, drug companies, non-governmental organizations. They can buy judges, journalists, politicians, publishing houses, television stations, bookshops and even activists.[28]

Her words will echo loudly when we discuss marketing to power in Chapter 8.

Not even a marketing revolution

This isn't even a marketing revolution, let alone a political one. The interactivity of new media and the supposed power of the digital audience takes us right back to Orson Welles and the nature of all mass media communications – digital or conventional. As we discussed in Chapter 4, in his day the preferred metaphor was the hypodermic syringe, framing the audience as quintessentially passive. In reality life is more complex than this, and communication, like beauty lies at least partly in the eye of the beholder. Welles showed the world how subterfuge, subtlety and shade can enable the insightful communicator to get through this subjectivity. Marketers used the same techniques, and coupled them with assiduous market research, to regain control of the syringe.

They are now repeating the trick for digital media. And this time around the market research data and communications technology are both infinitely more sophisticated. Corporate marketers have also learnt their trade well. As we saw with Carling's booze sponsorship in the last chapter, they are alert to the dangers of crass insistence; the 'logo-blindness' – and outright resentment – that can result from being too pushy. Corporate marketers have

> in a very short time, learned not to bombard us with their brands – they know that we don't go online in the first instance to warm our hands around the rosy glow of their logos – they know now to watch and listen to our behaviours online and map them very closely indeed.[29]

They understand the power of apparent choice and spurious agency. I *chose* to have a Facebook presence; and I *chose* to belong to my group of friends and acquaintances. But the gentle and regular reminders from Facebook 'Gerard, you have friend requests waiting; you haven't visited us for a while' (READ: you are holding vital data back and we need to collect it from you) feels like '"Why weren't you in Church on Sunday? Do you really want to risk ostracism?"'[30]

Thus, often unconsciously, as with brand communities, we willingly do the puppet masters' bidding. And the rosy emotional tinge attached to the whole process keeps us, once again, happy in our servitude.

Closing the net

Soft power delivers up hard power. The puppet masters are becoming ever bigger and fewer in number: Google, Apple, Facebook. Their power is immense and largely unchallenged. Why is it that Julian Assange, who gives us free access to private information about corporations is a villain, but Mark Zuckerberg, who gives private information about us to corporations, is man of the year?

Furthermore, the power we voluntarily give the puppet masters is being reinforced by the acquisition and control of the digital communication channels. Tim Wu's *The Master Switch*, quoted earlier in the chapter, puts paid to the very idea of an internet free-for-all. He presents a history of the communications industry from the earliest days of the telephone. Taking us through the development of telephony, then radio, film and television he shows that one after another the same pattern emerges. Each started with a 'Wild West' period, where anyone can join in with the new technology, setting up their own little media community. There is a lovely image, for instance, of farmers in the Mid-West running country music sessions on their fence-wire telephone systems, with musicians in different far-flung ranch houses. But in each case the same cycle kicks in, with this folksy engagement being corralled and swallowed by corporate interest: Bell Telephones, Universal Studios, the American Broadcasting Company.

This cycle now stalks the internet.

His Coke rewards

So rather than becoming our saviour, the internet is being co-opted by corporate marketers to reinforce our subjugation. As with traditional marketing, it makes us feel treasured with faux-friendship and illusory power, whilst distracting us from the toxic side-effects of what is a dangerous and deeply regressive system. The damage to the planet of over-consumption, the concentration of power in unaccountable corporations and gaping inequalities get overlooked and minimized in the rush to 'create value' – or more accurately to push consumption.

Boardroom remuneration provides just one illustration of this sleight of hand. As I am writing this, yet another report has emerged showing how CEO pay is rocketing up. The US trade union website, Executive Pay Watch[31] reminds us that CEO remuneration in 1980 outstripped that of the median worker by a factor of 42; by 2010 this had increased to 343. The same website informs us that Coke's CEO is riding the wave; 'Muhtar Kent received $24,782,017 in total compensation', which is '732 times the median worker's pay'. By comparison, in the much lambasted financial sector, the Bank of America CEO Brian T. Moynihan received a measly $1,940,069, which is only 57 times the median worker's pay.

Now that's what I call 'My Coke Rewards'.

Delivering Sennett's dystopia

In Chapter 3 we noted Richard Sennett's despondent observation that we now define ourselves, not in terms of what we produce, but what we consume. *Consumer Psychology for Marketing* begins with the same observation: 'We are consumers. Our primary economic significance derives from the purchase and consumption activities that take up so large a portion of our waking lives.'[32] The difference is that rather than regretting this turn of events the book goes on to spell out over two hundred pages of scientifically devised techniques for encouraging it. These are targeted at us from early childhood and follow us through to the grave.

The next chapter shows how marketing communication, hydra-headed and ubiquitous though it is, is actually just a fragment of this marketing effort.

Tesco

It's stressful down at Tesco, the stock is so extensive
You used to find me in the aisle looking lost and pensive
With twenty sorts of toilet roll: quilted, perfumed, fluffy
And forty sorts of herbal tea, I'd really had enoughy
So I started up a movement; this idol we'd defrock
By tracking down all those things that Tesco didn't stock
Then we would tell the world, their failure we'd betray
And so we'd show this retail God, had feet of callow clay

We got a hundred volunteers who fanned out through the land
With most unlikely shopping lists clutched firmly in their hands
Some looked for quails' eggs fricasseed in organic yak's milk butter
And some for arctic roses to make a young heart flutter
Coelacanth was on the list, along with curried wombat stew
And lark's tongue served in aspic; a ready meal for two
But each of them was on the shelf and there for all to see
We even found the Coelacanth was buy one get one free

Our hearts were growing heavy, and our spirits they were dropping
We couldn't find one human need that wasn't met by shopping
Every foolish foible, each addled whim and fancy
Was catered for and sanctified by Tesco's necromancy
We met in one last session, desperate to find
Just one earthly want to which Tesco's eye was blind
Then the penny tumbled down; so obvious, God damn it
You can't go down to Tesco and buy another planet

7

A VERY MIXED BLESSING

Actions speak louder than words

So far we have discussed only the corporate marketers' attempts to communicate with us. The real muscle is provided by three additional marketing tools: the price (the amount of money they can persuade us to part with in return for a given product or service); the place (the distribution network and point of sale activity); and the product or service itself. The task of the marketer is to ensure that the 'right' decisions are made about each of these: the 'right' price is set, the 'right' outlet is located and/or designed, the 'right' product or service is made.

The definition of 'right' takes us back to Chapter 2 and the core marketing idea of consumer orientation. On the face of it this means ensuring all three elements – price, place and product – are pitched so as to best satisfy us customers, which sounds most agreeable. However, a little thought throws up an inherent contradiction: as customers we would favour cheap prices, ready accessibility and high quality; but the marketer wants to make money. Specifically, the corporate marketer has an over-riding need to deliver increased shareholder value through higher profits, which in turn requires maximized margins and (especially) greater sales. Our consumption needs to be encouraged and accelerated. We have to be kept in the shops.

Each of the three marketing tools is, therefore, designed to stimulate our consumption: pricing is carefully calculated to maximize both the price we will pay and the number of us who will pay it; place, both in the sense of the distribution network and the configuration of each outlet, is designed to get us in with our wallets out; and the product itself is developed and tweaked to ensure it tempts us as seductively as possible.

Price, place and product, along with promotion, are together known as 'the four Ps of marketing' – or the 'marketing mix'. This collective identity is vital: the different elements need to be coherent and self-reinforcing to maximize effect, much as we saw with the marketing communications mix. Again great effort is put into getting the 'right' mix – and that is the one that will best encourage us to buy. Thus, the word 'satisfy' is quietly replaced with more muscular ones like 'impinge' and 'influence', and the focus moves from enhancing supply to increasing demand; from satisfaction to dissatisfaction.

The marketing mix forms the core of the marketing strategy, which is honed using the key functions of market research and targeting and segmentation, and is increasingly informed by relational thinking. Thus corporate marketing becomes endemic. Once again the purpose is to keep us consuming.

This multifaceted, strategic drive to stimulate shopping would be crass in an infinite world; it is catastrophic in a finite one.

The price of everything

Setting the price of a particular product or service sounds like a straightforward task. You work out what it costs to produce and add on your profit margin and away you go. Okay, it is a little more complicated because you need to factor in the expense of telling people about your offering and getting it to them (or the nearest shop), but again the principle is straightforward enough. However, to the corporate marketer such 'cost plus' thinking completely misses the point; as a leading text book puts it: 'it is not the cost that matters, but the perceived value'[1] – what we the customers think it is worth.

On one level this makes sense: if I am spending my own hard-earned money I am going to have very definite opinions on what represents good value, and these will not necessarily align with costs of production. For instance the Phillips-Van Heusen Corporation is unlikely to come up with a price for its Calvin Klein Obsession fragrance for men that I will think is good value because I am not interested in perfume. On the other hand, a bargain price for a new clutch for my defunct car will readily get my attention. In neither case does the cost of production really interest me.

On another level, however, pricing things on the basis of what we think they are worth is a disastrous recipe for disempowered fecklessness. It disempowers us because if we don't know what something costs to make we cannot judge whether or not we are being cheated. Without some notion of the production costs we have no idea of the mark-up. It encourages irresponsibility because we have a duty to consider how a product is made and especially who is paid what for doing the work. This underpins the concept of Fairtrade and, as we have discussed already, one of the few remaining powers we have is to shop responsibly; only a good knowledge of production costs (for all those involved) will enable us to do so.

More fundamentally still, it is an inability to recognize the broader costs of our consumption that is driving our unsustainable lifestyles and global warming. We drive our SUVs, fly to Thailand on holiday and overheat our houses because we manage to forget about the carbon footprint and ozone damage. Pricing built around our values actively encourages this purblind selfishness. It promotes the sort of behaviour we try to eradicate in five-year-olds: I want an ice cream now! (regardless of how far daddy has to drive to get it, the fact that the shop is shut or that it is made from union-busting pineapples). But for the corporate marketer none of this matters; just so long as we keep on shopping.

All that glisters

This way of pricing things, then, should more properly be called 'spoilt child' or 'selfish adult' pricing. Marketers, however, prefer the term 'market' or 'consumer oriented pricing', which has their familiar glister of seeming democracy; we can determine what we pay for our new car or washing machine. But as we have noted, corporations are not democratic, and in marketing, as in *The Merchant of Venice*, 'all that glisters is not gold'. Problems emerge for two reasons, both of which are now familiar to us. First, the corporation is driven by the need to increase shareholder value, not our value. Our desire for cheapness, for instance, will only be entertained provided it contributes to corporate growth. Profit is all; the perpetual search is for maximum sales and the highest possible margins. A corporate marketer who fails to manage these two competing agendas 'loses two sources of income: one is the revenue lost from customers who find the price too high and do not purchase; the other is the additional income they could have earned from customers who would have been willing to pay more'.[2] It is a tricky balancing act that has an immediate impact on the bottom line. Our ideas about value, just as with our needs more generally, only come into the picture because they help with these calculations.

The second problem comes with the all-important qualifying term *perceived* value. Perceptions can be adjusted and managed. 'One common marketing strategy' for instance, 'is to make a large expense look small by advertising it in terms of smaller amounts'[3] – the Christmas magazine subscription that builds into a book for just three dollars a week; a book that would cost far less than the necessary thirty $3 subs if bought outright. Similarly, we are bad at calculating 'partitioned costs' (separating out say delivery charges from the item price) so this tactic can 'decrease customers' recalled total costs and increase their demand'.[4]

Robert Cialdini's book *Influence*[5] shows we have bags of similar vulnerabilities because of the techniques we have devised to help us cope with a complex world, packed with too many decisions (not least thanks to corporate marketers) – and how easy it is for those in the know, including corporate marketers, to exploit these weaknesses to their advantage.

Thus car sales staff know we are more likely to purchase extras once we have made the much bigger commitment to buy the car, thanks to the 'contrast principle' which makes the radio or alloy wheels seem such trivial decisions. Similarly InBev corporation's famous 'reassuringly expensive' ad campaign for Stella Artois lager builds on the knowledge that we will actually buy some products more readily if the price is higher, because we have learnt to associate expense with quality (following something called the 'consistency principle') and can be tricked into using the heuristic when it doesn't apply. Cialdini identifies five other psychological drivers, and shows how, what he terms, the 'compliance professionals' exploit these with numerous examples, most of which have a queasy resonance to them. Just last Saturday I fell for the 'reciprocation principle' after accepting a free sample of expensive ham at the local market and then feeling obliged to buy a ludicrously expensive joint. And I've read Cialdini's book; I should have been forearmed.

The murky world of sales promotion

Corporate marketers populate this ghostly perceptual space with a vast array of sales promotions. One comprehensive text lists no fewer than twenty variations on the theme, including discounts, competitions, free samples, money-off coupons, loyalty cards and cashback offers. The multifaceted nature of sales promotion and its deployment in so many outlets makes it difficult to estimate expenditure, but sales promotion is a massive business, far outweighing marketing communications.

Marketers traditionally distinguish between 'above the line' adspend (that is all the things we discussed in the last three chapters) and 'below the line' promotions like the ones in Table 7.1, and the disparity is often illustrated using the metaphor of an iceberg. As Colin Harper, Head of Insight at the London-based Institute of Sales Promotion puts it:

> People only tend to notice the obvious marketing spend, on above-the-line advertising or obvious Point of Sale (POS) activity, for example. But sales promotion is a bit like an iceberg – there is far more going on below the surface than immediately meets the eye.[6]

The article in *Marketing Magazine* quotes his figure for the 2007/8 financial year of a £25.6 billion UK annual spend by branded-goods manufacturers on sales promotion with retailers – which it compares with the (relatively) modest £18.6 billion spent on conventional advertising. Meanwhile, in the United States, sales promotion expenditure topped $100 billion a year a decade ago.[7]

Although, as we've seen, these below the line promotions come in many different forms, their purpose is single-minded: 'the ultimate aim is always sales'.[8] I suppose the clue is in the name.

TABLE 7.1 'Below the line' sales promotions

Type of promotion	What this does	Examples
Discount pricing and sales	Gets us in the shop or online. Often incites price wars between competitors.	January sales; Asda Price campaign.
Money-off coupons	Encourages us to buy and start or continue to buy certain products.	Supermarket coupons; toy-shop coupons.
Refunds	Looks like a good deal. Often cheaper than giving discounts due to non-redemption.	Microsoft's offer of £50 cashback deal on Windows XP in early 2002.
Samples	Encourages us to start or continue to buy particular products.	Free shampoo samples.
Payment terms	Reduces the real cost rather than price. Helps to cope with seasonal demand.	Interest-free credit offers; buy-now-pay-later deals.
Multipacks and multi-buys	Gets us to buy and consume more than we intend in the short and long term.	Supermarket deals on frequently bought products; 3-for-2 offers.
Special features	Makes us think that if we don't buy the product or service now we won't get the chance again.	Often packaged as 'special' or 'limited' editions; cars with metallic paint; computers with extra memory.
Quantity increases	Looks like a good deal so makes us buy and consume more.	Canned beers frequently offer 25 per cent extra free.
In-pack premiums	Free extra item lures us into buying a certain branded product many times over.	Free toys in cereal boxes.
In-mail premiums	Chance of winning attracts us. Our details get added to their database.	Free movie tickets; limited edition T-shirts etc. – often must claim online.
Piggy-back premiums	Immediate increased sales for bought item and gives free item a trial leading to sales.	Free Gillette GII with Kleenex for Men.
Competitions	Lures us into buying and reinforces product's/company's ad campaign.	Win a car; win cash prizes; McDonald's $40 million Treasure Hunt.

Continued

TABLE 7.1 Continued

Type of promotion	What this does	Examples
Information	Brings the shop or service into our homes – a secure setting. We think we save time.	Catalogues; holiday brochures; investment guides.
Valued packaging	Added game, activity, recipe, etc. to packaging attracts us.	Games on cereal boxes; recipes on food items.
Loyalty cards	Keeps us loyal. Promos can be sent to us directly – our details go on their databases.	Supermarkets; Boots Advantage Card; Nectar cards.
Gift coupons	Gets us to repeat purchases. Our details go on their databases.	Offered in petrol stations, with draught beer etc. Often must go online to claim.
Product trials	Customers try product before buying – increases likelihood that they will buy it.	Home testing of computers. These are often combined with a competition.
Guarantees	We think we're getting the best deal. Relies on people not checking prices.	Supermarket 'Refund and Replace' offers; refund the difference deals.
Cashback offers	Cheaper than discounts if people don't redeem cashback – companies can insure themselves against 'over-redemption'.	Buyback pledges.
Clubs	Keeps us loyal. Makes us feel special and part of something. Our details go on their databases.	Marriott Hotels' Rewards scheme; Burger King's Kids Club.

Source: Adapted from table entitled 'Major forms of consumer promotions' in Michael J. Baker (ed.) (2003) *The Marketing Book*, pp.462–3 (Chapter 18 'Sales Promotion' by Sue Peattie and Ken Peattie).

Beware of the BOGOF

Achieving these increased sales calls for careful deployment and a good knowledge of Cialdini's insights. The BOGOF (Buy One Get One Free), which along with similar multi-buy offers makes up more than half of UK sales promotions, provides a good example. Marketers wax lyrical about the power of 'free'; we are all programmed to look for downsides in any transaction – but when something is free there is, seemingly, no downside. There are in fact many drawbacks to free – not least that in the world of corporate marketing it is as mythical as the unicorn. Newton's Third Law of Motion is that every action has a reaction; the first law of sales promotion is that every pitch has a payback.

We know this to be the case; the phrase 'there is no such thing as a free lunch' has become axiomatic. So we know that the free sample pulls us into the purchase; that the 'free' extra bag of Kettle Chips comes at the cost of our good dietary intentions; that a bargain is just something we wouldn't have bought at half the price we wouldn't have paid for it.

And yet the power of free holds us in thrall, and the corporate marketer uses the BOGOF to exploit it.

It needs some careful handling though. The danger for the marketer is that the promotion simply telescopes our shopping; we buy two today and none tomorrow, rather than paying the full price two days running. In the jargon of retailing, the promotion is 'mortgaging future sales'. The best bet from the marketers' perspective is therefore to go for products with 'elastic consumption' – that is ones we will use up as fast as we buy them, or at least faster than we would if we were to buy them one at a time. Non-essentials such as cakes, biscuits, soft drinks and alcohol are good examples; mundane necessaries like cleaning products are much less elastic. If a promotion encourages us to double our purchase of toilet rolls in our weekly shop the chances are that we will simply leave them off the list the following week. If it's a chocolate biscuit or beer promotion, on the other hand, we will just eat and drink twice as much and buy again next week.

This is 'store-cupboard marketing'; if the product gets into our house it is then available 24 hours a day – and proximity all too often encourages consumption. Any dieter knows that if you want to cut down on cakes, the best first step is to banish them from your larder. For the corporate marketer, then, an empty store-cupboard is anathema, and the BOGOF is a great way to combat it.

Sales promotions owe their power to the fact that they come into play in the shop just as we are making purchase decisions and the key mechanism is the impulse purchase. Apparently 85 per cent of us are impulse purchasers – that is we buy 'spontaneously, unreflectively, immediately and kinetically' and extensive business research has identified the 'key situational factors' 'such as the store atmosphere and display product novelty and attraction and the price promotion'[9] that can trigger this profitable inclination. Cialdini draws a comparison with jujitsu: mimicking the martial art, the 'compliance professional', he explains, uses our own weaknesses against us; the sales promotion takes this power to scale. And it works: more and more of our purchase decisions are being made in-store, and promotions have been shown to increase our 'spontaneous' buying by between 2 and 65 per cent. It's worth pausing to think about these figures: these are purchases we didn't mean to make, carbon we wouldn't have burnt, if it weren't for some marketing novelty messing with our perceptions of value.

Brand new

Sales promotions, though, are just the most direct manifestation of the corporate marketers' efforts to manipulate our understanding of value. In reality the whole marketing effort is dedicated to adding value, and this thrust is encapsulated by the brand. As one business academic explains: 'today, marketing professionals prefer to talk about brands rather than products. This reflects the recognition that consumers do not buy just physical attributes, but also the psychological associations associated with a supplier's offer.'[10] All in our best interests of course, as he continues: 'choice today is difficult for customers because of the myriad competitors seeking patronage'.[11] (In other words, corporate marketers are trying to sell us so much stuff they have had to invent branding to help us cope with the resulting cacophony.)

A pair of generic trainers multiplies in value once it acquires the Nike swoosh; Marlboro cigarettes can command a premium and Heinz beans are well worth the extra cost. As we noted in Chapter 5, the power of the brand is amply demonstrated by the fact that its worth is directly linked to shareholder value and corporate wealth.

So what is the problem? Surely value is being created and shared by both the customer and the marketer? We don't just get a pair of shoes – we also get a guarantee of quality, a stylish accessory, a fashion statement and a boost to our confidence. What is more this added value is ecologically sound: the carbon footprint of a Nike Air Max is not going to differ much from that of a generic trainer.

The problem is consumption; enhanced shareholder value means more sales: branding begets buying – our buying. It succeeds for three reasons:

1. The additional psychosocial benefits it seems to offer give us more reasons to buy. (I say 'seems to' because there is no evidence to show that buying stuff makes us any more content or well-balanced.)
2. Psychosocial benefits are much more ephemeral than physical ones; a shoe's capacity to keep our feet comfortable can last for years – it is only a cool fashion statement for a season. The brand builds in obsolescence.
3. All this is under the control of corporate marketers, who deploy everything from celebrity link-ups to cool in-store promotions to build and hone brand image, and they, as always, have a single-minded focus on selling us more stuff. From their perspective that built-in obsolescence is a glorious opportunity, and our vulnerability a fertile sales territory.

So functional products become lifestyle props, and consumption becomes a favoured route to happiness. Where once we would have impressed our peers by derring-do or innate cleverness, we now buy multiple pairs of trainers – and a skip-load of other emotional accessories. (Except if you are poor of course; no room for you in the marketplace of cool, as we will discuss later in the chapter.) And this materialism starts early: the Nike Air Max 90 2007 is aimed at toddlers.

Place

A smoker can tell you where she can buy cigarettes at any time of the day or night. Tobacco companies understand that an addictive habit needs constant feeding, so have deliberately gone for ubiquity in their distribution strategy. Like the empty store-cupboard, the cigarette-less smoker is to be avoided at all costs. Coke has traditionally adopted a similarly ambitious strategy – in the 1980s it famously had a one-line marketing strategy: to put a can of its sugar-water within arm's reach of everyone on the planet.

The idea was taken a step further in 2001, when the BBC reported 'The drinks giant … has plans to provide Coke on tap in its customers' homes … it would create a system to mix Coke syrup with carbonated water at the site of each customer's home.'[12] The then CEO, Donald Daft, the report continued, 'will only be happy when customers are turning on their taps to drink Coke rather than water'. This is not an April Fool: the report notes that Coca-Cola 'has invested venture capital money in the idea' and 'formed a joint venture with the consumer products group Procter & Gamble' (that is another corporation) which 'will focus on developing and marketing innovative juice-based drinks and snacks on a global basis'. It is just a logical extension of store-cupboard marketing.

Other corporate marketers adopt a more bespoke policy and deliberately keep their outlets exclusive. Porsche want their showrooms to be select rather than commonplace, airlines reserve their business lounges for a chosen few and the makers of Burberry were horrified when their elite fawn tartan was adopted by working class Scottish adolescents.

The two sets of strategies are diametrically different, but the objectives are identical: to increase sales. In the case of Burberry, for example, it may appear that the fashion house is trying to *discourage* sales to the Scottish youngsters, but this is only to preserve the exclusivity of the brand and hence to deliver much larger global sales.

The same profligate focus dominates the design of individual outlets. 'Slotting fees' are paid by producers to get prime shelf locations; the difference between being on an aisle-end or in the main drag of a supermarket is enormous. An industry presentation I was at recently showed that, compared with being in a side aisle, a position in the centre aisle of the supermarket could lead to a 400 per cent increase in sales.[13] Again this is worth thinking about: we will buy four times as much stuff just because it has been put on a different shelf. Coke's arm's reach policy makes a lot of commercial sense.

In-store display, labelling and shelf fascias each also play key roles in the ceaseless fight to stimulate our shopping. Nothing is left to chance. An extremely technical paper in the world-leading and highly academic *Journal of Marketing* (*JoM*) explains how careful eye-tracking studies are conducted to see exactly what we look at and pay attention to. Note the important distinction – the former is apparently necessary but not sufficient to secure a purchase; the latter will get us buying. The authors confirm the fickle and superficial nature of our decision making: 'a majority of brand choice decisions are made inside the store, yet consumers only evaluate a fraction of the products available'.[14] In a sane world this lack of consideration about a behaviour that is destroying our planet would be a cause for deep concern, but for the corporate marketer it's an opportunity. The *JoM* article continues: 'In this context, improved attention through in-store marketing activity should strongly influence consumer behavior at the point of purchase, and our results show that this is indeed the case' – adding, with a note of regret, 'but only to a certain extent'.[15] The authors then go on to suggest ways in which this unfortunate imperfection can be ironed out and our shopping behaviour can be properly controlled to maximize sales.

In similar vein a UK marketing textbook explains that 'models have been developed to allocate display space'.[16] It seems some items are 'space elastic', 'with sales increases in response to higher allocation of space, others are not'. Care is therefore taken to study our behaviour in great detail so as to 'allocate space to yield the best returns', always allowing for 'direct product profitability', 'estimates of shelf replenishment/frequency costs' and of course, impact on the 'image of the store'. The book also underlines the corporate marketers' penchant for nifty camera work:

> camera-based techniques, used by advertising agencies to track eye movements in response to advertising images, are now being used to examine responses to displays. Cameras are also used to track customer movements within the store as a whole, leading to major improvements in layout effectiveness. They pinpoint areas of high, possibly dysfunctional density, and 'cold' areas visited by few shoppers. They record where people stop to look and where they tend to ignore the displays. Sometimes, the store security system can provide sufficient detail: for more detailed analyses, tiny cameras can be built into the displays.[17]

So next time you see that in-store camera blinking at you, you don't just need to worry about the store detective feeling your collar, but the marketer meddling with your mind. And meddle they do in every conceivable way. There is, for example, a whole body of market research into what are termed 'retail atmospherics': how music, colours and even scents can be used to affect our mood states and hence shopping behaviour – an influence 'that often operates at the subconscious level'.

It is difficult, then, to over-state the amount of time and effort that goes into measuring and honing the minutiae of the retail environment. The studies are legion, the detail exhaustive and the options for optimizing the marketing effort seemingly limitless. And all to one end, and one end only: to get us to buy more.

And so to the product

Arguably the product is what it is all about; this is where the marketing ends and the focus turns to our real needs. We have done with the sizzle, now we are on to the sausage. I'm afraid not.

For a start we don't really know what we want. My first proper job was as a junior research executive in a small market research company called Purchaser and

Consumer Studies Limited. We got a lot of work in the new product development field. Clients wanted to know how they could expand their product portfolios, extend existing lines and/or get into whole new areas. I spent innumerable evenings in market research recruiters' front rooms doing focus groups with different sorts of people – from children to grannies; Welsh, Scots, Irish and English; model makers, chocoholics and drivers.

Sometimes the brief was open-ended and we went to enormous lengths to trawl people's hopes and fancies. We used lots of 'projective techniques' like the instant coffee one we discussed in Chapter 4, to dig down to emotional and unconscious levels. We played word games to open up their creative thinking. We asked them to imagine they were in charge of production at the Airfix factory and could make anything they wanted. We gave them shopping baskets full of groceries to play around with to see if there were any gaps in current provision. On reflection, it was often good mind-stretching activity; except it was all focused on finding ways to get us to consume more.

And we did succeed. This was the late seventies and pasta sauce mixes were a thing of the future, but our work on tinned tomatoes, showing how they could be a vegetable in their own right, a cooking ingredient or a substitute for the fresh variety, demonstrated their versatility and surely paved the way for the forty-one different variations on this theme that Tesco online now stock. And that's just in the supermarket's Italian range; it doesn't include its fresh pasta and pasta sauce (88 varieties), instant snacks (13 varieties) or British and Tex Mex (4 varieties).

The 'extruded savoury snack market' was also in its infancy (or at least adolescence) back then. In case this innovation is unfamiliar to you, a paper in *Food Research International* explains this exciting addition to our diets:

> Extrusion cooking provides the conditions for gelatinizing starch, poly-merizing proteins and cross-linking molecules to form expandable matrices. The addition of proteins to starches increases sites for cross-linking and affects textural quality. The source of milk protein, the concentration and processing conditions are significant factors in the cross-linking and complexing of the molten material in the extruder. Ideally, proteins are denatured, realigned, and complexed to form expanded matrices; however, the degree of expansion depends on the concentration of protein.[18]

In plain language, extruded savoury snacks are deep fried gobbets of reconstituted corn, potato or rice that can be loaded with any desired flavouring. Because the gobbets can be made into any shape you like, they provide the perfect way of getting kids to consume massive quantities of fat and salt. Our work on Monster Munch ("The Biggest Snack Pennies Can Buy") with four different monsters on the packs to match the novelty shapes (monster paws or tongues) and fun flavours (including the ever-popular pickled onion) was exhaustive. Innumerable focus groups were done with primary age children during which we fed them the product on its own and in liveried bags; showed them potential television ads to see which appealed; and provided a selection of competing products to make comparison. We played games, told stories, laughed and joked – all to uncover their consumption preferences.

Again our work seems to have formed a profitable launch pad: Tesco now has 346 different products listed under crisps and snacks (not including 99 sorts of nuts). Not all our doing of course; only a proportion of these will be extruded.

Try, try and try again

We also had many failures. Which is not surprising – the vast majority (around 80 per cent) of new food products do fail. This might evoke pity for the forlorn lot of the corporate marketer: who would want a job where four times out of five your efforts come to nought? Alternatively it can be seen as just another indication of profligate waste. Our 'needs' are so well pandered to that we yawn like Roman emperors as yet another tantalizing but pointless sweetmeat is dangled before us, and the marketers rush off to try and find some other means of piquing our jaded appetites.

Our failures were most apparent when we came in further down the new product development process, and got people trying prototypes like apple crisps (wrong expectations) or poussin branded as baby chickens (the heart-rending name nearly got me lynched). My favourite blooper was an attempt by Cadbury to combine its premium dairy milk chocolate with 'space dust' – a children's novelty product which exploded in the mouth like hyperactive sherbet. The focus group of thirty-something women began with a discussion of the joys of chocolate, which, it emerged, were almost sexual; I can still recall the languorous descriptions and sensual recollections of chocolate melting in the mouth. I was young and innocent, and had to hide my blushes. Then I gave them the new product to try, which looked like their usual semi-erotic treat but unbeknownst to them contained the mischievous space dust. It was like watching someone bite into a succulent sweet pepper only to discover that it is a bird's eye chilli.

But such failures did not deter, and Purchaser and Consumer Studies Limited continued to earn a good living doing all manner of new product development work. It was one of hundreds in London at that time, and of thousands globally. The new product development business has been growing ever since.

My early tinkering in the field is explained more formally by a present-day marketing textbook: prospecting for new products 'goes beyond merely asking customers what they are looking for' it involves 'creatively seeking to discover needs that customers cannot articulate because they are unaware of the possibilities offered by new technology and the changing environment'.[19] Again this is worthy of reflection. In a finite world, where the need to *reduce* our consumption is becoming ever more pressing, we have countless teams of corporate marketers devoting their careers to uncovering 'needs' that we consumers don't even know we have. My boss in the market research company had a favourite saying: 'the consumer doesn't know what they want until they get it'; if corporate marketers aren't restrained, what we are going to get is a planet burnt to a cinder – and I for one know I don't want that.

The old standbys

New product development is just a fraction of the effort that goes into product management; most of the corporate marketers' energy is focused on bolstering existing offerings. The principal problem here is differentiation. There is such a plethora of stuff out there that it is not just arduous for us to choose, as we have already noted, it is hard for the marketer to convince us that their product has any additional tangible benefits to offer. As a leading business academic puts it: 'unfortunately, today, with the speed with which technology travels, it is increasingly difficult to build brands, and certainly to maintain them, on the basis of demonstrable, superior functional benefits'.[20]

This problem stems, not least, from the fact that there rarely are any tangible differences between products, as he goes on to explain: 'Comparably priced washing powders, cars, computers or auditing firms are usually much alike in the performance they deliver.' The solution then, presumably, is some form of rationalization, some sifting of the obvious over provision – some move to a less profligate system. Not at all. He continues: 'consequently, firms must find other ways to differentiate themselves, to create awareness and recall among customers. Hence they turn to design, colour, logos, packaging, advertising and additional services.' But he warns, 'while differentiation creates recognition it does not necessarily create preference'. For this you have to dig deeper: 'increasingly it is the emotional or experience associations that a successful brand promises that creates customer value'. In other words, we are quite literally, buying hopes and dreams.

Thus we return to the field of perceptions and the potential of brands to influence and manage these. If there is no real difference between the washing powders, corporate marketers simply set about fabricating one – and the brand is their most powerful instrument. Bringing us full circle, it also greases the wheels of new product development: 'new products launched under a strong brand name are more likely to be trusted by consumers and to achieve a faster market penetration'. Brands get us to buy things we otherwise would not. They keep us shopping.

The marketing mix

The enormous effort put into managing price, place and product decisions is combined with that devoted to marcomms, which we discussed in the previous three chapters, to form the marketing mix. This combination of marketing tools creates powerful synergies: the Monte Carlo setting for the television commercial; the sponsorship deal with a Bond star; the pristine showroom in the best part of town; the eye-watering prices; the calf leather seats and high performance engine – all serve to reinforce the exclusivity of the car. By the same token, alcopops need to combine juvenile flavours, links to youth culture, cool imagery, competitive pricing and ready availability in youth venues. In both cases, the synchronization of every bit of marketing effort produces an increase in both effectiveness and efficiency, and the whole becomes greater than the sum of its parts.

Again, the challenge to the corporate marketer is to develop the 'right' mix. Many textbooks on marketing will, at this point, revert to the rhetoric of customer satisfaction. The right mix is that which best pleases us consumers. But this is patently naïve; we will typically be best pleased by low prices, easy accessibility and high quality – but making money out of such offerings is tricky and gaining the 'economic advantage which endures' (see Chapter 2) completely impossible.

With refreshing bluntness, one business academic dismisses such double-talk and proclaims outright that 'the key principle of the optimum marketing mix is that which maximises shareholder value',[21] thereby putting it in the frontline of the corporate mission. On this he agrees with *Business Week* that 'the fundamental task of today's CEO is simplicity itself: get the stock price up. Period.' He goes on to quote, in turn, the mission statements of Coca-Cola, the Disney Corporation and Cadbury Schweppes – each emphasizing the primacy of shareholder value.

Then to reassure us, lest we take fright at such transparency, he adds: 'these shareholders are not the bloated capitalists of socialist propaganda, but rather the pension funds and insurance companies responsible for managing the savings of ordinary people'. To be fair he was writing before the banks had imploded causing mass bankruptcy and home repossession; before the scandal of profligate boardroom remuneration had been fully exposed; and before the socialists had been joined by the 99 per cent in decrying the 1 per cent of 'bloated capitalists'.

Interestingly, when it comes to the application of the marketing mix, everybody's language becomes more muscular. Thus rather than a route to our satisfaction, it now becomes the set of 'controllable demand-impinging elements (instruments) that can be combined into a marketing programme used by a firm to achieve a certain level and type of response from its target market'.[22] These instruments 'influence demand to a greater or lesser extent'. Or, as our blunt business academic puts it: 'the marketing mix is the main way management seeks increases in sales'.[23]

Demand-impinging, achieving response, influence demand, increases in sales – there is no hiding the manipulative purpose. The aim is to get us consuming, to boost sales and thereby corporate growth. It is back to the shops with us.

Strategic planning

We discussed strategic planning in Chapter 2, and noted that its primary purpose is to 'recognise and achieve the economic advantage which endures' – not for us customers, but for the corporation. The marketing mix forms the core of this strategy, and the brand is its public manifestation.

Two additional tools play a particularly important role in building the strategic power of the mix. First, as we discussed specifically with marcomms and product development, assiduous market research is conducted to get a detailed understanding of our lives, priorities and needs. I won't repeat myself; suffice to say no research stone is left unturned. Every element of the mix and its deployment is the subject of constant scrutiny, as are our responses.

The second tool comes from the insight that we consumers differ from one another; not profound perhaps, but vitally important. If corporate marketers are to maintain the conceit that our needs are at the centre of their universe, they can't adopt an off-the-peg mentality and sell the same stuff to us all. Indeed if the idea of consumer orientation is taken to its logical conclusion, then corporate marketers should be producing bespoke offerings for every single unique one of us. This is too implausible even for a corporate marketer – and certainly uneconomic – so they compromise by 'segmenting' us into similar types (at least as far as our consumption is concerned) and then selecting particular 'target groups' on which to focus.

Given the rhetoric of consumer orientation and satisfaction, one might expect the most sought after target groups to be those with most need. The textbooks correct this confusion: the marketer's hunt is not for needy target groups, but ones which are accessible, responsive and (above all) viable. The key concerns are to be able to reach these people with persuasive marketing campaigns, and having done so, be confident that there is a good chance that they will be both willing and able to pay.

The massive scale of corporate marketing means this modus operandi causes three sets of problems. First, it exacerbates inequalities: to those who have is given more; whilst those who have not are completely ignored. On an international level the full horror of this is laid bare by Bakan's observation, which we noted in Chapter 2, that in the pharmaceutical market cures for baldness and erectile dysfunction have been prioritized over treatments for life-threatening tropical diseases. Simply because we in the rich developed world form 'viable target markets', trivial ills become pressing needs; whereas life-threatening diseases are overlooked because they lack buying power.

But closer to home there is also a big social cost to segmentation and targeting: it divides us into exclusive groups. I find myself feeling superior because I drive a certain car, or sneering at someone for buying what I see as a second rate clothing brand. I hate this condescending tendency, but somehow it insinuates itself. As I confessed in Chapter 3, coffee marketing has fed my over-blown belief in my discriminatory palate and turned me into a supercilious prig.

It's not that I think we should all wear uniforms, drink bad coffee or move to North Korea. The observation that we are all different is axiomatic, and indeed to be welcomed and celebrated. I just think that having a phenomenon as powerful and effective as corporate marketing focused on accentuating these differences is dangerous – especially when the only motive for doing so is to get us consuming more.

The second major problem with segmentation and targeting is that it institutionalizes the notion that being able to afford something justifies its consumption. The ludicrous wealth of corporate CEOs leads seamlessly to Learjets; bonus-happy city traders take us to jeroboams of vintage champagne; bejewelled despots provide the rationale for arms sales. Thus the pocket book pre-empts moral judgement or intelligent debate.

Third, and most fundamentally, segmentation and targeting hone and perfect the aim of the corporate marketer. It makes everything he or she does more powerful, just as a magnifying glass concentrates the power of sunlight. So everything we have been discussing in this book becomes turbo-charged; it accelerates and gains even more influence. And so we shop.

Building relationships

As we noted in Chapter 2, these strategic marketing efforts have increasingly been centred around the building of relationships with us customers. Over the last twenty-five years marketers have learnt that it makes sense to think beyond individual transactions. A whole new sub-genre has grown up called 'relationship marketing' where the focus is put on keeping us content over time. From this perspective the task of the corporate marketer is to ensure that the company does all it can to build, enhance and retain long term customer relationships. Customer satisfaction – rather than sales figures – becomes the arbiter of success. One measure of how well embedded relational thinking has become is in the area of performance indicators. Over a decade ago a survey conducted by the Economist Intelligence Unit found that customer satisfaction is 'becoming one of the top indicators of executive performance in Europe, Asia and North America … and is being rated above profitability and short-term investor return by companies around the world'.[24]

In essence the aim is to simulate the kind of service, and the resulting loyalty, that Michael the greengrocer and Mary the publican provide (see Chapter 1). This demands an intimate knowledge of us customers, covering not just our views of their products, but also our psychological profiles, past experience with the company, hopes and aspirations. It means making and keeping promises, accepting that some of the individual transactions that make up the relationship will be unprofitable and ensuring that the process, as well as the offering, provides customer satisfaction. As with other human relationships, trust and commitment are crucial. This approach to marketing has even been likened to marriage.

Initially the potential to meet these ideals was limited to businesses with small numbers of very valuable and highly involved customers: private banks, for instance, or luxury hotels. However, as we noted in Chapter 6, the digital revolution has greatly expanded its potential. Data from every keystroke, sophisticated loyalty schemes and electronic point of sale data have changed the face of consumer marketing. Tesco's remarkably rich Clubcard data means they know more about us than our mothers ever did. This has given birth to another marketing sub-genre: *e*CRM or electronic Customer Relationship Management.[25]

It's all so heart-warming I can almost feel a tear forming. Bless those kind and loving corporate marketers.

Marketer, you are no Tin Man

Sorry yet again to be the bearer of harsh tidings, but this is simply another instalment of the marketing fairy tale. Relationship marketing has taken business thinking by storm because it provides an even better way of feeding the bottom line, not because the corporate marketer has, like the Tin Man, at last found his heart. It is, for example, much cheaper to keep existing customers than continually win new ones. Knowing your customers better also makes your marketing more effective – as we have seen marketers have always put a high premium on researching us. A reduced return today is repaid a thousand-fold by a lifetime of brand loyalty, and anyway, research shows that if we are kept happy we actually become less price-sensitive. We also tell our friends and neighbours how happy we are – and we, of course, have great source credibility. And remember, if we enjoy the process of shopping, our 'retail therapy', then we are more likely to do it whether or not we actually need anything.

These self-seeking relationships can also be built around and above us customers – with government, policy makers, stakeholders and even competitors. As we will discuss in the next chapter, these 'upstream' relationships bring enormous benefits in their own rights for corporate marketers. But for now let us just simply note that they ensnare us in a web of influence. Think for a minute of the closeness of the financial corporations of the City of London to the UK Government that have vitiated our – the general public's – incessant demands to curb bank bonuses. Think of the 1980s when US tobacco companies were able to persuade the US Government to pressurize South East Asian countries to open up their markets to American cigarette brands;[26] great for shareholders and corporate wealth; lethal for the citizens of Thailand and Vietnam. Both highly profitable manoeuvres are the result of successful relationship marketing with our leaders.

Relationship marketing is, then, just another corporate marketing sleight of hand. And yet again the core aim is to get and keep us shopping.

My hobby is shopping

The billboards, television ads and social networking campaigns we discussed in the previous three chapters are just the communications tip of a much more muscular marketing effort. This combines the sophisticated management of distribution, pricing and product design guided by rigorous market research, concentrated by astute targeting and made endemic through relational thinking. All this to feed the bottom line and thereby boost executive salaries and shareholder value. All this to get and keep us shopping.

My friend Jennifer is a secondary school teacher. She works with 'high social needs' teens in Central Scotland, trying to get them interested in education and straightened out so that they have some prospect of getting a job when they leave school. One key focus of her work is helping them develop their CVs or résumés so that they can tell a compelling and attractive story about themselves. In doing so she has lost count of the number of kids who list their principal hobby as shopping. Given all we have discussed so far this is not in the least surprising, but it is ineffably depressing. From a planetary perspective it is calamitous.

Fortunately I live in a democracy and the leaders I have helped elect will come to the rescue. Sadly, the same thought has occurred to the corporate marketers.

With thanks to Olivier Renou for permission to reproduce this picture.

8

MARKETING TO POWER

The take-over

And so we come to the sinister chapter.

Corporations need power and influence to secure their continued growth, and for this they turn their attention to politicians, policy makers and other stakeholders. The more blatant attempts to get these groups onside – overt lobbying, donations to campaign funds, revolving door employment practices – already get considerable attention, but the work of the corporate marketer in this arena is less well known. 'Stakeholder marketing' uses the same flattery, faux-friendship and manoeuvring of the marketing aimed at us, but now the target is those who have power. The aim is to build and burnish corporate reputations; in stakeholder marketing, corporate identity is as important as the brand is in consumer marketing.

The two favoured and linked techniques are 'Cause-Related Marketing', where the corporation links up to a personable and self-evidently worthy issue such as child literacy and makes sure the world knows about its seeming bounty; and Corporate Social Responsibility, which wraps this specific beneficence in longer term commitments to good practice. Corporate marketers are open about the self-serving nature of this activity and clearly state that this is business not altruism. Nonetheless the purpose is to gain grace by association and fend off statutory regulation by talking a good voluntary game. This leaves the corporation free to grow the bottom line with much less let or hindrance.

More importantly it also paves the way for a proactive policy of gaining access to the power which governments have. Increasingly then, the talk and reality is one of partnership working, with government and the corporate sector being instrumental in developing and realizing the policy agenda. As markets tremble and democracy looks less secure than it has since the Second World War, the importance of being at the top table is becoming more apparent. Stakeholder marketing is mutating into the corporations' overt bid for power.

The implications for our way of life are profound.

In search of legitimacy

Thus far we have discussed how corporations use marketing to approach you and me, as customers and potential customers. It is familiar and has an obvious legitimacy; however warped our consumption behaviour might have become, we do genuinely need many of the products and services corporations provide for us. It is difficult to imagine, for instance, how the population of a modern conurbation like London or Los Angeles could be fed without the logistics of a Tesco or a Walmart. Similarly, it's easy to see how our lives are improved by the technical know-how of the pharmaceutical companies.

It is also true to say that the disappearance of some corporations would be an unalloyed blessing. Tobacco companies, for instance, are a straight debit. Arguably, the fast food and fizzy drinks companies are also of very dubious worth and we could do with a sight fewer people pushing booze. Then there's the arms trade.

Nonetheless the principle of the corporations selling us stuff has at least got face validity.

Now, however, we will turn our attention to how they interact with stakeholders – all those groups and individuals who aren't customers in the going-down-the-shops sense, but nonetheless have a big potential influence on corporate success because, in some shape, sense or form, they have power. Despite vigorous attempts to create it, here there is much less apparent legitimacy; just a lot of disturbing questions.

Only connect

As we have seen, corporate marketers understand that seemingly individual consumption decisions are greatly influenced by the social context in which they are made. That is why they put so much effort into store design and atmospherics (Chapter 7), and work so hard to get their brands knitted into iconic cultural events (Chapter 5). This broad understanding of our behaviour also extends beyond the immediate marketing context, to a recognition that wider social and cultural mores will also have a big impact on our consumption habits. Corporate marketers have absorbed the lesson of David Foster Wallace (Chapter 3) about the subtle but powerful influence of the 'water we swim in'.

It is tempting to think of such influences as givens, like the weather. The beverage alcohol industry is fond, for example, of blaming youth bingeing in the UK on a northern European culture of alcohol abuse. Erudite quotes are rendered from Beowulf and Shakespeare and palms are upturned in innocent protestation: it's not our marketing; it's just how things are. But this is disingenuous. In reality our relationship with alcohol – along with countless other aspects of our culture

– is changing all the time. What is more, many of these changes are deliberately engineered by those with power – especially governments and policy makers. Thus the UK's drinking culture has been transformed with licensing laws, the lot of children by health and safety legislation and the role of women by equal opportunity provisions.

So, while in our case corporate marketers crave access to our wallets and purses, in the case of stakeholders they want access to such power. The techniques they use are remarkably similar: careful planning, alignment of all the marketing effort and strategic relationship building. However, while for us they burnish the brand image, for stakeholders the weapon of choice is corporate reputation and this is built and honed by embracing goodness (or at least seeming to).

Doing well by doing good?

Corporate marketers have therefore developed a great interest in good causes. School books for British youngsters, indigenous rights in the Americas and child literacy in Malawi have, in recent years, all been rewarded with corporate beneficence. Welcome to the world of Cause-Related Marketing (CRM), where multinationals link up with charities and social projects to help them better achieve desirable outcomes such as improved education or better services. Confusingly this specific activity is typically embedded in a broader Corporate Social Responsibility (CSR) strategy, which adds in longer term commitments to behave well. Whatever label is used, it is essentially about cosying up to power.

None of this, then, represents a Damascene conversion to the Boy Scout code; it is much more in line with Tom Lehrer's dope peddler: 'doing well by doing good'.[1] The emphasis is put on the favoured marketing concept of the win–win: both the good cause and the corporation benefit. Corporate marketers are quite open about their self-interest; this is a business decision with the good cause chosen, not on its own merits, but on the benefits association it will bring to the corporation. Careful analysis is done to ensure that the values associated with the selected cause can be aligned with, and have the clear potential to strengthen, those of the brand or corporate image. Given sufficient business acumen, a well-chosen and managed link-up will bring multiple such benefits. According to one text, for instance, it is good at

> enhancing reputation, building image and brands, creating relationships and loyalty among customers and stakeholders, adding value, generating awareness and PR, driving trial and traffic, providing product and service differentiation, developing emotional engagement with the consumer and other stakeholders, and obviously increasing sales, income and volume.[2]

Obviously. The same author underlines this quid pro quo agenda: 'whatever cause-related marketing is, it certainly is not philanthropy or altruism'.[3]

Practitioners are equally candid. This is a spokesperson for Marks & Spencer talking about the company's ambitious plan to 'combat climate change, reduce waste, safeguard natural resources, trade ethically and build a healthier nation' which she explains is a matter of 'enlightened self-interest'. The reaction amongst customers had been to 'increase trust in the M&S brand more than any other ad campaign' and this had been 'very good for profits'.[4]

As we noted in Chapter 1 Christian Aid, in a highly critical report, notes and condemns this selfish foundation. The focus, the charity points out, is not on the needs of the much vaunted beneficiaries, but with the company's own reputation, threats to this from bad publicity 'and overwhelmingly, with the desire – and the imperative – to secure ever greater profits'.[5]

Even marketers are beginning to doubt the benefits of this double think. Business guru Michael Porter, writing in the *Harvard Business Review*, dismisses it as ineffectual image management: 'Corporate responsibility programs – a reaction to external pressure – have emerged largely to improve firms' reputations and are treated as a necessary expense. Anything more is seen by many as an irresponsible use of shareholders' money.'[6]

But, you might argue, if business is open about the selfish motives of its do-gooding, what is the problem?

There are many. For a start, CSR builds on a deception. Its power comes from the link with the good cause, with the hope that proximity to saintliness will result in some of it rubbing off on the company. While the business plan and the textbook pinpoint the self-interest, the public face is all about sharing the halo. It is the modern equivalent of buying indulgences. Supporting good causes provides grace by association; just as the sports and music festival sponsorship we discussed in Chapter 5 provides coolness by association. If it were not so, the corporate marketers would get a better deal spending their money on traditional advertising campaigns (and remember, given the fiduciary imperative, they always go for the better deal).

And just like with sponsorship, doing good is made more powerful because the overt sale pitch is disguised. 'Coke is working with WWF; that's nice, I do love that panda.' The selfish intent is masked – or at least made a little less obvious.

The eightfold path to profit

This is a complete inversion of normal ethical and religious teaching. If a young child shows seeming generosity by passing on the first piece of cake only because he knows the next slice will be bigger, he gets criticism rather than plaudits. Good intention is the second branch of the Buddhist eightfold path; Christ branded the Pharisees as 'whited sepulchres' because they obeyed the letter of the law, but ignored its underlying intent. Lawyers set great store by establishing an accused's motives and use these to determine the acceptability of his or her actions. Time and again wisdom tells us that it is not just what we do that matters, but our reasons for doing it.

The calculated nature of corporate benevolence gets its power by turning this insight on its head, and disguising selfish motives behind seemingly generous actions. Remember a cause is not chosen for its inherent goodness, but by cherry picking the one that best fits the business plan. Again this reverses civilized thinking; surely the essence of kindness is prioritizing the needs of others, not the benefit to the do-gooder? The Good Samaritan did not conduct a business appraisal before he intervened.

Tesco's efforts in this arena are a good example. They begin with consumer research, to identify which causes have most resonance with Tesco shoppers. If genuine social benefit were the motive, the starting point would be to try and identify the UK's most pressing social needs, perhaps through a consultation with experts. But this is about pleasing customers and in their eyes 'schools were identified as a key cause for concern for parents and communities' and 'IT equipment was a much needed resource'.[7] So the 'Computers-for-Schools' campaign was born. The mechanics of the scheme were straightforward: for every £10 they spent shoppers got a Computers-for-Schools voucher which they could donate to their school of choice.

Again the focus is on Tesco's benefit, not social good: 'the aim was to build customer loyalty, drive traffic into stores, increase spend and reinforce Tesco's proposition that Every Little Helps'.[8] Despite the campaign's selfish motives, its power comes from seeming benevolence – giving a little help. It's a popular corporate ruse; Tesco copied the idea from the States, and Nestlé have a similar 'box tops for education' scheme which involves school children collecting the tops of Nestlé cartons – in the process 'Nestlé demonstrates how nice it is by giving tax-deductible donations to schools and gets the schools to market its products'.[9]

And to make sure its kind-heartedness is fully recognized, Tesco's 'programme has been thoroughly supported since it began, with TV, press and radio advertising, as well as other significant communications in-store and on-pack'.[10] This is another reversal of sound ethical thinking: we are supposed to do good deeds for the sake of others, not to get maximum credit for ourselves. It's like a child who behaves well when he or she knows the adults are watching, or the Good Samaritan ringing the local paper before he crossed the road. This self-aggrandizement was taken to its natural conclusion by Philip Morris International a few years ago. The company decided to sponsor shelters for battered women in the US, and was then caught spending more on advertising its good deed than on the good deed itself.[11]

So getting into bed with a good cause enables the corporation to further its business aims by cherry picking personable issues and gaining goodwill by association. It then boasts shamelessly about this to maximize the recognition it gets and exploits the enhanced marketing effectiveness that comes with the disguised sales pitch. The result is both socially damaging and morally corrosive.

But this is not the half of the problem: the real purpose behind this currying of do-gooder favour is the power it enables corporations to exercise by enhancing their standing and influence in society. Both the good causes and society's system for selecting these are being channelled to boost corporate identity.

White-washing the sepulchre

The business partner is not alone in being narrowly focused about outcomes. The partnering cause is likely to adopt an equally circumspect view, judging the success of any link-up on benefits to their particular mission – whether it be school books or women's rights. This is perhaps understandable; monocular vision is an occupational hazard of the single issue organization.

But from the government's – and indeed everyone else's – point of view there is a pressing need to pan out and make much wider judgements.

Each of the three causes we highlighted at the start of this section is undeniably good; who could argue against school books for British youngsters, indigenous rights in the Americas and child literacy in Malawi? But just as a sale does not guarantee a profit, so a good deed (especially a self-serving one) doesn't guarantee a better world. It all depends on the costs; the externalities. These three eminently good causes were funded by News International, ENRON and British American Tobacco respectively. Is burnishing the image of these deeply flawed corporations a price worth paying? Is, for example, BAT's literacy programme such a good deed in light of exposés of their marketing practices and use of child labour in the same African country? Are Milly Dowler's family any less hurt by the *News of the World*'s phone hacking because Murdoch funded school books – stakeholder marketing that enabled him to build up the power and hubris that led to the hacking in the first place?

One of the most blatant attempts to whiten the sepulchre came from arms manufacturer BAE Systems, whose Bradley Family of armoured vehicles we noted in Chapter 2. In 2006 the company trumpeted its new ecological credentials – including a line of lead-free bullets. Spokesperson Deborah Allen told the BBC: 'We all have a duty of care to ensure that from cradle to grave products are being used appropriately and do not do lasting harm.'[12] I am not making this up.

Moving beyond individual countries, given our pressing need to contain consumption and live more sustainably, should we be allowing the very organizations that depend on us consuming more and more to garner goodwill in this way? Doesn't it just generate confusion and opacity? It seems like we are not just allowing the wolf to don granny's dressing gown, but inviting him in for a fitting with her dressmaker.

The effect is also morally corrosive. Helping our fellow creatures is the defining quality of a civilized society because it is done on a point of high principle. We might express this with complex political theories or sophisticated theological arguments or more simply just see it as a matter of fairness, but the point is we offer support and help to the less well off because it is right to do so. When we allow multinational companies to co-opt this quintessentially human urge we are all cheapened, while they, as usual, are enriched.

Corporate agenda setting for social improvement

The self-evident goodness of causes like child literacy also distracts attention from another fundamental issue: which causes get support and how are they selected? If public money is involved, this will be the subject of careful and transparent decision making and competent professional judgement. Think of the effort and public debates that go into establishing priorities for the UK's National Health Service, for instance; or the checks and balances that are in place to steer European funding into the right projects. Cases have to be proposed, priorities adjudged and strategic decisions made and justified. I am not saying it is always perfect, or that such decisions never get traduced, but at least the intent is democratic, fair and informed by some attempt at needs analysis. In the voluntary sector as well there is a degree of regulation and transparency, although more direct public involvement can lead to a beauty parade effect – so donkey sanctuaries frequently win out over less personable causes such as drug rehab or prison reform. Nonetheless the good cause is being judged primarily on its capacity to do good.

Once the corporate marketer gets involved, however, as we have noted, all decision making becomes the servant of corporate strategic planning. The causes that get support are those that best deliver to the business goals – to the bottom line. The needs of the illiterate child or the battered woman will always come second. The needs of society barely get a look in. This exactly matches the flaws with consumer marketing which we discussed in Chapter 2: the perpetual search for 'the economic advantage which endures' ends up determining political priorities; so exploiting the halo of good causes pre-empts the ethical agenda. Thus corporations are able to move from the secular to the sacred.

Not that the corporate marketers always get it right, mind. The Fabergé corporation specializes in luxury goods. Its Agathon Regulateur wristwatch – a snip at £26,778 – has pride of place on the 'How to Spend It' website for the stupidly rich (Chapter 3). The decision to link it up with a UK poverty alleviation effort was always going to be a stretch; about as sensitive as Mr Kipling's Cakes getting Marie Antoinette to do a celebrity endorsement. It didn't last long. Then neither did Marie Antoinette.

From one-off causes to long term strategy

This corporate exploitation of doing good becomes even more serious when we consider that the most pressing social problems need systemic change, not ad hoc intervention. Poverty alleviation, violence reduction and global warming demand changes to the way we live our lives and run society – not a self-serving campaign. Indeed, unless carefully thought through from a societal perspective, an ad hoc intervention might actually be counter-productive because its palliative effect reduces the apparent need for systemic change.

Alcohol again provides a good example of this. The recent Health Select Committee report began with the disturbing observation that in 1947 the English were drinking on average three and a half litres of pure alcohol each per year; at the time of the report (2010) this figure had risen to nine and a half litres.[13] People are simply drinking too much. Furthermore the public health evidence base shows that the best way of reducing this excess is for the whole population to drink less; per capita consumption must come down. Not surprisingly, given what we know about corporate marketing and its focus on the sales graph, the alcohol corporations hate this evidence base. They much prefer to focus on education and individual change, policies that the World Health Organization points out are completely ineffective.[14] They have therefore invested heavily in an entity called the Drinkaware Trust (DAT), which achieves little but looks good.

But DAT also has a more strategic purpose; it is there to help build relationships with policy makers and politicians. The alcohol industry has long sought to avoid the terrible fate of the tobacco companies, who are gradually being excluded from the corridors of power, and so in the UK DAT has become their vehicle for ensuring they are seen as part of the solution rather than part of the problem. The UK Government has succumbed to their charm and last year a new 'Responsibility Deal' was developed, giving the UK alcohol industry massive representation at the policy-making table. Many in the voluntary sector walked away in disgust.

A similar long term vision underpins Tesco Computers-for-Schools; the most important pay-back is political: 'the benefits have included enhanced reputation, image and profile' – not just with customers, but schools (who have to register with Tesco to benefit) and local politicians who are only too glad to bask in the positive PR when 'the store manager presents the equipment to schools'.[15] Furthermore, given the size of Tesco and the absolute amounts of money involved in these contributions (despite being a fraction of the company's profits), Computers-for-Schools also gets the attention of national politicians.

Let them drink Coke

Coke's link-up with conservation group WWF, which we touched on earlier in the chapter, provides another revealing illustration of where stakeholder marketing is taking us. In 2007 the two organizations announced a major collaboration aimed at 'safeguarding our global water supply'. For Coke this offered a gold-plated get-out-of-jail-free card from the high profile accusations that its water extraction practices were harming local communities in India. For WWF it would enable them 'to help set new industry standards and make meaningful impacts at a global scale'.[16]

Both the company and the NGO are clearly happy with the deal as it has now been extended to take in the plight of the polar bear. This new initiative includes a jointly branded fundraising Arctic Home website[17] which, thanks to some stunning IMAX photography, is chock-a-block with footage of gorgeous polar bears – much of which has also been posted on YouTube. Coke has made an initial $2 million contribution and has agreed to match every dollar donated up to the first million. $3 million is a lot of money, though the Rudd report (Chapter 6) shows that the company actually spends twice this amount every week just on television advertising and just in its US market.

And this is advertising, incidentally, that has featured the polar bear for nearly a century. As Katie Bayne, president and GM of Sparkling Beverages, Coca-Cola North America explains:

> The polar bear has been a beloved Coca-Cola holiday icon for decades. We first introduced the bears in our advertising in 1922 and today they remain one of Coca-Cola's most lovable symbols. They stand for ice cold refreshment and family and friends togetherness.[18]

This time though the state of the art promotional footage comes complete with fabulous co-branding from WWF. The NGO presumably knew it was signing up as sugar salesman in chief when it agreed the deal?

To publicize the campaign Coke also took the unprecedented step of producing their drink in white cans, instead of the usual red. Katie Bayne continues: 'we have come to realize just how much the polar bear needs our help in the Arctic and now we are taking our commitment to the bear to a new level'.[19]

This dramatic move was justified because, as well as providing a mass of reinvigorated polar bear advertising, the business case was compelling:

> We have built our partnership on targets, very specific targets for achieving growth at Coke while maintaining no growth in the CO_2 emissions. Pursuing the best practices in sustainable agriculture, and the partnership brings together two of the biggest brands in the world. We have two great networks that are coming together in places around the world, and it's interesting, business leaders I've talked to, they've commented on the importance of businesses becoming leaders in addressing the world's problems because the best and the brightest don't just want to achieve more market share they also want to be leaders in solving the biggest problems that face the world.[20]

These words are disturbing for three reasons. First, they provide an unnerving glimpse of the strategic purpose of CRM; it makes the corporation part of the solution and in the process airbrushes away the problems it generates – most especially the problems caused by assumptions of perpetual growth. Second, they conjure up a world where business leaders, because they are 'the best and the brightest', should and will take over a more general leadership role. We need not trouble our little heads about details like democracy; we can safely ignore Arundhati Roy's observation that 'the people who created the crisis will not be the ones that come up with a solution'.[21] We will revisit these wider political ambitions of big business later in the chapter. Third, this fulsome puff for the business sector sends shivers down the spine because it was not, as you might expect, delivered by Muhtar Kent, the $24 million a year CEO of Coke, but by Carter Roberts who runs WWF in the US. He is not just selling sugar, but corporate capitalism. Again I presume this was in the contract.

And, just in case we are still under any illusions about Coke's real motives and whether or not the corporation has genuinely been converted to the cause of conservation, the story has a final twist. American consumers did not take to the white cans, which some confused with Coke's diet products and others thought impaired the flavour, and complained to the company. Coke immediately grabbed the opportunity to reinforce the ecological message by explaining to the fault-finders that this was a very important and worthy cause and a trivial inconvenience was surely a price worth paying to save such a magnificent creature as the polar bear. If however the customer was not prepared to step up to the plate in this minor way they could jolly well find another brown sugar water to drink. No of course it didn't; it stopped using the white cans – because its love of the polar bear will always play second fiddle to its love of the bottom line. So when Katie Bayne says 'we are taking our commitment to the bear to a new level' she means a level that does not jeopardize our profits; that's not commitment, it is just business as usual.

Systemic change

Corporate (Social) Responsibility picks up this strategic approach, adding in ethical governance procedures and codes of good conduct to the trumpeting of good deeds. Again it has the patina of desirability: surely everyone should welcome corporations making their staff recruitment more inclusive or setting targets on waste management? Again an obscured business purpose increases effectiveness. Again the ultimate aim is power.

Just as calculatedly self-serving good deeds pre-empt decisions about societal priorities, and blur the line between marketing and altruism, so CSR does the same for regulation and accountability. As Christian Aid points out, a key benefit of CSR for corporations is that it helps them to avoid culpability:

> Business, moreover, has consistently used CSR to block attempts to establish the mandatory international regulation of companies' activities. Its basic argument is that CSR shows how committed corporations already are to behaving responsibly and that introducing mandatory regulation could destroy this goodwill. Business leaders are also constantly saying that regulation is bad for their profits – the two statements are, of course, not unconnected.[22]

The charity uses the notorious case of Shell in Nigeria to illustrate its concerns. In the early 1990s the oil giant wanted to quell discontent among the local Ogoni people, whose land in the Niger Delta it was despoiling, and called on Nigeria's military dictatorship for help. This resulted in savage repression, dozens of people being shot down and the subsequent execution of Ogoni leader Ken Saro-Wiwa.

Shell's response to the resulting outcry was to invest heavily in CSR. It was the first major company to do so, and arguably is responsible for taking the strategy into the mainstream of business thinking.

Predictably, however, the good deeds and fine promises have done nothing to improve the lot of the Ogoni people; over a decade later the Christian Aid report documented their continued suffering at the hands of Shell. And in 2011 a report by Amnesty International documented further egregious behaviour. Two oil spills happened in the Niger Delta in 2008, which between them were as big as the Exxon Valdez disaster. In both cases no clean-up has happened and there were extensive delays before any remedial action was taken:

> Eight months later, Shell finally appeared to recognize that people's food sources had been affected. On 2 May 2009, Shell staff brought food relief to the community. It included 50 bags of rice, 50 bags of beans, 50 bags of garri (a cassava product), 50 cartons of sugar, 50 cartons of milk powder, 50 cartons of tea, 50 cartons of tomatoes and 50 tins of groundnut oil.[23]

In the quarter July–September 2011 the company posted profits of $7.2 billion.[24]

The marketing of infant formula provides another appalling example of the failure of CSR and voluntary corporate action. These are the words of Jasmine Whitbread, Chief Executive Officer, Save the Children UK:

> I shouldn't be standing in front of you, on the 25 year anniversary of the Code, telling you so little has changed and that companies continue to encourage mothers to spend money they don't have on manufactured food most of them don't need. I shouldn't be standing in front of you because it shouldn't still be happening. But it is, because the voluntary code clearly isn't working, and children are dying as a result.[25]

It is perhaps little wonder, then, that Christian Aid concludes that what we need is not more voluntary responsibility from corporations but accountability and statutory regulation. Unfortunately, as it also notes, a key function of CSR is to fend off regulation. John Hilary, Director of Campaigns and Policy at War on Want, confirms this view pointing out that the Corporate Responsibility agenda had been 'created explicitly in order to get away from corporate accountability and regulation'.[26]

You don't regulate your friends

Doing good and promising to behave better helps to normalize the corporation, making it part of the solution and adding a patina of respectability to all its deeds. This contributes to the perplexing presumption that overshadows us all: marketing is a given. The default position is that anyone can market anything to anyone until such time as definite evidence of harm is produced. Thus regulation is always post hoc and hence too late, and usually too little.

It reminds me of the story about a woman who sought absolution from her priest for the hurt that her gossiping and lies had caused. For her penance she was instructed to go to the market square in the middle of the town and buy a goose, then return to the church plucking it as she walked. When she arrived back with her now naked goose, the priest then asked her to go and retrieve the feathers. Thus it is with regulation as afterthought: action only occurs after harm has been inflicted and rectifying it is all but impossible.

Sometimes the evidence of harm can emerge almost instantaneously and be utterly irrefutable. For example, the shooting dead of seventeen people in a Scottish primary school in 1996 generated an immediate consensus for stricter controls on the marketing of handguns, and government action swiftly followed. More typically the evidence base emerges far more gradually and action to constrain harmful marketing is equally slow. Thus, limitations on tobacco promotion have taken decades to emerge, and have only been introduced after the production of massive evidence of multiple harms.

There are two problems with this model. First, the default is extremely questionable. Given that marketing is such a powerful mechanism, and the harm consumption can cause at an individual, social and planetary level so great, this seems an inordinately liberal regime. Wouldn't a more precautionary approach be preferable? Rather than allowing a free for all and then picking up the pieces afterwards, wouldn't it make more sense to say to the corporate marketer: first demonstrate that your marketing will do no harm then you will be allowed to go ahead? Show us that your new cigarette packs will not encourage children to smoke or pull adult quitters back to the habit; that your BOGOF on beer will not encourage bingeing; that your new SUV's capacity to break the ton will not encourage speeding. Or more fundamentally, prove to us that your new product is satisfying a genuine and important need so it is worth the carbon it will consume, or your sales promotions will help in the fight against global warming because they are discouraging wasteful consumption. And when you have hard, peer-reviewed evidence, we will listen to your case.

The second problem is that the burden of collecting the evidence falls on the public sector. This is an obvious expense and therefore vulnerable to cuts and shrinking budgets. It can even be misrepresented as wasteful. A recent attack from the UK tobacco industry, for instance, lambasted a review of smoke-free legislation:

> I believe that, in general, the sorts of health report (researchers/scientists have found …) that daily fill our newspapers and that rely on the results of studies and surveys are pretty much a waste of effort. The money spent on such studies would be better spent trying to improve the lot, and especially the education, of young people of the poorest members of our society.[27]

This from an industry that was first in the queue demanding evidence when smoke-free public places were initially proposed, is still wilfully killing 80,000 Britons a year and, when we still had smoky pubs, was taking out one bar worker a week.

So the onus of proof is on society to establish that harm is being done, not business to ensure safety, and then encourage government to belatedly close the stable door. CSR encourages and reinforces this laissez-faire approach by pulling government into the marketing effort. As the marketing text we quoted earlier points out, the win–win between business and good cause is actually a win–win–win: adding government to the list of beneficiaries. They gain because social problems they should be tackling get sorted (or at least addressed) for them; they get the positive glow from the presentation of new schools equipment and they get to rub shoulders with captains of industry. Grateful governments, whether democratically elected or militarily imposed, are disinclined to regulate the hand that feeds them.

More importantly still, grateful governments give access to power.

The corporate hunger for this is palpable. Jean Ziegler, UN Special Rapporteur on the Right to Food was asked by a journalist: 'The UN Global Compact boasts that it is "the world's largest, global corporate citizenship initiative". Why are you so critical of it?' He responds by explaining that global corporations now have much more power than many nation states, the supposed beneficiaries of UN policy, and have taken over the Compact for their own marketing purposes:

> The Global Compact started from an idea by former UN Secretary-General Kofi Annan. The UN Conventions only address themselves to nation states, but with globalized capitalism all of a sudden there are transnational corporations who have much more financial, marketing and ideological power than governments. We need to address their activities if we want to universalize and implement human rights. This idea is good, but the execution has been a total fake.[28]

In 1999, when Annan launched the Global Compact, he was much applauded. 3,000 companies signed up, including Nestlé, Novartis, General Foods (Kraft) and Cargill. They can put on their letterheads 'Member of the Global Compact of the United Nations'. But it is not working because it places no constraint whatsoever on the 3,000 companies who have signed up. They are there to make profits, not to advance solidarity, social justice or human rights. There is no sanction if, for example, a company violates the right to strike. So the Global Compact serves the interests of the global corporations. They can do whatever they want, so they are really happy with it![29]

Who is in charge?

Despite its many successes, however, the gloss is beginning to wear off CSR. In particular, the recent financial crisis and controversy over excessive boardroom pay has made people much more sceptical about big business. Michael Porter in his HBR piece, which is entitled 'Capitalism Under Siege', argues that the strategy is actually backfiring on business: 'the more business has begun to embrace corporate responsibility, the more it has been blamed for society's failures'.[30] He goes on to argue though that this is not because CSR is hypocritical, self-serving, deceitful or defensive, but because it is not ambitious enough. In place of its cosmetic manoeuvring, he argues, we need a much more root and branch system, where corporations, government and civil society come together to 'Create Shared Value' – a balance between profit for the company and societal welfare. A migration from CSR to CSV (Creating Shared Value).

His proposals include the radical one of removing the corporate fiduciary imperative: 'The purpose of the corporation must be redefined as creating shared value, not just profit per se.' Many would welcome this as a step towards reforming the corporation, provided it is replaced by an equally clear cut and powerful control that ensures social performance. Here Porter sees a role for government regulation, but emphasizes that this should be designed 'to enhance shared value, set goals and stimulate innovation' not discourage it because it 'forces compliance with particular practices … mandates a particular approach to meeting a standard – blocking innovation and almost always inflicting cost on companies'.[31]

Thereby his arguments beg questions about who exactly would be in charge in this system, and the answer for Porter is quite clearly business. Its self-interest is the key driver, and this he sees as axiomatically in line with public interest and democratic integrity – which in turn leads naturally to government setting policies that foster and support business:

> It is not philanthropy but self-interested behaviour to create economic value by creating societal value. If all companies individually pursued shared value connected to their particular businesses, society's overall interests would be served. And companies would acquire legitimacy in the eyes of the communities in which they operated, which would allow democracy to work as governments set policies that fostered and supported business.[32]

The implications for our way of life are profound. In his paper, for example, he emphasizes that his new world will certainly not involve any equalizing of current wealth: 'Nor is it about "sharing" the value already created by firms – a redistribution approach. Instead, it is about expanding the total pool of economic and social value.'[33] This is a massive political statement which begs questions about relative rather than absolute poverty, the current inequities in society (ironically thrown into relief by corporate pay) and the sustainability of perpetual growth. But it suits the corporate agenda so he has no compunction in making didactic judgements about it. It is a startling straw in the wind, showing just how a wealthy corporate sector's capacity to pay the piper is resulting in some very discordant political tunes being played.

Porter sees his ideas as a replacement for a failing system of CSR, but they can more accurately be seen as its natural successor. Where CSR seeks to deliver power to the corporation through stealth and seduction, CSV would make it mandatory.

It is all too reminiscent of Higham's conclusion, following his exposé of corporate collaboration with Nazi Germany (see Chapter 2): 'the bosses of the multinationals had a six spot on every side of the dice cube. Whichever side won the war, the powers that really ran nations would not be adversely affected.'[34] 'The powers that really run nations', it seems, are still at it.

When charm fails

Sometimes even the most carefully devised marketing strategies fail to charm; policy makers refuse to listen and critics will not be silenced. Two complementary variants on stakeholder marketing then result: the workaround and the full-on attack. Both the examples we will discuss here – the exploitation of smuggling and the use of Freedom of Information legislation as a competitive weapon – concern the tobacco industry, but the techniques involved and the determination to succeed these reflect could apply to any corporation.

Bootleg benefits

Corporate marketers imitate water: if there is a way through they will find it; an obstacle triggers a workaround. For example, when Gallaher the tobacco company wanted to introduce a new brand into the UK market it discovered that much of the supply came from illicit, smuggled sources. Despite the tobacco industry's best stakeholder marketing efforts, government policy for some years previously had been to increase taxes so as to discourage consumption; a policy that worked well but had the side effect of incentivizing smuggling. Neither Gallaher nor its ad agency had any interest in respecting the will of Parliament; however, they just knew that the size of the illicit market stymied the usual launch strategy of promoting it to retailers and thereby smokers. Completely unabashed the ad agency simply produced a strategy for targeting bootleggers:

> Bootleggers (who account for over 70% of the market in most areas) only bother with big brands – Old Holborn and Golden Virginia. We need to *create a demand* for Amber Leaf among the newer, younger consumers to encourage both shop purchase and *a willingness among bootleggers* to sell Amber Leaf.[35]

The agency's PowerPoint presentation starts by breaking down the smuggled tobacco market on a company by company basis, demonstrating that Gallaher is languishing behind its competitors in this (illegal) market. You might think they would all be pleased to be so law-abiding. Not a bit of it. The presentation goes on to carefully identify bootleggers in Belgium as a key stakeholder, and suggests a marketing strategy for reaching them and thereby accessing UK smokers (see Figure 8.1).

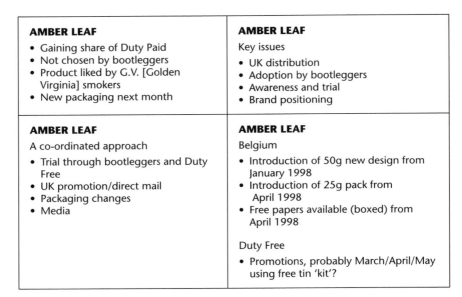

FIGURE 8.1 Marketing to bootleggers

Source: Hastings, G. B. and MacFadyen, L. (2000) *Keep Smiling No One's Going to Die.* CTRC & TCRC Report, p.13.

The illegality makes this particularly shocking, but the principle of using third parties to get round democratically determined public policy is a corporate commonplace. The tobacco industry is forever linking up with more respectable bodies to oppose public health measures. As I write it is being lambasted for doing this in Australia, as the government prepares to introduce plain packaging for cigarettes. We noted similar shenanigans from Diageo in Chapter 2 when it tried to resist minimum unit pricing in Scotland.

Of PINGOs and BINGOs

Indeed this hidden-hand approach to stakeholder marketing has become so common it has fuelled an apparently arcane – although in reality vital – debate between PINGOs (public interest non-governmental organizations) and BINGOs (business interest non-governmental organizations). The former are genuine organizations set up to pursue the good causes their names herald, such as Doctors without Borders, the International Confederation of Midwives, or Consumers International. The latter represent business interests such as the International Federation of Pharmaceutical Manufacturer Associations (IFPMA), or the International Federation of Dietetic Food Industries (IFSDI); they are essentially lobbyists.

The principle underpinning this concern is the blurring of the boundaries between business and society. It runs throughout stakeholder marketing like a fault line. Democracy demands accountability; stakeholder marketing evades it. Doing good demands genuine motives; stakeholder marketing institutionalizes deception. NGOs can get access to power because they are genuine in their concerns; corporations invent their own – as with their consumer marketing it is all about faking authenticity.

Journalist Jeff Ballinger explains how Nike used this ruse when it got into hot water over sweatshops in the late nineties. It set up a BINGO called 'Global Alliance for Workers and Communities (GA)' which got 'an "almost biological" process under way, by which major corporations co-opt those critical groups they can draw into partnership and isolate and marginalize those they cannot'.[36] In the light of his words, WWF's decision to partner Coke seems dangerously naïve.

Removing the gloves

In the absence of a workaround, corporate marketers go into attack mode. The World Health Organization, for instance, has suffered well documented attacks from the tobacco, alcohol and food industries when their interests were threatened by its championing of public health. In Chapter 4 we saw how our academic research on food marketing was the subject of sustained attack by food advertising interests.

Our work on tobacco has also been threatened. The tobacco industry has used Freedom of Information legislation to harass public health professionals and academics around the world to neutralize what it sees as a threat to its business. As a study in New Zealand concluded: 'Tobacco companies portray themselves as socially responsible corporate citizens. Yet they abuse legal avenues designed to protect the public's right to access to official information.'[37]

In September 2009, without any warning, it was suddenly our turn, and Philip Morris International (PMI) was the hit-man. As Box 8.1 describes we became the subject of a two-year campaign by the tobacco giant, working through its law firm Clifford Chance, to get access to our research with children. The research, which was conducted in absolute confidence with teens as young as eleven years old, looked in detail at their reasons for smoking and specifically their responses to tobacco marketing. In essence it would have been invaluable market research for an industry that, as we noted in Chapter 1, depends for its survival on children taking up smoking. Market research that PMI would never dare do for itself.

There ensued a series of meetings with the university's lawyers as we thought through what we should do. Our response, explaining why promises of confidentiality made to children carried more weight than any right to information was rejected by Clifford Chance, so it had to be reviewed by the senior officers of the University and then the Scottish Information Commissioner who proceeded to dismiss it on a technicality. PMI then came back with another request and the whole process started again.

This was all extremely stressful. The letters from Clifford Chance framed this as a request, but reminded us about UK Freedom of Information legislation, and that 'under the Act' we were 'obliged to respond to this request within 20 working

BOX 8.1 THE KEY STEPS IN THE PHILIP MORRIS FREEDOM OF INFORMATION (FOI) ATTACK

- In September 2009 we received a letter from Clifford Chance, asking for a vast array of information from our teen smoking study – including 'all primary data', 'all questionnaires', 'all interviewers' handbooks and/or instructions', 'all data files', 'all record descriptions' and 'all information relating to sampling, data collection, handling of non-response and post-stratification weighting and analysis'.
- Following detailed discussions with the University's lawyers, we responded with a sixty page explanation of why issues such as the young people's confidentiality prevented us from handing over the data.
- Clifford Chance challenged our response and the University was therefore required to undertake an internal review: a Deputy Principal had to examine our response in detail and check we had done everything we should according to the Act. This review upheld our initial response.
- The case then had to go to the Scottish Information Commissioner for adjudication. His response came back in July 2010 – some nine months after the initial request, which it rejected because Clifford Chance had failed to identify its client (PMI).
- Unabashed by this error, two months later PMI declared itself, repeated its request and added in another request on a different study.
- This time we argued that PMI was being vexatious, providing as evidence a dossier showing how it had used FOI legislation around the world to impede public health researchers and policy makers.
- Again there was an appeal, a review and – after a further nine months – an adjudication from the Commissioner. This time he said that he did not find the claim vexatious and we should rely on other exemptions in the legislation for our response – which, following further meetings with senior officers and lawyers, we duly did.
- The media picked up the story and a furore ensued.

days' – a compulsion that seemed completely at odds to the common-sense meaning of the word 'request'.

Furthermore, we are not lawyers and, like most civilians, find the law abstruse and the overt threat of serious punishment extremely disconcerting. And, while we are part of a university – and hence a public body under FOI legislation – we are in reality a small academic research unit entirely funded by external grants. This funding operates on a tightly costed project by project basis; the weeks of work we have put into this FOI process have inevitably been done at the expense of our day jobs. It is worth remembering that as academics, a key part of our day job is to disseminate our research through all the normal, properly policed channels. Ironically then, in this case, FOI is actually *hindering* public access to information.

None of this will raise a tear in the Philip Morris boardroom of course. They saw a threat from an academic research unit that was publishing inconvenient truths about tobacco marketing and sought to neutralize it using the best London lawyers and their massive resources. And they came close. Unfortunately for them they had not counted on public opinion and the power of good journalism to call it to arms.

Front page coverage in *The Independent*, a leading UK broadsheet, under the banner headline 'Smoked out: tobacco giant's war on science' produced a slew of media coverage and massive public support. Letters and emails poured in and the phone rang for days. 'Record Voice', the editorial page of Scotland's leading tabloid, captured the public mood perfectly when it concluded: 'hell will freeze over before a cigarette company are given help to kill more of our fellow Scots'. We have not heard from PMI or its lawyers since.

However without this public outcry the story might have had a very different ending, with repercussions not just for our small research unit, but for academic freedom more generally. How easy is it going to be to conduct and get funding to do critical research on corporate (mis)behaviour if the subject can use FOI to intimidate and harass the research team? And remember such legislation was brought in to help us little people keep an eye on overbearing government; not multinational corporations to throw their weight around.

Furthermore it was only past revelations about tobacco industry malfeasance, and their resulting lack of credibility, that enabled us to survive this attack. As we have seen, stakeholder marketing is explicitly devised to undermine such transparency by artificially boosting the image and power of the corporation. Fortunately PMI's own efforts in this field, such as the battered women shelters we touched on earlier in this chapter, did not stop the general public from seeing it for the rapacious corporate marketer it is.

Even with this happy ending, we now live in fear that PMI or another corporation will, at any moment, decide to attack us in this way if they judge our work to be a threat. This is an affront to academic freedom and eats away at the critical thinking which forms the foundation of any functioning democracy. If you combine it with Michael Porter's vision of a future where government has got so close to the corporation that it automatically sets policies which ensure that business is 'fostered and supported' the prospect is truly chilling.

Citizen, consumer, employee?

We are used to corporations attempting to seduce us; we are less familiar with the effort they put into winning over those stakeholders who they deem to have influence in the marketplace – especially governments. In our case they are after money; in the case of government they are after power.

This 'stakeholder marketing' began with face-saving and well-publicized good deeds to distract attention from the obvious failings of the corporation – whether tobacco deaths, oil pollution or plain old fashioned corruption. This calculated and self-interested benevolence is then combined with promises of good behaviour and formed into strategic Corporate Social Responsibility programmes. These not only spare corporate blushes and boost the corporate image, they promote the idea that voluntary codes of conduct will suffice. Fine words and vacuous promises replace much needed statutory regulation and full accountability.

This cynicism has begun to unravel with the financial crisis. It is difficult to pose as Florence Nightingale when you are trashing the world economy and stuffing obscene bonuses in your back pocket. Consequently, much as with consumer marketing, the focus is moving to relational thinking. Business is seeking to work in partnership with governments which will then learn to deliver the policies that will foster and support its needs.

Stakeholder marketing is then a simple grab for power.

The World Conference on Tobacco or Health takes place every three years, and this one was in Washington, DC. The speaker was an illustrious campaigning medic from the Midwest and he was concluding a talk on the power and success of the tobacco industry's stakeholder marketing. All the tricks and ruses discussed in this chapter had been identified and the underlying strategy of cosying up to power laid bare. His final slide contained just one sentence, and this is still etched on my mind: 'either we get this right or in ten years' time we will all be working for Philip Morris'.

The conference was six years ago; it is time we starting getting things right.

PART II

Solutions

A Man's A Man For A' That

1.   Is there for honest Poverty
   That hings his head, an' a' that;
   The coward slave – we pass him by,
   We dare be poor for a' that!
   For a' that, an' a' that.
   Our toils obscure an' a' that,
   The rank is but the guinea's stamp,
   The Man's the gowd for a' that.

2.   What tho' on hamely fare we dine,
   Wear hoddin grey, an' a that;
   Gie fools their silks, and knaves their
       wine;
   A Man's a Man for a' that:
   For a' that, and a' that,
   Their tinsel show, an' a' that;
   The honest man, tho' e'er sae poor,
   Is king o' men for a' that.

3.   Ye see yon birkie, ca'd a lord,
   Wha struts, an' stares, an' a' that;
   Tho' hundreds worship at his word,
   He's but a coof for a' that:
   For a' that, an' a' that,
   His ribband, star, an' a' that:
   The man o' independent mind
   He looks an' laughs at a' that.

4.   A prince can mak' a belted knight,
   A marquis, duke, an' a' that;
   But an honest man's abon his might,
   Gude faith, he maunna fa' that!
   For a' that, an' a' that,
   Their dignities an' a' that;
   The pith o' sense, an' pride o' worth,
   Are higher rank than a' that.

5.   Then let us pray that come it may,
   (As come it will for a' that,)
   That Sense and Worth, o'er a' the earth,
   Shall bear the gree, an' a' that.
   For a' that, an' a' that,
   It's coming yet for a' that,
   That Man to Man, the world o'er,
   Shall brithers be for a' that.

Robert Burns

9

IN SEARCH OF SOLUTIONS

Hopeful signs

So we have a massive problem. Our consumption behaviour is spinning out of control, causing immense harm to us as individuals, as communities and as a species. Individually the obvious manifestation is in physical illness caused by corporate marketing – obesity, lung cancer, liver cirrhosis and at a group level the social malaise of public drunkenness, sedentary entertainment or dying high streets. Meanwhile, the planet inexorably heats up. Underpinning all this is a corrosive passivity; we consume rather than produce, shop rather than create, and so become ever more dependent. Increasingly, it seems, we get our self-worth not from our achievements but from a packet.

However, saying what is wrong with society is relatively easy, especially when you are a man of a certain age. Coming up with solutions is more challenging.

In the opening chapters I invoked John Steinbeck to emphasize that our problems with corporate marketing have been long in the making, and that our blind eye to them is increasingly untenable.

Steinbeck's Dust Bowl farmers also demonstrate three crucial strengths that we need to regain – or at least strengthen – in ourselves. First, they had internal self-reliance. On the journey out from Oklahoma to California the family suffers numerous setbacks, not least with the perpetual breakdown of its dilapidated truck. Tom Joad, and especially his younger brother Al, have the skills and ingenuity to mend the truck time after time at minimal cost. In the process they not only keep the vehicle going, they gain immense self-worth. This internal validation cannot be bought, however much corporate marketers try and convince us otherwise.

Second, Tom and Al Joad's mechanical skills – along with the family's other all too meagre resources – are frequently shared with fellow travellers. Ma in particular knows the importance of collective action; of sticking together. Corporate marketing, with its self-centred, materialist foundations and divisive targeting, undermines this collective identity.

Third, and most importantly, Steinbeck's characters have a sense of purpose and durability: 'us people we go on living when all them people is gone … we're the people that live. They ain't gonna wipe us out. Why, we're the people – we go on.'[1] And as a direct result the novel, despite its bleak subject matter, carries a massive message of hope.

On these very broad and capable shoulders, therefore, I will rest my pitch for a way forward which is equally hopeful. It falls into three sections:

1. Unto thine own self (below): we have to learn from the Joads, build our internal resources and take action.
2. Power to the people (Chapter 10): marketing was not invented by corporations; it has in fact underpinned our capacity to cooperate for millennia – it has just been co-opted and industrialized by them in the last few decades to push completely unsustainable lifestyles for the benefit of excessive private profit; it should be reclaimed and used to encourage lifestyles that benefit us and our planet.
3. Marketing as if people mattered (Chapter 11): all this will come to nought unless we control the corporate marketer.

Ultimately though, the problems are profound and I freely confess that I do not have the answers. I am not sure any one person has. The urgent need is for us to start a conversation that might lead to a collective reappraisal of how we are leading our lives and thereby begin to uncover how we can make them more sustainable.

Unto thine own self

'It's all your own fault' is never an easy sell. Nor is asking people to give up all the little luxuries to which they have grown accustomed, especially when they have been told since the cradle that these baubles are the defining qualities of a happy and successful life. Similarly, suggesting that there is a need to sympathize with our parlous political leaders, as they scrabble to knit together our feckless double standards into a coherent strategy, is bordering on the foolhardy. Finally, arguing that our calamitously greedy bankers and CEOs are actually just as bewildered and lost as we all are, and therefore need pity rather than vilification, is positively suicidal.

Nonetheless, all of these things I will do in this chapter. Wish me luck.

Revitalizing the victim

I have been dreading writing this chapter ever since I thought of doing this book. It turns the spotlight on personal responsibility and hence opens me up to the multiple hazards of being patronizing (we are all adults), naïve (I am not a moral philosopher) and regressive (it's the system what did it). Furthermore, much of my working life has been spent in the company of public health professionals, an admirable bunch who put particular emphasis on the collective causes of ill health. They build on the truth that we get ill and die earlier than we should because of our lifestyles and behaviours, and that these causes now greatly outweigh the traditional demons of communicable disease as threats to our health and happiness. Across the world, it has become increasingly apparent that we now have far more to fear from bad living than bad bugs.

This does sound like the recipe for an individually focused 'it's-all-your-own-fault-so-pull-your-socks-up' sort of perspective. However all the evidence – and public health loves evidence – shows that our individual decisions are greatly influenced by what is going on around us. The thinking of David Foster Wallace and the two little fishes is well accepted (Chapter 3). Even with a behaviour like smoking, which seems quintessentially individual, the public health expert will point out that cigarette use is heavily socially patterned. In the UK for instance, the poorer you are the more likely you are to smoke – by a very long chalk.

The public health response is then to think systemically. What can we do to make the system better so that healthy choices become the obvious and easy ones? The founding story of the discipline epitomizes this approach. In 1854 John Snow, a public health doctor working in London, found convincing evidence that a cholera epidemic in the district of Soho was not being caused by bad air, as the contemporary wisdom had it, but by polluted water. When the authorities refused to listen, he took matters into his own hands and had the handle removed from the public pump which was delivering up sewerage contaminated drinking water. In this way he proved his point and resolved the problem all in one. He also hard-wired the public health discipline's focus on intervening upstream. The danger otherwise is that you end up blaming people for a predicament they find themselves in through no fault of their own. There was, for instance, little the individual Soho inhabitant could do about his or her poor quality water, even had they known it was toxic.

I respect Dr Snow and share the public health aversion to victim blaming. But equally I am sure systemic change is not enough. We are all perfectly capable of being miserable in paradise if we don't have internal balance. Kropotkin was right when he lauded humans' capacity to cooperate and work together, but that collective instinct is also dependent on robust individuals. So Burns was equally perceptive when he reminded us that 'The Man's the gowd (gold) for a' that.' Notice this is surely not gold in any material sense; the lyrics are reproduced at the outset of this chapter and you can see how he dismisses the trappings of wealth and privilege: 'rank is but the guinea's stamp ... gie fools their silks, and knaves their wine ... their tinsel show, an' a' that ... the honest man, tho' e'er sae poor, is king o' men for a' that.' Nor should we be diverted by his sexist terminology: people are the gold for all that.

George Orwell squares this circle by pointing out that both these 'two viewpoints are tenable' (I would say essential). 'The one, how can you improve human nature until you have changed the system? The other, what is the use of changing the system before you have improved human nature?'[2] Any recipe for change, then, has to address both the individual and the systemic.

The corporate marketers have acquired their astounding dominance over our lives because they have paid careful attention to both these dimensions. They simultaneously seduce us with their brands and specious solicitude, and our leaders with their lustrous corporate images and seemingly magical moneymaking abilities.

If we don't, who will?

This corporate double dealing partly explains the complete absence of leadership we are currently experiencing. Our political representatives are paralysed because we loyal marionettes of the corporate puppet masters demand the impossible. We want our SUVs and holidays in Thailand but we also want our leaders to save the planet; we want the products of unrestrained capitalism but reject its inevitable inequities; we bleat at the moat of bankers' bonuses but fail to acknowledge our own plank of unsustainable greed. Above all, like spoilt children, we insist we are worth it when all the evidence is we are not.

The unenviable predicament of our leaders was neatly summed up by Luxembourg's long-serving prime minister, Jean-Claude Juncker: 'we all know what to do, but we don't know how to get re-elected once we have done it'.[3] This is a terrible harbinger, because if elected leaders cannot cope, the alternative will be unelected ones.

The cycle, therefore, has to be broken and it is increasingly apparent that the impetus for change must come from us. Northern Ireland provides a shaft of hope. It has been deeply divided along sectarian boundaries for most of the last hundred years, and until very recently the conflict seemed completely intractable. But now an accord has been signed, divisions are starting to heal, peace is returning and the community is once again beginning to flourish. Tommy Sands, a musician who, along with his fellow citizens of the Province, lived through 'The Troubles', uses a revealing public transport metaphor to explain this remarkable success.

Two buses full of passengers meet nose to nose in the middle of a single-lane humpback bridge. An impasse results, with both drivers folding their arms and darkening their brows. Then the passengers of each bus take the initiative, approach their respective drivers and say that they are happy for them to reverse; that they understand the need to go backwards before you can go forwards. Only with this permission were the drivers – the political leaders – able to compromise.

We need to give our leaders permission to act. To reassure them that we understand that going backwards on material wellbeing is an acceptable and necessary price to pay if we are going to make progress on much more meaningful forms of wellbeing: that of our spirits, our children and our planet. We need to drown out the siren voices of the corporate marketers with their alarmist hints that we will get restive without our full complement of brands and shopping.

At this point, I confess, my nerve is beginning to wear thin. I really don't have the answers. What follows are just my own tricks for evading the corporate maw; they may or may not work for you. But I am sure that between us we can succeed; if we all think through the problem and share our ideas we can and will break out from our servitude. I also take comfort in Schumacher's intelligent words: 'Everywhere people ask: what can I actually do? The answer is as simple as it is disconcerting: we can each of us work to put our own inner house in order. The guidance we need for this work cannot be found in science and technology, the value of which utterly depends on the ends they serve; but it can still be found in the traditional wisdom of [hu]mankind.'[4] We are not alone in our task.

Snapping 'the mind-forged manacles'[5]

We have spent much of this book rehearsing the abiding cleverness of the corporate marketer; how they use every possible trick and tactic to catch us hapless flies in their profit-driven webs. Enough. We are not insects, but thinking, empowered beings who can question, analyse and challenge. We have to start using these critical faculties on corporate marketing. As we noted in Chapter 1, we need to follow the lesson of the Chinese general Sun Tzu, and get to know both ourselves and our enemies better. We have to assume the mantle of Eisenhower's 'alert and knowledgeable citizenry' if we are to check the advance of the military industrial complex and its hypermarket outriders.

The first step in escaping the marketing matrix, then, is to recognize and keep always in mind that the corporation is an inanimate organization, ruthlessly designed to serve the needs of its owners and, in the process, enrich its managers. This it will do at all costs; so however alluring the brand or attractive the sales staff, the psychopathic purpose prevails. Each of us should have these words tattooed on our hearts: this corporation does not give a damn about me; it wants my money and my spirit until death us do part; its brands and Corporate Social Responsibility campaigns are simply there to disguise its malevolent intent.

This strategic reading of enemy signals has to be matched with an analysis of our own priorities and vision. We have to think about what makes us happy, gives us a sense of purpose and ensures our lives are worthwhile. If the answers to these questions come anywhere near 'shopping, consuming as much as I possibly can and bedecking myself in evocative brands', the rest of this book is not for you. But as you have obviously got this far, I'm guessing that you are not prepared, quite yet, to accept the judgement of sociologists and marketers; that we have come to define our identity by what we consume. You have, I suspect, less materialistic priorities. Take the time to think through what these are, perhaps by writing down a list of the ten best things in your life. Now ask yourself exactly how much shopping has contributed to these.

Keep the list in your wallet or purse – preferably in a breast pocket, nice and close to those words you have just tattooed on your heart. Another quote from Mr Steinbeck might also help remind us that shopping really doesn't work: 'I ain't

FIGURE 9.1 'Time is Everything' poster. With thanks to ICE for permission to reproduce this picture

trying to preach no sermon, but I never seen nobody that's busy as a prairie dog collectin' stuff that wasn't disappointed.'[6]

This issue of resisting the temptation to buy arose at a recent seminar I attended in Liverpool. One of the participants almost pleaded with the group for help: how could she stop buying things she wanted and stick to those she needed? There was much discussion as a result, which resolved itself in the conclusion that all of us had to start turning L'Oréal's pernicious slogan on its head, and accept that we simply were not worth it – not worth the exploitation, the faux-treat, the planetary degradation. A graphic designer at the event was inspired to encapsulate the debate in a poster (see Figure 9.1).

Having armed ourselves with knowledge of corporate purpose, and contrasted it with our own, we can now turn to tactics.

Deconstructing the marketing mix

Corporate marketers, as we discussed in earlier chapters, think in terms of promotion, price, place and product. So will we.

Starting with *promotion* we should be on our guard against the subterfuge, subtlety and shade of all marketing communication. Even as it makes us laugh and melts us with its creativity, the ad campaign remains simply propaganda. When it moves beyond straightforward advertising, into sponsorship or Cause-Related Marketing, our critical antennae should be further sensitized; it's all too easy to fall for this melding of the brand with a cause we support or a person we admire. And, turning this around, the decision of an NGO to link up with a corporation, or an already well-remunerated celebrity to act as its paid spokesperson can provide a useful tool for parsing our allegiances. I for one will think much less respectfully of WWF now it has got into Coke's silk-sheeted four-poster.

All this is writ large with the internet, which is rapidly becoming a virtual mall, but without any of the warnings that we are entering a retail environment. The websites we browse, the friends we make on Facebook, the photos we post – all are being monitored and orchestrated. Our scepticism, therefore, has to be redoubled.

Turning to *price*, there is a need for particular caution, not just because this is where the rubber hits the road – the corporate marketer is preternaturally focused on our money – but because this is the fulcrum of our power. From an early age we are armed with the concept of *caveat emptor*; let the buyer beware. We are warned by our parents to be careful: to ascertain the full price before buying, to beware over-charging, and to check our change carefully before we leave the shop. This is what the proponents of advertising to children (see Chapter 5) laud as 'consumer socialization'; but it could be more accurately described as training us in materialism and selfishness. All the focus is on our own interests. This has to stop. We need to revolutionize how we think about price. Cheapness, the bargain, the special deal are not attractive prizes; they are warnings. They should cause us not to rejoice, but to raise a red flag and ask two important sorts of question.

First, do I need this? Given that we are so easily seduced by price promotions, as we noted time and again in Chapter 7, there is an immense risk that we will buy things unnecessarily. Such excess cuts to the quick of humanity's current predicament. Schumacher again expresses this with powerful clarity:

> the chance of mitigating the rate of resource depletion or of bringing harmony into the relationships between those in the possession of wealth and power and those without is non-existent as long as there is no idea of enough being good and more than enough being evil.[7]

The second sort of question is about who exactly is funding the good deal. One thing of which we can all be absolutely sure is that the corporation is not losing out; our seeming good fortune will never be at its expense. If a hit is being taken, it will be by someone much less powerful in the supply chain. The small farmers who are barely keeping their heads above water because of microscopic margins and ninety-day credit arrangements; the Costa Rican pineapple grower being drenched in pesticides; the non-unionized vegetable packer on two euros an hour. Time and again these abuses are the real price to be paid for the BOGOF and the bargain.

One guard against getting drawn unwittingly into such exploitation, as we noted in Chapters 2 and 3, is Fairtrade. If a Fairtrade option is available it should always be preferred; remember the obverse of fair trade is unfair trade. If there is no fairly sourced option available, ask why not, and demand that one is provided. This is not as easy as it might be for two reasons: the penetration of Fairtrade is disgracefully low and many corporations are jumping on the band wagon and producing their own version of fair trade. The first can be corrected by all of us demanding change. The second calls for caution. Check out the credentials of any scheme; you cannot take anything on trust. Ultimately the only really sure solution is to look for the Fairtrade logo, as this is guaranteed by Fairtrade International (previously known as Fairtrade Labelling Organizations International).[8]

Turning to *place*, the retail sector, as we discussed in Chapter 7, has become the shoppers' equivalent of shark infested waters. Every possible device is used to stimulate an almost automatic 'buy-it' response. If the water is full of sharks, we should keep our swimming to an absolute minimum. It also pays to use size as a guide: there are exceptions, but generally speaking the smaller the establishment the less manipulative the marketing. So if you are lucky enough, as I am, to still have small shops in your neighbourhood, treasure them, support them, use them. Do the same with any form of cooperative or mutual. And in either case, if they don't have what you need, think of possible alternatives.

In praise of bad service

If and when corporate shopping is unavoidable, gird your loins and keep that list close to your heart. And whatever you do, avoid places that give good service.

That's right, turn your back on all the 'can I help you sirs', 'certainly madams' and 'have a nice days'. Perpetual good service is a menace. It preens our egos, which are the source of so much woe. It makes us think we are terribly important; in reality we are no more important than the other people in our lives (who will waste little time correcting our misperception). Preened egos are also extremely perishable, so we need more and more good service to keep them in peak condition. Cloying customer service acts like a narcotic that creates dependence even as it delivers diminishing hits.

The other side of this coin is even more toxic: good service deadens our capacity for empathy. When we get a rude shop assistant we take personal affront, rather than remembering that the interaction is just as much about them as it is about us. They may be having a bad day because of their sleepless baby or being paid a pittance for their mind-numbing work or be under notice that their job is coming to an end. We are all in danger of becoming like Priestley's Sheila Birling as we sanctify our consumption needs and use them to assert specious authority.

These problems are much less prevalent with the small establishments. If I go down to the greengrocer's and Michael is lacking in his usual *joie de vivre*, I don't get sulky at his seeming indifference to me – I ask him how he is. If the service at my local pub is sullen, I don't take it as a personal slight – I assume life is being a bit more difficult for the bartender than it is for me and take my proper turn in the pecking order (either that or I just accept that it's Jack's shift). So in the corporate shop try to see bad service as your friend. It puts your ego safely back in its box, makes you more caring and reduces the chance of you succumbing in the future. Next time a shop assistant treats you like dirt, be grateful.

And now to the final P – the *product*; supposedly what it is all about. As we noted in Chapter 5, Joseph Heath and Andrew Potter teach us that in a society dominated by corporate marketers, the only effective rebellion is to stop shopping. As Marcus Aurelius might have said, had he ever experienced a twenty-first-century mall: to refrain from shopping is the best revenge. (He actually said: 'the best revenge is to be unlike him who performed the injury'.) Every other avenue will have corporate fingerprints all over it. OK, we can't stop shopping altogether; lots of the stuff we buy we do genuinely need. But we can reduce retail activity in two ways. First, we can perpetually check whether we need a given item. And to sift the needs from the wants and whims, set the bar high. Aldous Huxley, in his introduction to the 1946 edition of *Brave New World* suggests we should analyse all our behaviour by asking: 'How will this thought or action contribute to, or interfere with, the achievement, by me and the greatest number of other individuals, of man's (sic) final end?'[9] We could simply add shopping to 'thought or action'.

If we do need whatever it is, don't dismiss the possibility of furnishing it through self-production, which comes in numerous forms. Is there an old one I can repair? Can I borrow one from a friend? Check out the charity shop. Is there a greener alternative I could use? Leaving aside carbon saving, these more imaginative solutions are better for us. They stimulate and challenge; they slough off dependency. The default to shopping 'is standing truth on its head by considering goods as more important than people and consumption more important than creative activity'.[10] Like men who don't cook, people who get everything they need from the mall are not just increasing their dependency but needlessly diminishing their lives. Materialism is self-destructive.

Pity the merchant banker

This brings us back to the greedy CEOs. Following through the logic of our argument so far, the fight against corporate marketing is not just a worthy one, it is a self-enhancing one. Contrary to every ad you ever saw, every mall you ever darkened, consumption does not bring happiness. It's the same with wealth; an excess of it is not a measure of success, but of neediness and failure. The preacher in *The Grapes of Wrath* explains the millionaire's terrible dilemma:

> If he needs a million acres to make him feel rich, seems to me he needs it 'cause he feels awful poor inside hisself, and if he's poor in hisself, there ain't no million acres gonna make him feel rich, an' maybe he's disappointed that nothin' he can do'll make him feel rich ....[11]

It turns out that acquiring ridiculous amounts of money is as unsatisfactory as an overfilled shopping trolley or an excess of Kettle Chips. Or, recalling Schumacher, enough is good but more than enough is a corrosive evil. The banker is bewildered and confused rather than villainous. If you have any doubts about this, read Huxley's elegiacally entitled novel *After Many a Summer Dies the Swan*. For all his crass selfishness and overblown material possessions, Jo Stoyte, the preposterously rich central character is utterly wretched.

I heard the ecologist and broadcaster David Attenborough on the radio a couple of years ago talking about people driving SUVs (aka 'Chelsea Tractors') in London. He described how he had seen passers-by pointing and laughing at someone driving a particularly large model through the centre of the city, simply because it looked so out of place; so silly. He went on to explain that in his view this was marking a trend away from this particular form of marketing-driven foolishness. He may have been over-optimistic in the specific sense – SUVs still abound in our major cities – but I think he is right in the generality.

We have to stop pontificating about excess and start laughing at it. Excessive consumption is the hallmark of the sap, not the superman; likewise massive salaries betray foolishness, not ability. Bob Diamond's £10 million a year, for example, is so far beyond what any one person could sensibly spend it is effectively worthless. He must have to consult 'How to Spend It' on an hourly basis. Indeed he is probably so busy earning even more money that he cannot possibly need, that he pays somebody to do this for him.

So the merchant banker isn't a monster to be hated, but a needy, empty fool to be pitied, or, if we are feeling cruel, laughed at. This matters because demonizing corporate excess risks exacerbating its predations, which are driven by hubris. Like

Shelley's Ozymandias, captains of industry have a greatly inflated sense of their own power; they need to be deflated not pandered to. (Shelley's poem 'Ozymandias' tells of a traveller coming across the remains of a once glorious kingdom in the desert: it finishes with the haunting words: 'Round the decay/ Of that colossal wreck, boundless and bare/ The lone and level sands stretch far away.')

A few years ago there was a great Australian anti-speeding campaign aimed at young male drivers. Instead of using the tired old approach of depicting gory aftermaths, it showed young women reacting to boy racers by waggling their little fingers – street code for mocking their manhood. I think the same approach might work for stupidly greedy CEOs.

In deciding whether to mock or pity, however, we should be mindful that the only difference between the Bob Diamonds of this world and the rest of us, is that he has fallen for the vacuous marketing hype slightly more precipitously. Perhaps this is what Nye Bevan, the founder of the UK National Health Service, meant when he warned us: 'stand not too close to the rich man lest he destroy you'. Nor does any of this suggest greed should be forgiven or let be; Bevan's dictum continues: 'and not too far away lest he forget you'.[12]

The pith of sense

Corporate marketing has brought us to a pretty pass, and systemic change is undoubtedly needed. But progress also depends on our internal strength and determination; in Orwell's words: 'what is the use of changing the system before you have improved human nature?'[13] We also need to make a stand as a signal to our leaders that we want things to change; that they can reverse the bus. This stand necessarily casts us as Eisenhower's 'alert and knowledgeable citizenry' with a critical and abiding recognition that corporate marketers, despite all their charm, are not our friends. Their ceaseless aim is profit, and in its pursuit we are just as likely to be the collateral as the satisfied customer. The planet does not get a look in, unless invoking its welfare also feeds profits.

Despite this depredation, the greedy corporate executives need to be pitied not reviled. The threat to our future comes as much from their hubris as their greed, so a bit of deflating will go much further than a lot of demonizing. And the surest way of pricking the corporate marketers' balloon is to walk away from their offerings.

We can, we must and we will do all these things. Despite my unease at the outset of the chapter I am sure about this. I am confident because, in this case, the traditional wisdom recommended by Schumacher comes from no better source than Burns. In 'A Man's a Man', as we noted earlier, he dismisses wealth and privilege; he then goes on to reassure us in ringing tones that 'pith o' sense, an' pride o' worth, are higher rank than a' that'. I have every faith in our pith of sense and pride of worth.

However, just in case they fail us, the next two chapters argue for much more support for enlightened consumption behaviour through social marketing, and a root and branch reconfiguration of the corporate sector's marketing.

Wise Words

India has millions of internally displaced people. And now, they are putting their bodies on the line and fighting back. They are being killed and imprisoned in their thousands. Theirs is a battle of the imagination, a battle for the redefinition of the meaning of civilisation, of the meaning of happiness, of the meaning of fulfilment. And this battle demands that the world see that, at some stage, as the water tables are dropping and the minerals that remain in the mountains are being taken out, we are going to confront a crisis from which we cannot return. The people who created the crisis in the first place will not be the ones that come up with a solution.

That is why we must pay close attention to those with another imagination: an imagination outside of capitalism, as well as communism. We will soon have to admit that those people, like the millions of indigenous people fighting to prevent the takeover of their lands and the destruction of their environment – the people who still know the secrets of sustainable living – are not relics of the past, but the guides to our future.

Arundhati Roy (2011)[1]

Before our white brothers arrived to make us civilized men, we didn't have any kind of prison. Because of this, we had no delinquents. Without a prison, there can be no delinquents. We had no locks nor keys and therefore among us there were no thieves. When someone was so poor that he couldn't afford a horse, a tent or a blanket, he would, in that case, receive it all as a gift. We were too uncivilized to give great importance to private property. We didn't know any kind of money and consequently, the value of a human being was not determined by his wealth. We had no written laws laid down, no lawyers, no politicians, therefore we were not able to cheat and swindle one another.

We were really in bad shape before the white men arrived and I don't know how to explain how we were able to manage without these fundamental things that (so they tell us) are so necessary for a civilized society.

John (Fire) Lame Deer, Sioux Lakota (1903–1976)[2]

10

POWER TO THE PEOPLE

We can do this

Marketing was not invented by the corporations; it was co-opted by them. Marketing is in fact as old as human civilization itself: it underpins our ability to cooperate, to come to mutually beneficial arrangements, to organize ourselves into societies. Our first task then is to liberate it from its bondage in the corporate sector and change its focus from consumption behaviour to social and health behaviour: 'if marketing can encourage us to buy a Ferrari, it can also persuade us to drive it safely – or resist the temptation to steal one'[3] – or, better still, swap it for a bicycle.

'Social marketing' campaigns have become a commonplace on the back of this thinking. However, ad hoc interventions risk being patronizing, are frequently unsustainable and can never bring about the root and branch changes the world now needs. For this we will have to harness the very real power and commitment of ordinary people – and especially indigenous people – by melding marketing skills with community development and going to scale with digital media. That way we can move from piecemeal behaviour change to full-on social change.

To complete the circle though, this social marketing must be balanced with the reining in of the corporate sector. Why waste resources discouraging the purchase of Ferraris? It is much cheaper and more effective to stop them being marketed in the first place.

Reclaiming marketing

Business schools teach that marketing emerged somewhere in the middle of the last century, as the post-Second World War boom took production beyond demand. As we noted in Chapter 1, this might have been a good point at which to rethink the model; supply was, after all, only outstripping demand in the rich North.

Instead of producing ever more arcane stuff and selling it to us jaded patricians of the world, perhaps a bit of redistribution would have been in order. But corporate capitalism instead co-opted and industrialized marketing and has used it remorselessly ever since, in all the ways we discussed in the first eight chapters, with utterly predictable and devastating consequences.

I say co-opted because although the business texts imply that the discipline was invented in the 1950s, it is in fact as old as humankind. Its core principles of mutually beneficial exchange, doing deals and seeking to identify the win–wins that make cooperation pay for multiple parties are the essence of collective living. Richard Layard takes this thinking way back to the origins of our species, arguing that cooperation and mutually beneficial exchange were key to our success on the African savannah:

> If human beings had not been able to cooperate in this way they would probably not have survived the rigours of the savannah – or subsequently of regions much colder. At best our lives would have been, as Thomas Hobbes put it, solitary, poor, nasty, brutish and short. We survived because our genes gave us the ability to cooperate.[4]

Marketing is the timeless protocol behind this vital human cooperation. Yes, it has been spirited into the MBA syllabus and, in corrupted form, has pole position in the corporate arsenal, but in reality it has a much older and more important role in our lives. It oils the wheels of cooperation. We saw in Chapter 1 how in the hands of a skilled publican (Mary at the King's Head) or shopkeeper (Michael the greengrocer) – neither of whom has ever been near a business school – it can help a community run more smoothly, improve people's lives and even bring marital harmony.

It is time, then, to reclaim marketing.

Social marketing

Fortunately, I am not the first person to think that marketing can work beyond the marketplace. There is in fact a burgeoning discipline called 'social marketing', which takes the principles and practice that have been honed by commercial marketers to craft our consumption behaviour and applies them to our social and health behaviour. Or as two American academics expressed it: 'Social marketing is concerned with the application of marketing knowledge, concepts, and techniques to enhance social as well as economic ends.'[5]

This productive union has been most widely seen in public health.

To see how it works, we should turn back to Mary the publican. It may seem counter-intuitive to seek public health wisdom in a bar, but Mary does have a crucial common agenda with those working in infant immunization, obesity prevention and, as the example below illustrates, smoking cessation: she too is dealing in voluntary behaviour change. She wants – needs – people to visit her pub, buy her beer, tell their friends and family what a good pub it is, visit her pub again, organize their wedding receptions with her … And she knows they have a choice; she cannot compel them to do these things, so she has to seduce them. This means she has to understand their needs absolutely, and cater to them at every opportunity. Bethany's hairdo and her husband's late arrival are core business for her. She has to avoid the trap of taking refuge in the technicalities of her work, focusing purely on the science of good beer or the minutiae of stock management. These things matter, but only in so far as they help her meet her customers' needs.

As with Mary's pub, so with smoking cessation. Box 10.1 shows how a service in the north east of England succeeded in building links with pregnant smokers from very low income communities and persuading them through its doors. The first step was qualitative research to dig down and understand the perspective of the women and how they felt about their smoking and the possibility of quitting. This revealed a remarkable degree of ambivalence in both areas. They knew smoking to be harmful for them and their baby, but they also valued the indulgence, affirmation and 'me-time' it provided – rewards that were only enhanced by their constrained lives. Corresponding research with health professionals revealed that they fully understood this ambivalence among the low income smokers, and it made them reluctant to broach the idea of quitting and reticent in their approach when they did. The resulting initiative built on these insights and comparison with neighbouring providers demonstrated their striking success – attendance at the local cessation service shot up.

BOX 10.1 USING SOCIAL MARKETING TO HELP PREGNANT SMOKERS QUIT

The problem

The impacts of smoking in pregnancy are well documented but when the United Kingdom city of Sunderland set up a service to help women quit, few were using it.

The stakeholders

Pregnant smokers; their 'significant others' (partners, parents, friends); health professionals (obstetric, medical, health promotion) and service providers, clinical managers and support groups.

Objective

To increase the number of women who were using the service, and thereby their success in quitting.

Consumer research

In-depth discussions with the women showed they were keen to quit but that the services were difficult to identify and access, and health professionals were unsympathetic. Research with health professionals revealed an ambivalence about raising this sensitive issue with their clients.

The strategy

Product	A cessation service designed around the women's needs
Price	Ease of access for the target (including free of charge)
Place	Go to the women's preferred locations
Promotion	Enthuse and skill up key health professionals

Outcomes

Recruitment of pregnant (and non-pregnant) smokers to the new smoking cessation intervention increased tenfold during the intervention phase, and the Sunderland stop smoking service is now one of the top performers in the UK: Sunderland pregnancy stop smoking service was highlighted in the Department of Health's "Best practice in smoking cessation services for pregnant smokers" (November 2005), is one of the top three beacon services in England and is the *most cost effective* (quitters per member of staff, clarity of data collection and reporting procedures).

Avoiding top-down ad hockery

So the key principles of marketing can successfully cross the profit divide and provide some solutions to our market driven problems. All we need is enlightened leaders who will adopt this thinking and use it to get us all doing the right things. Not just quitting smoking, but taking exercise and eating healthily – even living sustainably. Given the massive social changes brought about by corporate marketers, social marketing can do enormous good. Our leaders just need to hone their focus group skills, and start swotting up on the 4 Ps.

For the most part, this is where social marketing is today; a kind of enlightened social engineering with a built-in tendency to operate top-down. Under the guidance of our leaders, experts determine priorities, budgets are allocated and well-meaning interventions follow. However, given the problems we face, especially the imminence and calamitous consequences of climate change, this is patently failing.

Putting in more resources – even were they available – is not the solution. We do not have a problem of 'how much?' but of 'how?' Apart from sounding like a recipe for hell on earth, calling for more of this intermittent do-gooding would make three untenable assumptions:

- That our leaders know what needs to be done and have the courage and calibre to promote it. As we discussed in Chapter 10, while they may be up to speed on the former, they are patently failing on the latter.
- That we have the budgets. Because corporations are selling stuff, their budgets are perpetually being replenished (as long as they get the marketing right) – social marketers are not self-financing; they depend on governments, foundations and ordinary people giving them money.
- That it is possible to micro-manage our lives. Corporations do it, but only in the very narrow sphere of shopping and the result, as we have seen, is a cultural desert. Applying this process to the complex reality of what it is to be a fulfilled human being is impossible to even contemplate – outwith the realms of nightmarish science fiction.

So running a perpetual coterie of Sunderland-style interventions would never be better than a piecemeal, sticking plaster solution. A much more joined-up approach is needed. The job of social marketing then is not to provide the powers that be with more sophisticated means of social control. Rather it should be a facilitator of action; a means of empowerment for ordinary people so that they can live in harmony with their fellow creatures and their environment.

Community activism

Fortunately, social marketing is custom-made for such grassroots thinking. As we have noted it starts by listening to and learning from the people rather than being precious about expertise or making assumptions.

In my early years in social marketing this took the form of the then revolutionary idea of public health communications being pretested with audiences as well as scrutinized by medics – and then changed in response to the former as well as the latter. For the first time since the birth of modern medicine there was official recognition that the doctor did not always know best. Since then the idea has remained at the core of social marketing and continues to provide its essential strength because it recognizes the power of we ordinary people. The power that both Steinbeck and Eisenhower, from opposite ends of the political spectrum, invoked.

This power takes two forms. Firstly, in a conventional sense, people can and will resist change if they feel it does not meet their needs. Smokers will continue to smoke in the teeth of stark health warnings and motorists will drive too fast despite ubiquitous speed cameras not just because they are ignorant or recalcitrant (though they may be both) but because they can. Secondly, more subtly, social change is a process not an outcome. It happens because people use their personal and collective power to make their own and their communities' lives better. This hankering after progress is a definitively human characteristic: we are need-directed beings with a built-in inclination to try and improve our lot. Solutions to our current predicament need to recognize the role of this organic process and make further adjustments to the balance of power between the expert and the citizen.

Strength of spirit

The potential of ordinary people to make a difference was brought home to me by Simon. We had been friends for a number of years but both of us are in late middle age so we had lots of past life that neither knew about. One night Simon was round at mine for a meal when his phone rang. We were about to eat but he apologized, said something had cropped up, and left. I was taken aback and a little hurt; I had spent most of the afternoon preparing the curry we were about to eat. The following evening Simon rang me to apologize again and said he would like to come round to explain his peculiar behaviour.

When he arrived I made a cup of tea; Simon doesn't drink alcohol – a fact that I had noted but had never really thought about before. He sat down and there was an unusually long silence (we are both pretty garrulous) before he cleared his throat and spoke.

> I used to drink. A lot. It got to the point when I would have to stop at three different bars on my drive home from work. A half and half [Glaswegian for a single measure of whisky and a half pint of beer] in each. Then when I got home I could break open a bottle of vodka. Did this for years before I woke up to the fact I was killing myself. So I got help [a massive step for a west of Scotland male]. I went to Alcoholics Anonymous (AA) and it pulled me through.

It was not an easy or rapid process though.

> After my first AA meeting it took me 3 years to stop drinking. My life just got worse and worse. The redeeming feature was that I always went back to AA, probably 20 comebacks in 3 years. The same people were always there to help. They took me to meetings when I was unable to drive. I had constant panic attacks. I finally gave AA the chance to give me a chance. (I'm paraphrasing a UCS [Upper Clyde Shipbuilders] shop steward here.) Some 40 to 50 people must have tried to help me in the 3 years before my last drink. I often wondered why they hadn't given up on me. People don't really give up on one another in AA. There's no formal arrangement. From their first meeting people are encouraged to obtain the phone numbers of AA members and to use them no matter the time of day (or night).

The previous night, when we were about to have dinner, it had been Simon's turn to be the support. Indeed he ascribes his success in escaping from the drink to the profound feelings of responsibility and paying back that AA gives him. No, escaping is the wrong word; this is about change; profound and permanent personal change.

A sobering story. And it continued a month later when Simon invited me to his AA twentieth birthday. Twenty years without a drink. The meeting, organized by members – AA has no hierarchy – was a deeply impressive experience. Everyone, except me, was there because they had a problem with alcohol. Some like Simon hadn't had a drink for decades; others were still recovering from their last hangover – but all were equally welcome and accepted. They came from all walks of life – public school to public housing – but the mutual respect was palpable. Each told his or her own story in simple and deeply moving terms. Each took another step on the journey.

Three things live with me from these events. First, even in our darkest hour we have enormous internal resources. Second, we will respond collectively and effectively to a shared external threat. Third, we will do this on a long term, even perpetual basis if it gives us a sense of purpose and self-worth. From so many tales of despair there emerged enormous hope. Society needs to access this power and this hope.

More important than all this, though, is the clear proof – which Simon's story proves – that we are capable of change. I'll leave the last word to him:

> There can be no progress without change; and change from a basis of honesty. The same person who came through the doors of AA is the person who will take you back out. The whole concept of change is central to your project and if a bunch of drunks can do it, then … .

Community mobilization

Work at the University of South Florida is helping to do just this by blending social marketing with community mobilization. Communities can be defined in many ways – geographically, by sexuality, their particular enthusiasms and so on. Social marketers approach them with a completely open agenda asking them to select the social problems they want to tackle, set programme goals, and become partners in the research, strategy development, and delivery of the activities used to reach those goals. In particular, the Florida team teach community social marketing skills like market research, objective setting and strategic planning based on marketing's 4 Ps. This approach provides valuable information about local problems and the assets available to resolve them, enhancing the fit between programme strategies and local institutions and customs. By working together, network ties are strengthened and new problem solving skills acquired.

Importantly, then, communities are treated as agents and partners instead of the 'passive consumers of messages and programs'.[6] This approach also leads naturally to the idea of relationship building, which we discussed in its much less functional commercial guise in Chapter 7. By contrast with the exploitative synthetic relationship of a profit driven corporation with a needy punter, community based social marketing produces mutually respectful partnerships around shared goals.

As a result of their participation throughout the planning and implementation process, then, community members gain the skills needed to address other issues and work together to sustain and institutionalize solutions. This approach has now been used in numerous settings and has been shown to work. For example, one poor urban community decided that its particular public health concern was obesity and the poor provision of exercise opportunities. Working with the Florida team they were able to map out the problem – specifically a lack of play facilities and organized activities in the school summer holidays – and start developing solutions. Importantly these combined grassroots volunteering around very local events with lobbying of local authorities for better statutory provision. Thus community based social marketing can not only help improve the lot of individual fish, but change the water.

Similar thinking has been applied around the world. Amnesty International's work in the Northern Territory of Australia shows that giving Aboriginal communities greater control of their own health services in and of itself enhances outcomes.[7] And across the Pacific in Peru a development NGO called Intermediate Technology Development Group (ITDG) has recognized the value of replacing external experts with indigenous citizens trained as *kamayoqs*, which in the local Quechua tongue means knowledge bearers.[8]

As with the South Florida team, the process 'began by simply talking to the local people'. These conversations were in Quechua, which is typically disparaged by officialdom, and the development workers put 'great emphasis on local culture' because, they argue, change 'has to be rooted in campesino institutions otherwise it won't be sustainable'. Nonetheless

> to begin with, people were mistrustful. They were used to a vertical relationship with state agencies, even with development agencies. For them, a vet was someone who turns up in a car wearing good boots and a new jacket and says: 'This is what we're going to do.'[9]

But cultural sensitivity combined with partnership working succeeded in removing these barriers. For example, the irrigation system, which dated back to the Incas, was renovated with due deference to its powerful religious significance and by team work: ITDG provided the materials and 'the campesinos did the work, they invested their labour' and so 'now they're managing the irrigation system themselves. They've made it their own – that's what makes it sustainable.'[10]

ITDG took the same approach to agriculture. Rather than parachuting in expensive external experts they helped local people access training in animal husbandry. The resulting system of *kamayoqs* has three major advantages: it avoids expensive consultants' wages; it is sustainable because the *kamayoqs* are and will remain locally based and it sets in train a process of self-improvement. To use a well-worn metaphor this was not a matter of providing people with fish, but of enabling them to fish for themselves. The last word should go to one of the *kamayoqs*, a woman called Vicenta Cahuana:

> I used to take orders from my husband and sometimes he was violent. In the past women didn't have rights. I began to think this has to change. I started

to respect myself more. My husband got very uncomfortable. He said: 'Whatever you're learning, it's no good for this household because you're answering me back. You're not respectful any more since you've been running around.' In a friendly way, I told him I'm taking better care of the animals. I don't waste money getting them cured. Now he says carry on.[11]

Nga hapori hokohoko

None of this, however, is easy or quick. Putting people at the centre of things never is; ask any teacher or social worker. This dilemma was writ large for me a few years ago in New Zealand; I was there for a social marketing conference. The organizers were very keen to involve Maori in the event, but knew they would have to do much more than issue an invitation to what was a *pakeha* (European) event. Indeed even the term 'social marketing' smacked of cultural imperialism. Discussion with the Maori community led to the idea of organizing a '*Hui*', a traditional coming together of the community to discuss shared problems and opportunities. This *Hui* would 'provide a unique opportunity for discussion and debate on the role and relevance of social marketing to Maori'. The key objectives (see Box 10.2) included its relevance to the 'Te Tiriti o Waitangi' (the crucial 1840 treaty between the Maori chiefs and the British Crown which became the 'founding document of New Zealand as a nation'); the traditional role of marketing for Maori (reinforcing the point that this is not a twentieth-century business school invention); and 'what the future role of social marketing in Aotearoa (New Zealand) should look like'.

BOX 10.2 THE OBJECTIVES OF A MAORI *HUI* ABOUT SOCIAL MARKETING

- What is the social marketing paradigm?
- What is the role of the Te Tiriti o Waitangi/Treaty of Waitangi in relation to social marketing?
- How effective are social marketing initiatives and activities in reaching Maori?
- What are the critical elements and processes involved in marketing with, or to, Maori?
- What expectations and issues should be considered when developing and designing effective marketing interventions with Maori?
- What is the traditional role of marketing to Maori? (Marketing and traditional Maori practices.)
- What should the future role of social marketing in Aotearoa (New Zealand) look like?

It was a powerful event. Maori do not pull their punches, as anyone who has experienced the Haka (warlike dance) can attest. There was concern that this was yet another attempt to manipulate; that this was just one more shot from an alien culture that had already caused many of the community's problems – not least in public health. But there was also a palpable respect for the process; for the effort at inclusion that was being made. The day culminated in a highly respected Maori elder and *tohunga* (cultural leader) presenting his view that social marketing does have something positive to contribute to Maori – and, crucially, offering a translation of the term into the Maori tongue: *Nga hapori hokohoko*. Literal translation is difficult so suffice it to say that this Maori phrase describes the notion of mutual or reciprocal exchange between people either as individuals or as sections of a *whanau* (family), community, tribe or society.

This says it all really, and provides an apt reminder that in social marketing the concept of 'mutually beneficial exchange' is not the rhetorical sleight of hand it is for the corporation, but a vital reality. I was at the *Hui* as an 'expert' in social marketing, but I learnt just as much as I taught. I had been exposed to what Arundhati Roy calls 'another imagination – an imagination outside of capitalism as well as communism'.[12] 'An imagination that has an altogether different understanding of what constitutes happiness and fulfilment.'[13] She goes on to argue for greater recognition for indigenous peoples, 'the people who still know the secrets of sustainable living' and 'are not relics of the past, but the guides to our future'.[14] Schumacher's traditional wisdom again, plus the reinforcement of the obvious truth that no one has all the answers: we have to pool our resources to make progress. Just like we did on the savannah.

Participatory media

In Chapter 6 I was pretty rude about digital media, not least because they are rapidly being corporatized. Nonetheless, the internet does offer some hope in the fight back. Its phenomenal reach, even into the most remote parts of the world, is one cause for optimism. People can connect, arm themselves with accurate information and express their views. Tales of African farmers using their phones to check wholesale commodity prices and so defeat attempts to cheat them are intuitively heart-warming.

A second reason to be hopeful is provided by the active nature of digital communications: we don't just passively absorb them as with traditional media – we can interact. This 'participatory'[15] quality has the most fundamental implications for social marketing. It provides an electronic and ubiquitous platform for grass-roots activism. This has the power to transform ordinary people and community groups from passive message recipients into fellow storytellers, network builders and co-activists. We are now able to search for, or 'pull', information we want instead of waiting for it to be 'pushed' to us.

Thirdly, despite the corporate marketers' success in colonizing hyperspace they are hitting resistance. We don't want to use participatory media to create or enter communities populated with commercial brands; we want to meet like-minded people, help each other, develop ourselves and gain status.[16] We do maintain a critical distance from commerce and its products, even if it's simply at the level of pointing our peers towards better deals – as with Paddy and his Ford Galaxy in Chapter 6. Facebook is a corporation making money by selling our data to other corporations, but its success is built on a genuine desire for ordinary people to connect with other ordinary people.

I want to tell you a story

The prospects of participatory media are indeed exciting, and the greatest potential will come, it is argued,[17] when we begin to absorb some of the storytelling skills of traditional culture (think back to the *Hui*) and pre-digital media (perhaps best exemplified by commercial cinema). Interactive storytelling allows people not just to participate but to perform in a journey of their own making. Cinematic storytelling has the ability to structure and evoke powerful emotions – pride, self-worth, identity, belonging, status and validation: it will make it possible for people to experiment with whole new lifestyles in safe and self-asserting, life-affirming contexts. Refusing a cigarette from your mate can be very challenging in real life – and it is unlikely to deliver any greater status or rewards – but as an avatar such possibilities can be tried out, tested and rewarded:

> By combining interactivity and reward structures – as evolved by the computer games industry – with storytelling and emotional structuring – as evolved by commercial cinema – Social Marketing can help clients to experiment outside of their local, real world familial and peer group milieu – as many young people around the world are beginning to do and enjoy. By embracing participatory media and emergent storytelling forms, Social Marketers can collaborate with and help to co-create identities, environments, behaviours and life styles. It can help participants rehearse real-life challenges, take on real-life antagonists and experience rewards and emotions unavailable anywhere else. We can be heroes.[18]

The last sentiment was recognized fully by game designer Jane McGonigal who in collaboration with the World Bank ran an initiative last year called 'EVOKE: A crash course in changing the world'.[19] Participants were given the opportunity to take on the role of hero and experiment with the challenges of real world development scenarios played out online. Real world financial rewards and opportunities were given to those who were able to empower others and collaborate to collect real world evidence. No formal evaluation has been released at the time of writing, but the weblogs are certainly very positive. Participatory media clearly have much social marketing potential, offering as they do the opportunity to take partnership working and the *kamayoqs* to scale. In addition, they give more power to the people and push towards a further rebalancing between expert and citizen. Humility and power is a potent mix.

We have a movement

We have an enormous potential to respond to the challenges we all face. When our internal strengths are combined with social marketing skills and community activism, tangible improvements to our lives can be achieved. Add to this a marrying of traditional wisdom and storytelling with digital reach and interactivity and the potential for sustained social change is palpable.

A few years ago California organized a statewide conference to discuss the rapidly unfolding threat from obesity. We were coming to the end of a discussion on the role that social marketing might play and we had explored its capacity to empower grassroots action, enable policy change, marshal advocacy, constrain the fast food industry and mobilize the population. Then a tall, gaunt septuagenarian rose slowly to his feet at the back of the hall. The phrase 'distinguished hippy' would probably best capture his appearance – distinguished enough to bring the hubbub of the large meeting to a respectful silence; hippy enough to defy prediction. No one could tell what was coming next, but we somehow knew it would be worth hearing. He cleared his throat and in a sonorous Californian burr declared:

> My name is Vince and I'm a veteran of the fight to stop the Vietnam War. Now, for the first time in the thirty-eight years since our direct action ended that conflict, I feel able to use the 'M' word.

I thought for a gratifying moment his 'M' word was marketing, but he continued:

> I mean we have a movement – and it is movements that make a difference, that change things. We needed a movement then to stop the War, and we need a movement now to fight obesity; we have one.

Vince was telling us that social marketing could help to tackle obesity because it was taking on the multifaceted, engaging and strategic qualities of a movement.

It was a profound insight. If we are to push back on the depredations of corporate marketing we too need a movement.

But positive action will only succeed in a sympathetic environment; we have at the same time to rein in commerce. The definition of social marketing I quoted earlier is actually incomplete. In its full version it reads: 'Social marketing is concerned with the application of marketing knowledge, concepts, and techniques to enhance social as well as economic ends. *It is also concerned with analysis of the social consequence of marketing policies, decisions and activities.*'[20] Even Vince and his colleagues didn't succeed until the hawks in the White House and the Pentagon had been constrained.

Building a House in Old Europe

I was building a house, a small, yellow-and-white one like a hard-boiled egg. You have no idea how complicated such a thing is in Europe. Before the house was finished, we had been through strikes by bricklayers, carpenters, joiners, parquet-layers and roof-tilers. The building of the house unfolded itself as a two-year social struggle. If work was done at all, people had, in between the laying of two bricks, enough time to have a little chat, enjoy some beer, spit and scratch their backs. For two years I went regularly to watch how my house was coming to light. It was part of my personal history. My relation to the house grew into an endless intimacy. During those two years I got to know a host of details about the work and life of bricklayers, joiners, canteen-keepers and other hairy, serious and jocular men. All this got cemented into the bricks and joists of my house. You must see that after so many drawbacks I cling to it with a certain fierce patriotism, and that I wouldn't change it for anything.

Now, you in America would build such a house within perhaps three days. You would come in your Fords with a ready-made iron construction, tighten a few screws, pour in several sacks of cement, nip into your Fords again, and go and build somewhere else. It would be far cheaper and quicker; it would have all the technical and economic advantages. But I have the feeling that I would be less at home in my house if it had sprung into being at such an unnatural speed.

Karel Čapek[1]

11

MARKETING AS IF PEOPLE MATTERED

The return of the citizen

Given all we have learned about the harm being done by corporate marketers, it is tempting to simply make this final chapter a call for stringent regulation. This, however, risks understating the problem, as it implies we are broadly getting things right, and just need to make a few running repairs. In reality we need a much more fundamental review, not just of lifeboat provision, but of the purpose of the voyage. Schumacher's book *Small is Beautiful*, which we have already referred to on several occasions, has the subtitle: 'a study of economics as if people mattered'. In this last chapter then we will do a study of marketing as if people (and the planet) matter.

This analysis must start with us. The concept of consumer sovereignty, which is in any case the unicorn in the corporate marketplace, has to be replaced by the concept of consumer responsibility – an obligation on us to consume less and do so more ethically and sustainably. Corporate marketing, and the management of each of the four Ps of promotion, price, place and product, should be focused not on boosting sales, but encouraging this responsibility.

This will inevitably lead to corporate shrinkage, which is much to be desired. Too big to fail has become an ominous invocation in the current economic crisis; in the process it has blotted out a more fundamental truth: corporations have become too big to succeed in all but the narrowest of senses. Their sheer size removes them from the lives of ordinary people, a distance that is evocatively illustrated by ludicrous corporate salaries but is in reality an inevitable result of a system that lionizes profits and growth to the exclusion of all other concerns. This change of direction will require statutory regulation. It took the force of law to make factories safe; it will take the same firmness of hand to detoxify corporate marketing. This legislative action should actively encourage reductions in size, returning businesses to a human scale.

In and of itself though, this will merely contain the corporation, and reduce the harm it does. The need is also for positive and more fundamental change that gives ordinary people much more say, recognizes the importance of collective action and reasserts ethicality in our way of life. We are not consumers, we are citizens.

What is the point of marketing?

Let us return to the textbook definition of marketing we started with in Chapter 2: marketing is 'the achievement of corporate goals through meeting and exceeding customer needs'. We have rehearsed long and hard how this serving of two masters, the corporate goals of the shareholder and our consumption needs, will always culminate in the interests of the former being preferred. The fiduciary imperative – the requirement for corporations always to put the interests of their shareholders first – makes this outcome both legally binding and inevitable.

One response to this dilemma is to challenge the validity of the fiduciary imperative as Porter does (see Chapter 8) and argue that corporations should be given a broader remit which prioritizes other outcomes – such as social good or sustainability. Thus far, attempts to do this have met with only marginal success. This is partly because corporate marketers have been so good at using techniques like Corporate Social Responsibility to both deflect criticism and simulate change. Give a corporate marketer a problem and time and again he or she will provide a response that looks good and provides plenty of reassurance, but produces no tangible change – and as a result ends up making things worse. As with the tobacco industry and low tar cigarettes, which turned out to be more harmful than the standard product, it is almost impossible to provide a solution when you are completely wedded to the problem.

More fundamentally, the fiduciary imperative plays a vital role in controlling corruption. It is there, as we noted in Chapter 1, to ensure that corporate executives, who are spending other people's – shareholders' – money, do so in the interest of those shareholders. Flawed though this process clearly is, given the obscene levels of boardroom remuneration, removing the focus on profits and the discipline this imposes could cause major problems. Not least, what are the other priorities that a corporation should address, who will decide when they are being successfully achieved and how will they do so? At least the financial bottom line, crass though it is, is reasonably easy to measure.

A complementary approach is to challenge not just the corporation's goals but how these are achieved. This brings us to the second half of our definition of marketing – 'meeting and exceeding customer needs' – and begs questions about legitimacy.

Deposing the consumer

Much of this book has derided the notion of consumer sovereignty as a myth perpetrated by corporate marketers to disguise their unstinting self-interest. My purpose in repeating it now is just to note that it works: pretending that they are looking after our consumption needs justifies corporate marketers' existence and methods. Our shopping confirms their legitimacy; consumption is sacrosanct. Thus retail sales become a barometer of a country's economic success; poor Christmas shopping turnouts have politicians wringing their hands. Maximizing consumption is a respectable ideal. Box 11.1 shows headlines on both sides of the Atlantic invoking despair when we stop shopping, and hope when we start again.

However, this, as Schumacher points out, is actually the reverse of what a healthy society should do: 'the aim should be to produce the maximum of wellbeing for the minimum of consumption'.[2] Corporate marketing, as we have seen, does the exact opposite – maximizing sales and promoting perpetual dissatisfaction.

BOX 11.1 SHOPPING AS A MEASURE OF ECONOMIC PERFORMANCE[3]

Concern as Scots retail sales tumble

The value of Scottish retail sales tumbled last month at its fastest annual pace since comparable records began in 1999. The fall is revealed in figures published today by the Scottish Retail Consortium (SRC), which show the value of sales in November was down 1.3% on the same month last year. These numbers signal conditions on the high street continue to be much worse in Scotland than in the UK as a whole.

Ian McConnell and Jody Harrison, *The Herald*
14 December 2011

Concern as Eurozone retail sales fall

Eurozone retailers saw sales drop 0.7pc in September as households reined in their spending amid the ongoing debt crisis. The bigger than expected slump in their performance reinforced concerns that the region is hurtling into a recession.

Emma Rowley, *The Telegraph*
7 November 2011

U.S. Retail Sales Rise More-Than-Forecast 1.1%, Easing Recession Concern

Retail sales rose in September by the most in seven months, showing American consumers are helping the world's largest economy fend off a slump.

Timothy R. Homan and Bob Willis, *Bloomberg*
14 October 2011

The obvious need, as Schumacher also underlines, is to rethink our priorities and question this blatant preference for materialism.

> Needless to say, wealth, education, research and many other things matter for any civilization, but what is most needed today is a revision of the ends these means are meant to serve. And this implies above all else, the development of a lifestyle which accords material things their proper, legitimate place, which is secondary and not primary.[4]

For our purposes he also neatly highlights the insanity of allowing corporations, some of the biggest and most powerful organizations on our planet, to use every scrap of their massive marketing effort to promote this very materialism. And remember he was writing in the 1970s, before global warming became such a clear and present danger; before the global financial crisis showed how insecurely the wheels of corporate capitalism are attached; and before boardroom pay demonstrated just how divisive 'the idea of conducting the entire economy on the basis of greed'[5] can be.

Greed is not good; it is personally corrosive and ecologically catastrophic.

This thinking chimes with the work of Czech author, Karel Čapek, whose story of house-building starts this chapter. He set great store by the importance of recognizing the full person in any economic system. He wrote the piece for the *New York Times* Sunday edition, and in it contrasts the speed and efficiency of mass production and modern, 'Fordist' business methods then coming to the fore in America with the slow, 'complicated' ways of old Europe (this is way before Donald Rumsfeld's time).

The underlying point which emerges from the work of both writers is that we are people, not consumers, and blurring this distinction, as corporate marketing perpetually does, is deeply problematic. A key step in our journey away from the marketing matrix, then, is to recognize that this confusion is dangerous and that the notion of consumer sovereignty – even in the make-believe sense of corporate marketing – is very unhelpful.

Marketing is not a given

This strips away the corporate marketers' fig leaf, and opens their activities to much greater critical scrutiny. If consumption itself is devalued, then a discipline whose principal purpose is to encourage consumption becomes equally questionable. The legal to sell, legal to advertise default, which was always dubious, becomes completely unacceptable. The starting point, to recall Schumacher, should be wellbeing: the wellbeing of individuals, communities, the planet. It should not be with the marketer who has something to sell, or the customer who has the means and desire to buy it. And there should certainly not be any assumed right to market, to use the 4 Ps of promotion, price, place and product and all the variations on that theme which we discussed in earlier chapters, in order to encourage consumption.

Instead the default should be no corporate marketing at all until a convincing case has been made to show that it will contribute to the collective wellbeing: that the individual will be healthier and happier as a result, that the community will benefit, above all that less carbon will be consumed. And the job of marketing should be to enhance the capacity of the product or service to bring about these ends, not just to secure the sale. It should only be there to help us all make better, more responsible consumption decisions.

This thinking easily transposes to the four Ps.

People-centred advertising

Marketing communications should be designed to help us make better informed decisions about our purchases: what, and crucially whether, we buy. To do this we need factual and verifiable information about the tangible characteristics of a given product or service. Forget the celebrity endorsements or manicured brand images; stop attaching enticing symbolic meanings to consumption. Just give us the facts that we need to decide if your product is for us.

As we noted in Chapter 4, the French introduced just such a provision, the 'Loi Evin', for alcohol advertising in 1991, and it has worked well for the last twenty years. If you want to promote booze in France you have to restrict yourself to making verifiable statements about the characteristics of your wine, beer or spirit – such as its alcoholic strength, grape variety, ingredients, flavour and place of origin. All the information in fact that, as possible customers, we would want to know.

We need, then, a Loi Evin not just for alcohol – but for all products and services. Marketing communications should stick to provable facts. Not a big demand you might think, given that, as we also noted in Chapter 4, all advertising is supposed to be 'legal, decent, honest and truthful'. In reality it would, of course, dramatically change the face of advertising. Just think how little straight, factual information there is in the average commercial break. And the sort of sport and cultural sponsorship we discussed in Chapter 5 would vanish, as would the borrowing of beat poetry and Dow Chemicals' 'wrapping' of the Olympic stadium. Facebook stalking would be a thing of the past.

No doubt, as with the French alcohol regulations, corporate marketers will hate this idea – a response that is instructive in itself. It is a little disconcerting is it not, when there is resistance to telling the truth and sticking to facts? More fundamentally, they will resist any measure that stands in the way of sales and their ceaseless quest for 'the economic advantage which endures'; thereby confirming the conclusion we drew in Chapter 8, that having corporate marketers anywhere near the levers of political power is a catastrophically bad idea.

In their haste to defend their ad budgets, corporate marketers will remind us of how endearing and clever commercials can be, how we even have our favourite ads, as the TV shows and websites devoted to them demonstrate. Of course they are and we do; seduction works because it is enjoyable. But should we really be burning precious carbon consuming products that we otherwise wouldn't simply because a clever piece of emotional manipulation has triggered us to do so? In any case all the creative energy that goes into advertising could then be diverted to the arts and entertainment sector where it really belongs; so nothing would be lost.

Corporate marketers will also wave shrouds about the loss of sponsorship money to sport and culture. But why should these vital human endeavours be dependent on corporate business planning? Surely the sign of a civilized society is that it prioritizes the arts because they matter, not because they provide a platform for selling us stuff? In any case, in sport as in life, having lots of money bears little relation to success achieved or contribution made. The French have managed without alcohol sponsorship since 1991 and their football team has won both the World Cup and the Euro Championship; in the alcohol-sponsored UK the four home countries have, between them, only managed one semi-final appearance in either tournament.

But, as Schumacher and Čapek remind us, this issue needs to be seen not from the perspective of the corporate marketer, but from the perspective of the people. We urgently need to reduce our collective ecological footprint; our children's future depends on us doing so. We understand that this is no longer a matter of taste or choice; the warnings of scientists are too trenchant and unanimous. We know in our hearts that the ludicrous abundance in our supermarkets is exactly that, ludicrous; that, as the UNICEF report discussed in Chapter 5 showed, our children are not made any happier by an excess of stuff; that obesity is not a sign of contentment.

So, just as the focus on consumer sovereignty must go, a focus on consumer responsibility needs to emerge. And one of our first responsibilities is to make consumption decisions on hard-nosed rational grounds – not emotional whims. Requiring corporate marketers to stick to the facts in their communications campaigns will greatly assist us in this.

Furthermore they should not just be required to tell the truth, but the whole truth. When they are devising a campaign advertising agencies will typically make a note of what they call 'mandatories' – items such as the client's logo or mission statement that have to be included in the proposed ad. These mandatories should not, henceforth, be required to focus on the needs of the advertiser, but of us people and our obligation to shop responsibly. For every potential purchase decision we should have to be given full information on such things as the extent to which the goods are fairly traded, whether the producers have been properly treated (where relevant), what were the animal welfare provisions and, above all, what is the product's carbon footprint. Only when we are armed with this information can we make responsible consumption decisions.

Price and place

We need to approach price and place with exactly the same clarity and determination. Both these marketing tools should also be devoted to helping us become more responsible: to consume less and do so more ethically. It is clear from Chapter 7 that we are not good at judging prices, and are readily fooled by price promotions; corporate marketers can manipulate our shopping baskets with relative ease. This being the case, there is no justification for using these methods to promote products or services that are undesirable either individually or collectively. So BOGOFs should be on apples but not on donuts and special deals should be offered on low emission cars not gas guzzlers. And the onus should be firmly on the marketer to prove that his or her efforts will have these socially beneficial outcomes. Marketing that does not have such provenance should be treated with the same leery reticence as an unknown snake, and kept in a box until it is shown to be harmless.

Exactly the same arguments apply to point-of-sale activity and store design. Shops should be designed with people and the planet in mind, not the shareholder's returns or the CEO's bonus.

Product

There is a long tradition of controlling what products can be developed and launched on to the market. In different parts of the world, for instance, guns are tightly controlled, drugs and alcohol are completely prohibited and pharmaceuticals are heavily regulated. These constraints exist because the products in question are deemed to have high collateral costs or 'externalities'. They cause disease, offend religious sensitivities or threaten real harm if not used with great care. Given the problem of global warming we have to start defining these externalities much more broadly. Specifically, any consumption decision uses up carbon, and therefore has implications for our planetary health. Consequently any new product needs to be justified: is it worth the carbon it will cost?

There are two ways of proceeding from here. One is simply to calculate the full externalities of any product and make sure these are fully paid for by the producer. Last year the European Commission conducted a review of its options in the future fight against tobacco. One very straightforward solution which the consulting group suggested was to calculate the external costs of smoking – hospital admissions, days lost to work, litter clean up and so on – and then to charge this to the tobacco companies on a pro rata basis according to market share. Once a year Philip Morris *et al.* would get a bill for their share of billions of euros that these externalities comprise.

The other option is to calculate the externalities and decide which are worth paying and which not. Tobacco is again a good example. It might be adjudged that any industry that gets its profits from addicting children and then killing one in two of those who don't manage to quit is simply not worth having and should be closed down forthwith. Note this is not a proposal to ban tobacco – such prohibitions rarely work – it is just one to stop multinationals exploiting and profiting from it; to decide that using the full arsenal of corporate marketing to actively encourage the consumption of such a damaging product so that a small number of people can get extremely rich is a really bad idea.

As for the smoker's lungs, so for the planet: we should calculate the externalities and make sure the producer pays them or decide they are simply not affordable.

Health and safety

These suggestions may seem dramatic and far-reaching, but actually they are nothing new. The idea of controlling our economic system and ensuring that it is really working for the common good is as old as industrialization.

The risks taken in the early foundries, mines and factories would today make our hair stand on end. Highly dangerous practices that were barely even recognized as such, let alone guarded against, were common.

'Coming back brockens'[6] is a case in point. In the early days of the Durham coalfields in the north east of England, the pits comprised a central vertical shaft which, as it was sunk, passed through horizontal seams of coal. The miners worked out along these seams leaving in place columns of coal to hold up the roof. Once they reached the limits of the seam they returned to the central shaft, removing the columns as they came, because the mine owners wanted every scrap of coal they could get. This was called 'coming back brockens'. The miners' great skill was to judge just how much pillar they could remove without the roof collapsing. The dangers involved are demonstrated by the fact that 'coming back brockens' was only practised in coalfields with no habitation up above.

This hazardous method of working has, along with child chimney sweeps, been completely outlawed by modern health and safety regimes. Now, in the early years of the twenty-first century, we are just becoming aware of the full hazards of corporate marketing. Our equivalents of child chimney sweeps and coming back brockens are becoming more apparent, and we need to take action swiftly and resolutely.

Some years ago I met a senior executive from PepsiCo, who was, as he modestly explained, in charge of Russia. It turned out that he was not, in fact, Vladimir Putin, he just ran the Russian arm of Pepsi's empire. In spite of his immense power, he complained bitterly of his vulnerability to unfair competition from local producers. When PepsiCo built a factory, he explained, they had to obey all the statutory health and safety legislation – hard hats, machine guards, safe manning levels and so on – and would get severely treated by the authorities if they cut corners. ('Not that Pepsi would ever cut corners,' he hastily added.) Meanwhile the locals, who knew the mayor or whom to bribe, got away with all sorts of things.

Far from occasioning my sympathy, he just made me wonder why health and safety regulations are founded on statutory provisions but marketing regulation, where it exists at all, is time and again left to voluntary codes. If someone were to propose that the UK should repeal the Factory Acts and replace them with a voluntary code on child labour he or she would be a laughing stock; yet the beverage alcohol industry argues that children are perfectly well protected from its marketing by just such voluntary codes.

Beyond regulation

Regulation on its own however is never going to be sufficient. The massive problems that now face us will not be solved by the marketing equivalent of hard hats and machine guards, important though these are. As we have noted, we don't just need to contain corporate marketing, we need to re-engineer it so that its focus is on people not profits. This will take immense determination and resolution.

It will also, inevitably, result in a power vacuum. Corporate influence has become the hallmark of rich capitalist economies, and it will have to be replaced by power from a more benign and civilized source. In a democracy the obvious and legitimate place to turn to is to us: ordinary people. All the great thinkers, poets and leaders we have consulted in this book – Huxley, Steinbeck, Roy, Eisenhower, Schumacher, Burns, Bukowski, Neruda, Čapek, Orwell – are, in their own ways, agreed on this.

So how do we give power back to the people?

This will require a combination of all the ideas we have considered in the last three chapters: personal responsibility and ethicality; individual and collective resilience and action sustained by grassroots social marketing; and the containment, redirection and shrinkage of the corporation and its marketing. Others have come to very similar conclusions. In a detailed review[7] on how to motivate sustainable consumption, funded by the UK Government, Professor Tim Jackson concluded that progress will depend on movement on four key fronts: statutory measures, education to change people's attitudes, small group/community organization and ethical appeals – along with some robust controls of the commercial sector.

Nancy Roberts, in a more focused analysis of citizen participation, also argues that regaining an active part in the direction and flow of our own lives is crucial. The option of passive consumption is not just stultifying, it is an abdication of responsibility. She also points out that exercises in citizen participation, when done well, can be marvellous: 'many who witness them are awed by the fundamental wisdom of people, who, when given the chance, are able to rise to the occasion and publicly deliberate about the common good'.[8]

'When done well' is an important rider. Neither Roberts nor Jackson is in any doubt about the challenges of doing this. Both call for a cautious and carefully monitored approach. They are both right; these are critical issues and it would be foolish not to take precautions. Nonetheless the need for change is urgent, and the change will have to be great.

In April 2009 Gordon Brown, the then UK prime minister, called together a Summit of the G20 countries to try and address the financial crisis. It was a bold move, involving dashes to three continents to try and reach a consensus. Despite some early tensions – France and Germany for instance expressed concerns about the process – the meeting did produce some real hope. As the BBC reported,[9] for example, it drew a vital acknowledgement from the US of a need for change: 'President Barack Obama ... acknowledged that the "Washington consensus" of unfettered globalization and deregulation was now outmoded, and called for a more balanced approach to regulating markets rather than letting them run free.' It took some small steps towards the global regulation of financial markets.

Nonetheless with the benefit of hindsight, the Summit was not a success: the financial crisis has continued unabated; Obama's call for balance, echoing those of Eisenhower back in 1961, has had the same lack of impact. Arguably it failed for three reasons. First, it was too rushed – the Summit only lasted a weekend and, even allowing for the background work of civil servants, this is not enough time to rethink the enormous complexities of the financial sector. Second, it only included an elite; a much broader constituency is needed to bring about significant change. Third, it addressed the wrong question: we don't need to fix the banks, we need to completely rethink our way of life.

Business as unusual

Now imagine if you will that Brown, who then had just over twelve months left in office, had acknowledged this much more fundamental malaise and the need for systemic overhaul, and had announced that he would be devoting the rest of his prime ministerial term to facilitating a debate about how we alter course. Suppose he hadn't just invited a leadership elite to London, but a broad cross-section of NGOs, grassroots organizations, faith groups, trade unions, academics, climate scientists, youth groups, indigenous people. Suppose we had all been given a voice. Suppose that the only ones excluded had been the vested interests. The result would no doubt have been chaotic. There would have been setbacks and fallings-out. But at least we would have started the journey.

On a much more limited level I had my own experience of the power of such inclusive, bottom-up thinking a few years ago. Colleagues and I were working with the European Commission on a campaign to combat smoking. As part of the project we were required to work with the European Youth Parliament (EYP) which wanted to produce its own tobacco control manifesto. As 'experts' we were a little uneasy about this; what would these young people know about the technicalities of the smoking epidemic and the political machinations of tobacco multinationals? There was an obvious danger for naïvety and woolly thinking. These fears were reinforced when the president of the EYP turned out to be a smoker, whose first concern was not public health, but smokers' rights.

Our concerns and our conceit were completely misplaced. The Youth Parliament is a quintessentially inclusive organization made up of sensitive and intelligent individuals. The president proceeded to consult with all twenty-seven of his EC-based national committees. Each one held its own two-day conference where members were able to engage with the key issues and learn, for instance, that notions of freedom and addiction do not sit comfortably together; that the tobacco industry has lied and cheated for decades; that most smokers desperately want to quit – and all of them hate the idea of their own children starting. These conferences each comprised hundreds of delegates yet were able to develop a consensual tobacco control plan. These twenty-seven documents were brought together at a Europe-wide conference and, again with hundreds of delegates and again consensually, were successfully melded into one three-page manifesto. This proved to be more radical and forward-thinking than anything then being debated by us 'experts' (it anticipated plain packaging for cigarettes, for instance, which is only now becoming a reality in Australia) and its impeccable provenance meant that it was readily accepted by the European Commission. It turned out that the Youth Parliament had both the wits and the muscle to make a difference.

What can be done for public health can also – must also – be done for our way of life. The challenges are immense, but the consequences of inaction, of business as usual, are unthinkable.

NOTES

Preface

1 Steinbeck, John (1993 – first published 1939) *The Grapes of Wrath*. London: Everyman's Library, pp.38–9.
2 Thomas, M. J. (1999) 'Thoughts on building a just and stake holding society', paper presented at 20th Anniversary Conference, Alliance of Universities for Democracy, Budapest (Hungary), 7 November.
3 2010 data taken from annual reports.

1 The soft power of marketing

1 This is adapted from Baggini, J. (2005) *The Pig That Wants to Be Eaten: And Ninety Nine Other Thought Experiments*. London: Granta, Chapter 22.
2 Steinbeck, *The Grapes of Wrath*, op. cit., p.39.
3 Ibid., p.40.
4 Bakan, J. (2004) *The Corporation: The Pathological Pursuit of Profit and Power*. Toronto: Penguin (Canada).
5 www.scientificamerican.com/article.cfm?id=what-psychopath-means (accessed 9 December 2011).
6 http://www.who.int/tobacco/mpower/mpower_report_tobacco_crisis_2008.pdf (accessed 9 December 2011).
7 http://www.who.int/mediacentre/news/releases/2011/alcohol_20110211/en/index.html (accessed 9 December 2011).
8 http://www.usatoday.com/yourlife/fitness/2010-10-18-obesity-costs_N.htm (accessed 10 January 2012).
9 Eisenhower, Dwight D. (1961) 'Farewell Address'. http://www.youtube.com/watch?v=8y06NSBBRtY (accessed 9 December 2011).
10 Forster, E. M. (1995) *Howard's End*. Bath: Bath Press, p.245.
11 Schumacher, E. F. (1993) *Small is Beautiful: A Study of Economics as if People Mattered*. London: Vintage.
12 Baker, M. J. (2003) 'One More Time – What is Marketing?' in Baker M. J. (Ed.) *The Marketing Book*. (Fifth Edition.) Oxford: Butterworth-Heinemann, p.5.
13 Miller, A. (1949) *Death of a Salesman*. New York: Viking.

14 Packard, V. (2007) *The Hidden Persuaders*. Brooklyn, New York: IG Publishing.
15 Baker, op. cit., p.5.
16 http://www.aegisplc.com/media/grouppressreleases/2011/2011-08-25a.aspx
17 http://www.publications.parliament.uk/pa/cm200910/cmselect/cmhealth/memo/alcohol/al81memo.pdf
18 Ibid., p.5.
19 Bradshaw, T. (2011) 'Facebook Strikes Diageo Advertising Deal' in *Financial Times*, 18 September 2011. http://www.ft.com/intl/cms/s/2/d044ea24-e203-11e0-9915-00144feabdc0.html#axzz1irtgC58l (accessed 9 December 2011).
20 Christian Aid (2004) *Behind the Mask: The Real Face of Corporate Social Responsibility*, p.5. http://www.st-andrews.ac.uk/~csearweb/aptopractice/Behind-the-mask.pdf (accessed 9 December 2011).
21 http://www.brainyquote.com/quotes/keywords/hundred.html (accessed 9 December 2011).
22 Eisenhower, op. cit.
23 Steinbeck, *The Grapes of Wrath*, op. cit., p.48.

2 The customer always comes second

1 Jobber, D. (2001) *Principles and Practice of Marketing*. (Third Edition.) Maidenhead: McGraw-Hill, p.4.
2 http://www.marketingweek.co.uk/analysis/features/creating-a-new-roadmap-for-one-ford%E2%80%99s-marketing/3019775.article (accessed 9 December 2011).
3 Huxley, A. (1958) *Brave New World Revisited*, Section VI: The Arts of Selling. New York: HarperCollins.
4 Wensley, R. (2003) 'The Basics of Marketing Strategy' in Baker, M. J. (Ed.) *The Marketing Book*. (Fifth Edition.) Oxford: Butterworth-Heinemann, p.53.
5 Scottish Government (2008) *Changing Scotland's Relationship with Alcohol: A Discussion Paper on our Strategic Approach*, p.25. http://scotland.gov.uk/Resource/Doc/227785/0061677.pdf (accessed 9 December 2011).
6 Schumacher, *Small is Beautiful*, op. cit., p.215.
7 Bakan, *The Corporation*, op. cit., p.49.
8 http://senate.ucsf.edu/2002-2003/NicotineIsNotAddictive-2.mov (YouTube: http://www.youtube.com/watch?v=A6B1q22R438) (accessed 9 December 2011).
9 'Smoking is a Habit of Addiction', p.1. http://www.henrywaxman.house.gov/UploadedFiles/Smoking_is_a_habit_of_addiction.pdf (accessed 9 December 2011).
10 Schumacher, *Small is Beautiful*, op. cit., p.215.
11 Levs, J. (2008) 'Big Three Auto CEOs Flew Private Jets to Ask for Taxpayer Money' in *CNN*, 19 November 2008. http://articles.cnn.com/2008-11-19/us/autos.ceo.jets_1_private-jets-auto-industry-test-vote?_s=PM:US (accessed 3 October 2011).
12 CAAT (2011) 'UK Arms Sales to Middle East Include Tear Gas and Crowd Control Ammunition to Bahrain and Libya' in *Campaign Against Arms Trade*, 17 February 2011. http://www.caat.org.uk/press/archive.php?url=20110217prs (accessed 9 December 2011).
13 Higham, C. (2007) *Trading with the Enemy: The Nazi-American Money Plot 1933–1949*. Lincoln: iUniverse, p.xv.
14 Mosher, James F. (2012) 'JD Joe Camel in a Bottle: Diageo, the Smirnoff Brand, and the Transformation of the Youth Alcohol Market' in *American Journal of Public Health*, 102(1), January 2012, pp.56–63.
15 Hastings, G. B. and Angus, K. (2009) *Under the Influence: The Damaging Effect of Alcohol Marketing on Young People*. BMA Board of Science.
16 http://www.diageo.com/en-row/ourbusiness/ourpeople/Pages/default.aspx (accessed 9 December 2011).
17 Eisenhower ('Farewell Address' 1961), op. cit.

18 Jack, I. (2011) 'Dinner at Downton Abbey Has Livelier Debates than Party Conferences Today' in *The Guardian*, 30 September 2011. http://www.guardian.co.uk/commentisfree/2011/sep/30/conference-season-alessio-rastani-goldman-sachs/print (accessed 9 December 2011).
19 Hastings and Angus, op. cit. (accessed 9 December 2011).
20 Solley, S. (2005) 'Diageo Backs Bourbon RTD Debut with Direct Activity' in *Marketing Magazine*, 24 August 2005. http://www.marketingmagazine.co.uk/news/492180/Diageo-backs-bourbon-RTD-debut-direct-activity/?DCMP=ILC-SEARCH (accessed 9 December 2011).
21 Giuliani, R. W. (2007) 'Toward a Realistic Peace. Defending Civilization and Defeating Terrorists by Making the International System Work' in *Foreign Affairs*, September/October 2007, p.10. http://gees.org/documentos/Documen-02566.pdf (accessed 9 December 2011).
22 Zimmet, P. (2000) 'Globalization, Coca-Colonization and the Chronic Disease Epidemic: Can the Doomsday Scenario Be Averted?' in *Journal of International Medicine*, 247(3), March 2000, pp.301–10. http://www.ncbi.nlm.nih.gov/pubmed/10762445 (accessed 9 December 2011).
23 Neruda, P. (1950) 'La United Fruit Co'. Trans. Jack Schmitt in Tapscott, S. (Ed.) *Twentieth-Century Latin American Poetry*. Austin, TX: University of Texas Press, p.214.
24 Lawrence, F. (2010) 'Bitter Fruit: The Truth About Supermarket Pineapple' in *The Guardian*, 2 October 2010. http://www.guardian.co.uk/business/2010/oct/02/truth-about-pineapple-production (accessed 9 December 2011).

3 A tyranny of choice

1 Whitman, W. (1881–2) 'Song of Myself' in *Leaves of Grass*. Boston: James R. Osgood, p.54.
2 Haire, M. (1950) 'Projective Techniques in Marketing Research' in *Journal of Marketing*, 14, pp.649–56.
3 Sennett, Richard (2006) *The Culture of the New Capitalism*. New Haven: Yale University, p.161.
4 The NHS Information Centre, Lifestyles Statistics (2011) *Statistics on Obesity, Physical Activity and Diet: England, 2011*. 24 February 2011. http://www.ic.nhs.uk/webfiles/publications/003_Health_Lifestyles/opad11/Statistics_on_Obesity_Physical_Activity_and_Diet_England_2011_revised_Aug11.pdf (accessed 9 December 2011).
5 http://www.abs.gov.au/ausstats/abs@.nsf/Lookup/by%20Subject/1370.0~2010~Chapter~Obesity%20(4.1.6.6.3) (accessed 9 December 2011).
6 Wallace, D. F. (2008) 'Plain Old Untrendy Troubles and Emotions' in *The Guardian*, 20 September 2008. http://www.guardian.co.uk/books/2008/sep/20/fiction (accessed 9 December 2011).
7 The Dalai Lama (and many other Buddhists).
8 Wallace, op. cit.
9 http://www.olay.com/skin-care-products/total-effects/fragrance-free-daily-moisturizer?pid=075609001772 (accessed 9 December 2011).
10 Miller, *Death of a Salesman*, Act 1, op. cit.
11 Sennett, op. cit., p.171.
12 Quote from Huxley's *Ape and Essence* (1948) in the essay 'Aldous Huxley' by David Bradshaw in Huxley, A. (1994) *Brave New World*. London: Flamingo Modern Classics.
13 Shah, A. (2010) 'Poverty Facts and Stats' in *Global Issues*, 20 September 2010. http://www.globalissues.org/article/26/poverty-facts-and-stats (accessed 9 December 2011).
14 http://www.youtube.com/watch?v=Ezk0e1VL80o (accessed 9 December 2011).

4 Not exactly lying...

1 http://www.rbs.com/media/brand-communication/sponsorship.ashx (accessed 26 April 2011).
2 http://www.scottishrugby.org/content/view/55/47/ (accessed 26 April 2011).
3 http://www.tobacco.org/News/9910tobaccowars.html (accessed 18 October 2011).
4 Stewart, D. W. and Kamins, M. A. (2006) 'Marketing Communications' in Weitz, B. and Wensley, R. (Eds) *Handbook of Marketing*. London: Sage, p.283.
5 Ibid., p.287.
6 Forster, E. M. (1995) *Howard's End*. Bath: Bath Press, p.434.
7 Goldacre, B. (2011) 'Bad Science: Cherry Picking Is Bad. At Least Warn Us When You Do It' in *The Guardian*, 24 September 2011. http://www.badscience.net/2011/09/cherry-picking-is-bad-at-least-warn-us-when-you-do-it/#more-2385 (accessed 9 December 2011).
8 Hastings, G., Stead, M., McDermott, L., Forsyth, A., MacKintosh, A., Rayner, M., Godfrey, C., Caraher, M. and Angus, K. (2003). *Review of Research on the Effects of Food Promotion to Children – Final Report and Appendices*. Prepared for the Food Standards Agency. Stirling: Institute for Social Marketing. http://www.ism.stir.ac.uk (accessed 9 December 2011).
9 *Financial Times*, 26 September 2003, p.7.
10 *The Times*, 27 September 2003, p.3.
11 Ibid., p.3.
12 Young, B. (2003) *Advertising and Food Choice in Children: A Review of the Literature*. Report prepared for the Food Advertising Unit.
13 Paliwoda, S. and Crawford, I. (2003) *An Analysis of the Hastings Review*. Commissioned by the Food Advertising Unit (FAU) for the Advertising Association. http://www.adassoc.org.uk/hastings_review_analysis_dec03.pdf (accessed 19 June 2006).
14 Food Standards Agency (2003a) http://www.food.gov.uk/multimedia/webpage/academicreview (accessed 9 December 2011).
15 Food Standards Agency (2003b) http://food.resultspage.com/search?p=R&srid=S2%2d2&lbc=food&w=paliwoda&url=http%3a%2f%2fwww%2efood%2egov%2euk%2fmultimedia%2fpdfs%2fpaliwodacritique%2epdf&rk=1&uid=171613895&sid=2&ts=v2&rsc=qFgSz0DVJSuCqC5T&method=and&mainresults=mt%5fmainresults%5fyes (accessed 9 December 2011).
16 http://www.aclsrecertificationonline.com/acls-online-library-tobacco-resources-online-fact-sheets.html (accessed 9 December 2011).
17 NCI http://www.cancer.gov/ (accessed 9 December 2011).
18 http://www.1stapproach.com/about.html (accessed 9 December 2011).
19 All these quotes and the details can be found in this paper: Moodie, C. and Hastings, G. B. (2010) 'Making the Pack the Hero, Tobacco Industry Response to Marketing Restrictions in the UK: Findings from a Long-term Audit' in *International Journal of Mental Health and Addiction*, 9(1), pp.24–38.
20 Ford, A. (2011) *The Importance of Tobacco Packaging for Young People*. Presentation made to the Scottish Tobacco Control Alliance. University of Edinburgh, May 2011.

5 Suffer the little children

1 Schumacher, E. F. (1993) *Small is Beautiful: A Study of Economics as if People Mattered*. London: Vintage, p.63.
2 Huxley, Aldous (1994) *Brave New World*. London: Flamingo Modern Classics, p.25.
3 Foxall, G. R. and Goldsmith, R. E. (1994) *Consumer Psychology for Marketing*. London: Routledge, p.203.
4 UNICEF (2007) *Report Card 7*. http://www.unicef-irc.org/publications/http://www.unicef-irc.org/publications/pdf/rc7_eng.pdf (accessed 9 December 2011).

5 Nairn, A. (2011) *Children's Wellbeing in the UK, Sweden and Spain: The Role of Inequality and Materialism*. London: Ipsos MORI, p.1. http://www.unicef.org.uk/ http://www.unicef.org.uk/Documents/Publications/IPSOS_UNICEF_ChildWell Beingreport.pdf (accessed 9 December 2011).

6 Ibid., p.3.

7 Ibid., p.4

8 Ibid.

9 Ibid., p.2

10 Ibid., p.1.

11 Ibid., p.2.

12 Pine, K. T. and Veasev, T. (2003) 'Conceptualizing and Assessing Young Children's Knowledge of Television Advertising within a Framework of Implicit and Explicit Knowledge' in *Journal of Marketing Management*, 19, pp.459–73.

13 Schumacher, op. cit., p.63.

14 Foxall and Goldsmith, op. cit., pp.111–12.

15 http://www.publications.parliament.uk/pa/cm200910/cmselect/cmhealth/memo/ alcohol/al81memo.pdf (accessed 9 December 2011).

16 Hastings and Angus, *Under the Influence*, op. cit.

17 http://www.nuts.co.uk/magazine (accessed 9 December 2011).

18 R. Fuke of Brey Leino (2009) *Uncorrected Transcript of Oral Evidence. House of Commons Minutes of Evidence Taken before Health Committee 'Alcohol' Thursday 9 July 2009*: Q699.

19 Millward Brown (2009) *FHM Reader Analysis*. 1 April 2008. Prepared for Diageo GB Smirnoff F08 Research, Document #17, pp.2–3. Diageo, 21 May 2009.

20 http://marketing.about.com/cs/brandmktg/a/whatisbranding.htm (accessed 10 January 2012).

21 Lane Keller, K. (2006) 'Branding and Brand Equity' in Weitz, B. and Wensley, R. (Eds) *Handbook of Marketing*. London: Sage, p.169.

22 Ibid., p.170.

23 DiFranza, J. R. (1991) 'RJR Nabisco's Cartoon Camel Promotes Camel Cigarettes to Children' in *JAMA*, 266(22), pp.349–53.

24 Robinson, T. N., Borzekowski, D. L., Matheson, D. M. and Kraemer, H. C. (2007) 'Effects of Fast Food Branding on Young Children's Taste Preferences', in *Archives of Pediatrics & Adolescent Medicine*, 161(8), pp.792–7.

25 Huxley, *Brave New World*, op. cit.

26 Molson Coors Brewing Ltd (2009) *Primary Purpose Behind Each Platform*. Document S7, Folder 1, Music Strategy Documents Brand Plans 2006, rfids slide 1 of 12. Molson Coors Brewing Company (UK) Limited, 14 May 2009.

27 Molson Coors Brewing Ltd (2009) *Carling AMG Venues Activity 2006. Emotional Connections Opportunities*, p.5 of 20. Document S3, Folder 1, Music Strategy Documents Brand Plans 2005. Molson Coors Brewing Company (UK) Limited, 14 May 2009.

28 Ibid.

29 Ibid., p.9.

30 Mobious (2009) *Carling Objective: Evolve Passive Respect to Active Preference*. Slide 5 of 11. Document S10, Folder 5 Sport Strategy Documents 2006. Molson Coors Brewing Company (UK) Limited, 14 May.

31 Hastings, G., Brooks, O., Stead, M., Angus, K., Anker, T. and Farrell, T. (2010) 'Alcohol Advertising: The Last Chance Saloon' in *British Medical Journal*, 340, 20 January 2010, p.186.

32 Ibid.

33 Advertising Standards Authority (2007) *ASA Adjudications Coors Brewers Ltd t/a Carling*. 2 May 2007. http://www.asa.org.uk/ASA}action/Adjudications/2007/5/Coors–Brewers–Ltd/TF_ADJ_42658.aspx (accessed 8 September 2009).

34 Ibid.

35 Ibid.

36 http://www.youtube.com/watch?v=pnNblizjuEK (accessed 9 December 2011).
37 Bukowski, C. (1996) 'The Laughing Heart' in *Betting on the Muse: Poems and Stories*. Santa Rosa, CA: Black Sparrow Press.
38 http://www.levi.co.za/Press/PressDetails.aspx?id=1255 (accessed 2 July 2012).
39 Whitman, W. (1881–2) 'Song of Myself' in *Leaves of Grass*. Boston: James R. Osgood and Company, pp.29–79.
40 The Olympic Charter, http://www.olympic.org/Documents/olympic_charter_en.pdf, p.10 (accessed 9 December 2011).
41 Whitman, 'Song of Myself', op. cit.
42 http://www.olympic.org/sponsorship (accessed 9 December 2011).
43 Jobber, *Principles and Practice of Marketing*, op. cit., p.506.
44 The Olympic Charter, http://www.olympic.org/Documents/olympic_charter_en.pdf, p.10 (accessed 9 December 2011).
45 Foxall and Goldsmith (1994) *Consumer Psychology*, p.114.

6 Digital redemption?

1 Harris, J. L., Schwartz, M. B. and Brownell, K. D. (2011) *Evaluating Sugary Drink Nutrition and Marketing to Youth*. New Haven: Yale Rudd Center for Food Policy and Obesity, November 2011.
2 Ibid., p.76.
3 Ibid., p.87.
4 http://www.youtube.com/watch?v=FEpFlymH6RQ (accessed 9 December 2011).
5 http://www.innocentdrinks.co.uk/us/ (accessed 3 November 2011).
6 Eleftheriou-Smith, L.-M. (2011) 'Innocent Kids Launches Apps for Children' in *Marketing Magazine*, 28 September 2011. http://www.marketingmagazine.co.uk/news/1095718/Innocent-Kids-launches-apps-children/ (accessed 9 December 2011).
7 Harris et al., op. cit., pp.34–5.
8 http://www.innocentdrinks.co.uk/us/our_vehicles/index.cfm (accessed 3 November 2011).
9 Wu, Tim (2011) *The Master Switch*. New York: Vintage.
10 Swedberg, C. (2010) 'RFID Helps Make Friends for Israeli Teens' in *RFID Journal*, 25 August 2010. http://www.rfidjournal.com/article/view/7830/1 (accessed 9 December 2011).
11 Ibid.
12 Ibid.
13 http://knol.google.com/k/rfid-technology-in-marketing# (accessed 9 December 2011).
14 Ibid.
15 http://www.rfidjournal.com/article/view/7830/2 (accessed 9 December 2011).
16 Ibid.
17 Gold, T. (2011) 'The Deification of Steve Jobs is Apple's Greatest Marketing Triumph to Date' in *The Guardian*, 21 October 2011. http://www.guardian.co.uk/commentisfree/2011/oct/21/tanya-gold-steve-jobs-deification-apple?INTCMP=SRCH (accessed 9 December 2011).
18 Fournier, S. and Lee, L. (2009) 'Getting Brand Communities Right' in *Harvard Business Review*, April 2009. http://www1.hbr.org/products/R0904K/R0904Kp4.pdf (accessed 4 November 2011).
19 Ibid.
20 Ibid., p.107.
21 Anker, T. B. and Cappel, K. (2011) 'Ethical Challenges in Commercial Social Marketing' in Hastings, G., Angus, K. and Bryant, C. (Eds) *The Sage Handbook of Social Marketing*. London: Sage, p.294.

22 Schau, H. J., Muñiz, A. M. and Arnould, E. J. (2009) 'How Brand Community Practices Create Value' in *Journal of Marketing*, Vol. 73, September 2009, pp.30–51.
23 http://hbr.org/2009/04/getting-brand-communities-right/ar/1 (accessed 9 December 2011).
24 Reynolds, J. (2010) 'Radox Signs Up as First Sponsor of Mumsnet Book Club' in *Marketing Magazine*, 28 October 2010. http://marketingmagazine.co.uk/news/1037501/Radox-signs-first-sponsor-mumsnet/3028152.article (accessed 9 December 2011).
25 Longton, C. (2011) 'Viewpoint: Carrie Longton, Co-Founder, Mumsnet' in *Marketing Week*, 6 July 2011. http://www.marketingweek.co.uk/sectors/industry/viewpoint-carrie-longton-co-founder-mumsnet/3028152.article (accessed 9 December 2011).
26 Greenwood, C. (2011) 'The Battle of Tesco' in *Mail Online*, 26 April 2011. http://www.dailymail.co.uk/news/article-1379581/Riot-Bristol-Tesco-petrol-bombed-160-officers-swoop-arrest-4-squatters.html (accessed 9 December 2011).
27 Fournier and Lee, op. cit.
28 Gupta, A. (2011) 'Arundhati Roy: The People Who Created the Crisis Will Not Be the Ones Who Come Up with a Solution' in *The Guardian*, 30 November 2011. http://www.guardian.co.uk/world/2011/nov/30/arundhati-roy-interview (accessed 9 December 2011).
29 Grindle, M. (2011), personal communication.
30 Ibid.
31 Executive Pay Watch (2011) *CEO Pay: Feeding the 1%*. http://www.aflcio.org/corporatewatch/paywatch/index.cfm (accessed 9 December 2011).
32 Foxall and Goldsmith (1994) *Consumer Psychology*, p.1.

7 A very mixed blessing

1 Brassington, F. and Pettitt, S. (2003) *Principles of Marketing*. (Third Edition.) Harlow: Pearson Education Limited, p.392.
2 Doyle, P. (2003) 'Managing the Marketing Mix' in Baker M. J. (Ed.) *The Marketing Book*. (Fifth Edition.) Oxford: Butterworth-Heinemann, pp.304–5.
3 Ofir, C. and Winer, R. S. (2006) 'Pricing: Economic and Behavioral Models' in Weitz, B. and Wensley, R. (Eds) *Handbook of Marketing*. London: Sage, p.271.
4 Ibid. p.271.
5 Cialdini, Robert (1984) *The Psychology of Influence*. New York: William Morrow.
6 *Marketing Magazine* (2009) 'Inaugural Study Claims Brand Owners Spend £25.6 billion on BOGOFs and Other Sales Promotions' in *Marketing Magazine*, 19 October 2009. http://www.marketingmagazine.co.uk/news/946464/ (accessed 9 December 2011).
7 Peattie, S. and Peattie, K. (2003) 'Sales Promotion' in Baker M. J. (Ed.) *The Marketing Book*. (Fifth Edition.) Oxford: Butterworth-Heinemann, p.458.
8 Ibid. p.459.
9 Shu-Ling, L., Yung-Cheng, S. and Chia-Hsien, C. (2009) 'The Effects of Sales Promotion Strategy, Product Appeal and Consumer Traits on Reminder Impulse Buying Behaviour' in *International Journal of Consumer Studies*, 33(3), May 2009, p.274.
10 Doyle, op. cit., p.298.
11 Doyle, op. cit., p.300.
12 BBC News (2001) 'Coke on Tap at Home' in *BBC News Online*, 18 March 2001. http://news.bbc.co.uk/2/hi/business/1228266.stm (accessed 9 December 2011).
13 Holmes, C. (2011) 'Is that an Elephant in the Room?' Presentation at *Marketing to Children: Implications for Obesity*, UK Association for the Study of Obesity (ASO) Conference, University College London, 7 June 2011.
14 Chandon, P., Hutchinson, J. W., Bradlow, E. T. and Young, S. H. (2009) 'Does In-Store Marketing Work? Effects of the Number and Position of Shelf Facings on Brand Attention and Evaluation at the Point of Purchase' in *Journal of Marketing*, Vol. 73, November 2009, p.15.

15 Ibid.
16 McGoldrick, P. J. (2003) 'Retailing' in Baker M. J. (Ed.) *The Marketing Book*. (Fifth Edition.) Oxford: Butterworth-Heinemann, p.796.
17 Ibid. p.796.
18 Onwulata, C. I., Smith, P. W., Konstance, R. P. and Holsinger, V. H. (2001) 'Incorporation of Whey Products in Extruded Corn, Potato or Rice Snacks' in *USA Food Research International*, 34, pp.679–87.
19 Doyle, op. cit., p.288.
20 Ibid. p.300.
21 Ibid. p.291.
22 Baker, Michael and Saren, Mike (2010) *Marketing Theory: A Student Text*. London: Sage, p.189.
23 Doyle, op. cit., p.295.
24 Richardson, F. (2001) 'Packages: The Money or the Options' in *Business Review Weekly*, 23(20), 25 May 2001.
25 O'Driscoll, A. and Murray, J. A. (1998) 'The Changing Nature of Theory and Practice in Marketing: On the Value of Synchrony' in *Journal of Marketing Management*, 14, pp.391–416.
26 http://sftfc.globalink.org/internat.html (accessed 10 January 2012).

8 Marketing to power

1 http://www.sing365.com/music/lyric.nsf/The-Old-Dope-Peddler-lyrics-Tom-Lehrer/4C1F7B5A27436FAF48256A7D0024C395 (accessed 9 December 2011).
2 Adkins, S. (2003) 'Cause-Related Marketing: Who Cares Wins' in Baker M. J. (Ed.) *The Marketing Book*. (Fifth Edition.) Oxford: Butterworth-Heinemann, p.674.
3 Ibid., p.670.
4 Worth, J. (2007) 'Corporate Responsibility: Companies who Care?' in *New Internationalist*, December 2007, pp.5–6.
5 Christian Aid, *Behind the Mask*, op. cit. p.5.
6 Porter, M. E. and Kramer, M. R. (2011) 'Creating Shared Value' in *Harvard Business Review*, January–February 2011, p.64.
7 Adkins, op. cit., p.686.
8 Ibid., p.686.
9 Spencer, R. (2007) 'Spinning Out of Control' in *New Internationalist*, December 2007, p.8.
10 Adkins, op. cit., p.686.
11 http://www.alternet.org/story/10129/ (accessed 9 December 2011).
12 BBC News (2006) 'BAE Goes Big on "Green" Weapons' in *BBC News Online*, 26 September 2006. http://news.bbc.co.uk/go/pr/fr/-/2/hi/technology/6081486.stm (accessed 3 December 2011).
13 http://www.publications.parliament.uk/pa/cm200910/cmselect/cmhealth/memo/alcohol/al81memo.pdf, p.5. (accessed 9 December 2011).
14 Babor, T., Caetano, R., Casswell, S. et al. (2003) *Alcohol: No Ordinary Commodity. Research and Public Policy*. Oxford: Oxford University Press.
15 Adkins, op. cit., p.687.
16 http://www.worldwildlife.org/what/partners/corporate/Coke/ (accessed 9 December 2011).
17 https://www.arctichome.com/web/index.html#// (accessed 9 December 2011).
18 http://www.youtube.com/watch?v=kK3rb41c8yE (accessed 9 December 2011).
19 Ibid.
20 http://www.youtube.com/watch?v=lkR0WDvFK1Q (accessed 9 December 2011).
21 Gupta, Arundhati Roy interview, op. cit.
22 Christian Aid, op. cit., p.2.

23 Amnesty International and CEHRD (2011) *The True 'Tragedy': Delays and Failures in Tackling Oil Spills in the Niger Delta*, 10 November 2011. London: Amnesty International, p.11.
24 Rowley, E. (2011) 'Never Mind the Euro Bailout, Worry About Growth, Says Shell' in *The Telegraph*, 27 October 2011. http://www.telegraph.co.uk/finance/newsbysector/energy/oilandgas/8852496/Never-mind-the-euro-bailout-worry-about-growth-says-Shell.html (accessed 28 November 2011).
25 Save the Children and The Corporate Responsibility Coalition (2007) *Why Corporate Social Responsibility is Failing Children*. London: Save the Children and CORE, p.3. http://www.savethechildren.org.uk/sites/default/files/docs/Why_CSR_is_failing_children_1.pdf (accessed 30 November 2011).
26 Worth, op. cit., p.7.
27 Gay, G. (2011) *Tobacco Reporter*, October, p.94.
28 'The United Nations' "Partnership" with Corporations Is a Travesty, Argues Jean Ziegler, UN Special Rapporteur on the Right to Food'. Interview by Jess Worth in *New Internationalist*, December 2007, p.10.
29 Ibid.
30 Porter and Kramer, op. cit., p.74.
31 Ibid., p.64.
32 Ibid., p.77.
33 Ibid., p.65.
34 Higham, *Trading with the Enemy*, op. cit., p.xvii.
35 S&C Saatchi. Amber Leaf: Gallaher Brief, 4 December 1997.
36 Ballinger, J. (2007) 'Just Don't Do It!' in *New Internationalist*, December 2007, p.11.
37 Wong, Grace, Youdan, Ben and Wong, Ron (2010) 'Misuse of the Official Information Act by the tobacco industry in New Zealand' in *Tobacco Control*, 19: pp.346–7. Originally published online 7 July 2010.

9 In search of solutions

1 Steinbeck, *The Grapes of Wrath*, op. cit., p.359.
2 Orwell, G. (1970) *Collected Essays*. (Second Edition.) London: Secker & Warburg, p.48.
3 Baker, P. (2010) 'Euro Crisis' in *Slugger O'Toole*, 18 May 2010. http://sluggerotoole.com/2010/05/18/euro-crisis-%E2%80%9Cwe-all-know-what-to-do-but-we-don%E2%80%99t-know-how-to-get-re-elected-once-we-have-done-it-%E2%80%9D/ (accessed 9 December 2011).
4 Schumacher, *Small is Beautiful*, op. cit., p.252.
5 Blake, William (1792) *London*. For the full poem consult any good anthology.
6 Steinbeck, op. cit., p.265.
7 Schumacher, op. cit., p.250.
8 Fairtrade International http://www.fairtrade.net/ (accessed 9 December 2011).
9 Huxley, *Brave New World* (Foreword), op. cit.
10 Schumacher, op. cit., p.41.
11 Steinbeck, op. cit., p.264.
12 www.brainyquote.com/quotes/authors/a/aneurin_bevan.html (accessed 9 December 2011).
13 Orwell, op. cit., p.48.

10 Power to the people

1 Roy, Arundhati (2011) http://www.guardian.co.uk, 30 November 2011 (accessed 9 December 2011).
2 http://www.unitedearth.com.au/tipiwisdom.html (accessed 9 December 2011).

3 Hastings, G. (2006) 'Building Social Relationships' in Saren, M. (Ed.) *Marketing Graffiti*. Oxford: Butterworth-Heinemann, pp.53–8.
4 Layard, P. R. G. (2005) *Happiness: Lessons from a New Science*. London: Allen Lane, p.98.
5 Lazer, W. and Kelley, E. (1973). *Social Marketing: Perspectives and Viewpoints*. Homewood, IL: Richard D. Irwin, p.ix.
6 Lefebvre, C. (2009) 'Social Models for Marketing: Building Communities' in *On Social Marketing and Social Change* (Weblog), 20 October 2009. http://social marketing.blogs.com/r_craiig_lefebvres_social/2009/10/social-models-for-marketing-building-communities.html (accessed 26 January 2011).
7 http://www.amnesty.org.au/poverty/comments/22681/ (accessed 9 December 2011).
8 Open University and BBC (2000) 'Looking for a Future: Sustainability and Change in the Andes' in *U213 International Development: Challenges for a World in Transition* (DVD recording). Milton Keyes: The Open University.
9 Ibid.
10 Ibid.
11 Ibid.
12 Roy, Arundhati, *The Guardian*, op. cit.
13 Roy, Arundhati (2011) quoted in *New Internationalist*, October 2011, p.30.
14 Roy, Arundhati, *The Guardian*, op. cit.
15 Grindle, M. (2004) 'At What Stage is our Understanding of the Interactive Entertainment Development Industry in Scotland?' Paper presented at The Scottish Media and Communication Association Annual Conference, 3 December 2004, University of Abertay, Dundee.
16 Moran, E. and Gossieaux, F. (2010) 'Marketing in a Hyper-social World: The Tribalization of Business Study and Characteristics of Successful Online Communities', *Journal of Advertising Research*, 50(3), pp.232–9.
17 Grindle, M. (2010) personal communication.
18 Grindle (2004) op. cit.
19 Hawkins, R. (2010) 'EVOKE – A Crash Course in Changing the World' in *EduTech A World Bank Blog on ICT Use in Education* (Weblog). http://blogs.worldbank.org/edutech/evoke-a-crash-course-in-changing-the-world (accessed 27 January 2011).
20 Lazer and Kelley, op. cit., p.ix.

11 Marketing as if people mattered

1 Čapek K. (1926) A letter published to the New York Sunday Times, 29 April 1926.
2 Schumacher, *Small is Beautiful*, op. cit., p.42.
3 http://www.heraldscotland.com/mobile/news/home-news/concern-as-scots-retail-sales-tumble.16151863?_=73dc8f5748a14c821e64febc5e461a606f6bf7b1 http://www.telegraph.co.uk/finance/financialcrisis/8874912/Concern-as-eurozone-retail-sales-fall.html http://www.bloomberg.com/news/2011-10-14/retail-sales-in-u-s-rise-more-than-forecast-1-1-easing-recovery-concern.html
4 Schumacher, op. cit., p.249.
5 Schumacher, op. cit., p.214.
6 Holden, M. (1994) *Coming Back Brockens: A Year in a Mining Village*. London: Jonathan Cape.
7 Jackson, T. (2005) *Motivating Sustainable Consumption*. A Report to the Sustainable Development Research Network. London: Policy Studies Institute.
8 Roberts, N. (2003) *Direct Citizen Participation: Building a Theory*. Paper presented at the 7th National Public Management Research Conference, 9–11 October 2003, Georgetown University, Washington, DC, p.35.
9 Shifferes, S. (2009) 'G20 Leaders Seal $1tn Global Deal' in *BBC News Online*, 2 April 2009. http://news.bbc.co.uk/2/hi/business/7980394.stm

INDEX